PROBLEMS OF ANCIENT INDIA

PROBLEMS OF ANCIENT INDIA

K. D. SETHNA

ADITYA PRAKASHAN
New Delhi

First published 2000

ISBN 81-7742-026-7

Published by Aditya Prakashan, F-14/65, Model Town II,
Delhi – 110 009 and printed at
Rajkamal Electric Press, Delhi – 110 033

CONTENTS

THE LOCATION OF KAMBOJA

When doctors disagree, the patient often dies. Dr. D.C. Sircar and Dr. V.S. Agrawala are at variance over the location of Kamboja[1] and as a result the historical truth about this ancient Mahājanapada appears to fade out. The irony of the situation is that both the doctors are right - and both are wrong.

Agrawala puts Kamboja in the region of the Pāmīrs. He has the clear support of Kālidāsa (*Raghuvaṁśa*, IV.60 ff) as well as of Kalhaṇa (*Rājataraṅgiṇī*, IV.165-66). Some passages of the *Mahābhārata*, which we shall specify later, are also on his side. Then there is the fact that, as Jayachandra Vidyālaṅkāra showed on the basis of Grierson's Linguistic Survey, the root *śava*, which Yāska long ago noted as used only in the Kamboja dialect among the dialects of the Aryans, is still current in the Ghalcha-speaking parts of the Pāmīrs. This fact, of course, is not quite determinative of the Kambojas' location, because *śava* with its Irānian affinity is likely to have been used wherever the Irānian influence on a dialect was strong. Its currency today in the Pāmīrs cannot decide where the Kambojas, as members of a national or racial group which Yāska had in mind, were located in his ancient age. However, the fact creates a fair presumption that the Kamboja country may have once been in the modern Ghalcha-speakers' territory. And what finally clinches Agrawala's point is the testimony of the geographer Ptolemy (*c.* 140 A.D.), which is completely omitted by both Agrawala and Sircar.

It was Sylvain Lévi[2] who drew attention to the place which Ptolemy locates to the south of the Oxus under the name of Tambyzoi. Lévi identified it with Kamboja on the ground that Tambyzoi is only a Greek transliteration of the Austro-Asiatic spelling of Kamboja.

Yes, Agrawala is not off the mark at all. But several statements he makes in support of his thesis seem unacceptable. Thus, apropos of Kālidāsa, he says that all the area from

1. *Purāṇa*, July 1963, pp. 251-57, 355-59.
2. *Indian Antiquary*, 1923, p. 54.

the Sindhu to the Oxus, including Balkh (Bāhlīka, Bactria), was under the Guptas. First, even if Kālidāsa did imply such sway by the king who was his contemporary, we could not confidently apply it to the Guptas: we are not yet certain that any Gupta was his contemporary. Secondly, the Meherauli Pillar inscription of King Chandra, who was either Chandragupta I or Chandragupta II Vikramāditya, unmistakably mentions that the Bāhlīkas were conquered after a crossing of the mouths of the Indus by King Chandra. Agrawala makes no comment on this specific detail, even when he refers to it. As Allan[3] correctly remarked many years back, the inscription cannot mean that "Chandra's arms penetrated to Balkh, the route which would not be across the mouths of the Indus". Neither can the inscription be looked upon as merely marking by the Indus-delta and the Bāhlīkas two terms of a conventional fourfold definition of a *chakravartin*'s achievement: we cannot ignore the close-knit grammar of the inscription's sentence, by which the conquest directly and intimately depends upon the crossing. Apart from Allan's own suggestion that the term "Bāhlīka" in the time of King Chandra may have been employed in a general sense to indicate foreigners, the only plausible idea offered so far is Raychaudhuri's,[4] pointing to a tribe not very distant from the Indus-delta: "The Vāhlīkas beyond the seven mouths of the Indus are apparently the Bactrioi occupying the country near Arachosia in the time of the geographer Ptolemy."

Another statement of Agrawala's, which is impossible to accept, is that the Yavanas of Aśoka's inscriptions, who are mentioned along with the Kambojas, are the Bāhlīka-Yavanas of the Brahmāṇḍa Purāṇa (Uttarabhāga, Upodghāta Pāda, Ch. 16. 18) and that therefore Aśoka's Kambojas can very well be in the Pāmīr region. It is plain history, as Sircar urges, that Bāhlīka (Bactria) in Aśoka's day was part of the Seleucid empire until *c.* 250 B.C. (or *c.* 256 B.C., according to Newell) when its governor Diodotus revolted and made the province

3. *Catalogue of Coins, the Gupta Dynasty*, etc., Introduction, p. XXXVI.
4. *The Political History of Ancient India* (3rd ed., 1938), p. 364, fn. 1.

independent. It could never have been under Aśoka at any time. So the Bāhlīka-Yavanas could not have had Aśoka's Kambojas as their neighbours. What is more, Aśoka's Yona-Kamboja, as Sircar reminds us, is closely associated in Rock Edict V with Gandhāra, whose two chief cities, Takshaśilā and Puśkarāvatī, are about the Indus and not near the Oxus.

Sircar's two points go to prove that there was a Kamboja country in the vicinity of the Indus, most probably somewhere in Afghānistān and perhaps wide enough to take in Rājapura which is mentioned by the *Mahābhārata* (VII.4,5) as the scene of Karṇa's victory over the Kambojas and which Raychaudhuri[5] considered, with the help of Hiuen Tsang's Ho-lo-she-pu-lo (Rājapura, modern Rajauri), as the central clue to the location of Kamboja.

Sircar's further argument that the Aramaic version below the Greek in the recently discovered Kandahār edict of Aśoka must be for the Kambojas whom Aśoka (R.E. XIII) groups with the Yavanas is not at all negligible. But Agrawala is right in observing that we cannot connect Aramaic with the Kambojas exclusively or, merely on the strength of it at Kandahār, locate them in Southern Afghānistān. For, two other Aramaic inscriptions of Aśoka exist – at Takṣaśīlā and Lampāka (Laghman). Sircar's strong point is Aśoka's *yona-kambojeṣu*. If the Greek text was meant for the Yavanas, it is difficult to resist the conclusion that the Aramaic here was for the Kambojas.

Sircar, however, writes about the latter: "They appear to have lived side by side with the Yavanas." Does this mean that the two peoples formed a single province? If that is the implication read in Kandahār's bilingual text, it goes against Aśoka's other edicts. In those edicts, not only are the Yonas put with the Kambojas but both are put with the Gandhāras and once (R.E. XIII) the Yonas are mentioned by themselves. The clear suggestion is that each people formed a province on its own and that the three peoples formed contiguous pro-

5. *Ibid.*, pp. 125 ff.

vinces. Sircar himself at one place speaks of their living in contiguous areas of Uttarāpatha in the age of the Mauryas. In view of this, I suppose we should take his "side by side" to mean nothing more than contiguity. In that case the Kandahār epigraph cannot be said to stand in the Yavana country but only at the common boundary between the Yavana and the Kamboja countries. Attending to the Aśokan sequence Yona-Kamboja-Gandhāra, we should say that Yona stood south of Kandahār and Kamboja north of it, extending right up to the point where Gandhāra started and perhaps marching with its borders further north.

Now we may sum up. Sircar is right about his Kamboja on this side of the Hindu Kush. Agrawala is right about his Kamboja on the other side of that mountain. Both are wrong in ruling out each other's Kamboja. The historical truth is that there were two Kambojas. We have explicit evidence of it in the *Mahābhārata*. The epic does not direct us only to a Kamboja in the Rājauri region. It has a later reference (II.27.25-26) describing not the conquests of Karṇa but those of Arjuna, and here we have the Paramakambojas as distinguished from the Kambojas. The latter are grouped with the Daradas* who are to be put on the right bank of the Upper Indus, whereas the Paramakambojas are said to have allied their forces with the Lohas and "the Rishikas of the north".** In fact, it is the Paramakambojas whom Vidyālaṅkāra identifies with the Ghalcha-speaking peoples while identifying "the Rishikas of the north" with the Yuëh-chis (Kushāṇas). These Paramkambojas are the same as the Kambojas whom Vidyālaṅkāra finds often associated in the epic with the Bāhlīkas. But this association, which fully supports Agrawala, must not lead us to overlook the association with the Daradas nor the third associative formula, first emphasised by Raychaudhuri, which the *Mahābhārata* (XII.207.43) gives – Yauna-Kamboja-Gandhāra – in the closest possible agreement with the one in Aśoka's R.E. V, which fully supports Sircar.

* II.27.23. *Daradān saha Kāmbojaiḥ.*

** II.27.25. *Lohān Paramakāmbojān Ṛśikān uttarān apī.*

There is no need for the two eminent doctors to disagree. B.M. Barua[6] – no less a doctor – could have reconciled them with the double diagnosis he made quite a time ago. And a further truth which Barua[7] brought forward may interest Sircar and Agrawala, especially the latter. Just as the *Mahābhārata* speaks of Kamboja and Paramakamboja, the *Mahāniddesa* (pp. 155, 415) speaks of Yona and Paramayona.

Where shall we locate Paramayona? Only two possibilities present themselves. Bāhlīka, from where the Bāhlīka-Yavanas of Agrawala came, may have been known by an alternative name, Yavana. Or Ferghāna (Sogdiana) was the place we want. It was named Ta-Yuan by the Chinese and, as René Grousset[8] suggested, the component "Yuan" may be the same as the Irānian "Yauna" and the Indian "Yona" or "Yavana". As both Bāhlīka and Ferghāna can be considered contiguous to the Pāmīr-region, Agrawala no less than Sircar can legitimately have a Yona-Kamboja, but the heavy odds against its being Aśokan must be admitted.

We may add that Kālidāsa, on whom Agrawala leans a great deal, does not permit any combination of the Yavanas with the Kambojas. No alternative *yonakambojeṣu* to Aśoka's can be based on him. For, while his Kambojas are in the Oxus-area, his Yavanas are pretty far from it. The *Raghuvaṁśa* (IV. 61) clearly suggests that in moving towards Persia from Western India (*Aparānta,* Northern Konkan) Raghu had to cross the land of the Yavanas. Kālidāsa's Yavanas are not Bāhlīka-Yavanas. They are not northern enough to be anywhere near Bāhlīka, much less near a Pāmīrian Kamboja.

Here a final question must be posed and answered. Which of the two Kambojas was counted in ancient times as one of the Mahājanapadas of India? All depends on what limits we assign to Bhāratavarsha. Sircar speaks of Kālidāsa as describing Raghu's subjugation of "the countries in the northern areas of Bhāratavarsha" and as mentioning in this region "the

6. *Aśoka and His Inscriptions* (Calcutta, 1946), I, pp. 92-96.
7. *Ibid.*, pp. 94, 96.
8. *L'Empire des Steppes,* p 75, fn.

Hūṇas on the banks of the Vaṁksu (Oxus), *i.e.* in the Bāhlīka country or Bactria", and "the Kambojas" and "the Himālayas". If Bhāratavarsha can be thought of in such wide terms, there is no objection to making the Pāmīrian Kamboja a Mahājanapada of India. But, as none of the old lists of Indian Mahājanapadas includes Bāhlīka, it may not be proper to go beyond the Kamboja which neighboured Gandhāra.

Now we may make a few remarks on certain declarations by both Agrawala and Sircar, which strike us as insufficient. Not in his present article but in his admirable *India as Known to Pāṇini,*[9] Agrawala repeats what many others have stated before him: "The Kambojas are known as Kambujiya in the Old-Persian inscriptions." May we ask where in these inscriptions Kamboja is mentioned as a tribe or a country? The term "Kambujiya" occurs only as the name of the Persian king whom the Greeks called Cambyses. And even this term E. Benveniste,[10] disagreeing with J. Charpentier, refuses to affine in any way with the Indian designation "Kamboja". Benveniste plainly says: "The name of the Kambojas does not yet appear in any Irānian source."

This fact should make us pause before asserting too categorically that the Kambojas were of Irānian extraction. The root *śava* itself, we may remember, is commented on by Yāska because it occurs in the *Nighaṇṭu* (II.14) which is a collection of Vedic words. *Śava* must have been part of Vedic usage, even if we have lost the passages where it occurred, and it does not by itself prove Irānian extraction in the speakers. It only proves Irānian influence, either linguistic or racial. As A.D. Pusalker[11] writes: "The earliest mention of Kāmboja occurs in the *Vaṁśa Brāhmaṇa* of the *Sāmaveda* where a teacher Kāmboja Aupamanyava is referred to. The sage Upamanyu mentioned in the *Ṛgveda* (I.102.9) is in all probability the father of the Kāmboja teacher.... The speech of the Kāmboja is referred to by Yāska as differing from that of other

9. Pp. 48-49.
10. *Journal Asiatique*, Vol. CCXLVI, I, p. 48 with fn.
11. *The Vedic Age* (London, 1952), pp. 259-260.

Aryans and Grierson sees in this reference the Irānian affinities of the Kāmbojas, but the fact that Kāmboja teachers were reputed for their Vedic learning shows them to have been Vedic Aryans, so that Kāmboja was an Aryan settlement. Later on Kāmbojas settled to the north-west of the Indus..."

In regard to their historical status as compared with that of the Yavanas, it is hardly right to say, as Sircar does, that they and not the Yavanas were important in the age of Buddha. No doubt, the *Aṅguttara Nikāya* (VII.5.3 and 5), which Sircar quotes, enumerates among Mahājanapada Kamboja as well as Gandhāra and omits Yavana. But the *Majjhima Nikāya* (43.1.3), which too he draws upon and which is as old as the *Aṅguttara Nikāya,* makes Buddha himself mention the Yavanas together with the Kambojas in exactly the same form as Aśoka: *yona-kambojeṣu*. So the Yavanas were as prominent as the Kambojas or the Gandhāras in Buddha's age. Besides, as B.C. Law[12] tells us, the *Chullaniddesa* (which is included in the Buddhist canon and is therefore one of the oldest Pali commentaries) omits Gandhāra and mentions Yona no less than Kamboja in its list of the Mahājanapadas which flourished before the time of Buddha. Yona and Kamboja are absolutely on a par in the period of which Sircar speaks.

Here a problem arises. What are we to make of the references to a Yona state having existed in India's north-west in such antiquity? Must we revive that old favourite of Bhandarkar and Jayaswal – a pre-Alexandrine Greek colony in India? Or shall we accept the ancient Indian tradition which regards the Yavanas no less than the Kambojas as degraded Kshatriyas? Then we shall have to say that in ancient India, before the Greeks came to be called Yavanas, there were non-Greek Yavanas – just as in medieval India, though in a different way, the label "Yavana" was not confined to the Greeks. This is a theme well worth discussing at some length, and the more we explore it the more surprises we are likely to encounter, prompting changes in several aspects of ancient Indian history.

12. *The Age of Imperial Unity* (Bombay, 1951), p. 1.

One of the surprises Sircar himself has touched on in passing: the Purāṇic description of both the Yavanas and the Kambojas as having "shaven heads". And what renders this description all the more a challenge to the exclusive Greek-Yavana equation is that it merely reiterates what the *Gaṇapātha* on Pāṇini's rule II.1.72 says of these two tribes: *kāmboja-muṇḍaḥ yavana-muṇḍaḥ*. If this is authentic Pāṇinian material, what happens to the usual interpretation of that grammarian's *yavanānī* as an allusion to the Greek script? Here are deep waters indeed and we cannot launch on them at the moment. It is an enterprise to which we may well invite Sircar and Agrawala – particularly Agrawala who has not mentioned this part of the *Gaṇapātha* in his famous book.

THE ARYANS, THE DOMESTICATED HORSE AND THE SPOKED CHARIOT-WHEEL

In 1950 Stuart Piggott,[1] voicing a wide-spread opinion, wrote: "...apart from cattle, the really characteristic domesticated animal of the Aryans was the horse." In 1963 Frederick E. Zeuner, in his admirable book, *A History of Domesticated Animals*,[2] writes: "The people who brought the horse across the mountains to the Near and Middle East appear to have spoken Indo-Germanic languages."

The domesticated horse, therefore, may carry us straight into important problems connected with the Aryans. Its provenance and chronology should help us answer at least two questions: (1) Where did the Aryans have their homeland? (2) How far back in time can we trace them?

In association with the domesticated horse there is the light chariot of war moving on two spoked wheels, and this chariot takes us to the general subject of wheeled vehicles, their invention and spread. Zeuner touches on that subject with a reference to V. Gordon Childe who has made a good deal of research in it. We shall make use of his information wherever it is relevant, and inquire on our own into the origin of what is almost as characteristic of the Aryans as the domesticated horse: the spoked chariot-wheel.

1

Historically, the horse and the two-wheeled war-chariot come into prominence, according to Zeuner,[3] in about 1700 B.C., or slightly later, in all countries of the Near and Middle East. This is the most active phase of the Aryans' sweep from their homeland – a movement which, in Zeuner's words,[4] "started about 2000 B.C. or somewhat earlier". But did the

1. *Prehistoric India* (Pelican Books, Harmondsworth, 1952, 1961), p. 266.
2. *A History of Domesticated Animals* (Hutchinson of London, 1963), p. 315.
3. *Ibid.*, p. 318.
4. *Ibid.*, p. 315.

Near and Middle East – the part of Asia which first felt the shock of the horse-driving charioteers – know the domesticated horse for the first time in the second millennium B.C.?

Piggott[5] tells us: "...the horse... is not an original inhabitant of Mesopotamia, but is given the significant Sumerian name of the 'ass of the mountains' when it first appears, probably in Jamdet Nasr times. It was presumably imported from 'the mountains' of Highland Persia or Turkestan, which with Baluchistan formed a common geographical province within which the earliest evidence of horse-taming comes."

Jamdet Nasr times, by the chronological tables of both Piggott[6] and Zeuner,[7] are *c.* 3000 B.C. So, if we may accept the above statement of Piggot's along with his other one that the horse is the really characteristic domesticated animal of the Aryans we should conclude that the homeland of the Aryans covered Highland Persia, Turkestān and Balūchistān and that they tamed the horse there fairly before 3000 B.C. at whatever early date the archaeologists assign to the sites where the first evidence of the tamed horse has been found.

But Piggott himself fails to draw the same conclusion. To him[8] "the most reasonable hypothesis... is that originally put forward by Professor J.L. Myers and the late Harold Peake, and developed by Professor Childe, which sees the Indo-European languages evolving among the earliest agriculturists of the South Russian steppes and the lands eastwards to the Caspian Sea". His vision[9] of original Aryanism is: "by about 2000 B.C. ... a loose confederacy of tribes, stretching from South Russia to Turkestan, who shared certain elements of culture... and who spoke closely related dialects within the Indo-European framework". Piggott thus adds South Russia to Turkestān and omits both Persia and Balūchistān. In the context of the tamed horse his total view, with its special

5. Piggott, *op. cit.*, p. 158.
6. *Ibid.*, p. 65.
7. Zeuner, *op. cit.*, p. 16.
8. Piggott, *op. cit.*, p. 248.
9. *Ibid.*, p. 249.

emphasis on South Russia, is expressed in the passage:[10] "The horse appears to have been domesticated in South Russia by Middle Kuban times (between 2000 and 1500 B.C.) and representations of Przewalski's horse appear on a silver bowl from the rather earlier Maikop tomb. But the evidence from Anau and Sialk shows that an apparently domesticated horse was known in Persia and Turkestān in very early times, and it again appears in Balūchistān in Rana-ghundai I and, though rarely, in the Harappā Culture. One cannot, therefore, hold that the Aryans were the first people to domesticate the horse in India or on its western borderlands, but they were certainly among the first to introduce the idea of rapid transport made possible by its use. For their farmwork, ox-drawn four-wheeled carts seem to have been used, and horses bred solely for use with the light two-wheeled chariot for sport or warfare".

One need not deny the presence of Aryans in South Russia at *c.* 2000 B.C. But to lay special emphasis on this area and include it in the central region from which issued the horse-charioted movement of Indo-Germanic (or Indo-European) speakers over various parts of Asia and Europe flies in the face of the chronological scheme which Gordon Childe has worked out for the spread of wheeled vehicles. Zeuner[11] sums up this scheme: "He believes that the wheeled cart and the potter's wheel are both inventions of the Uruk culture of southern Mesopotamia and that this happened before 3500 B.C. There is evidence that the wheeled cart was preceded by the sledge, and sledges have been found in the royal tombs of Ur which are at least 1000 years younger. The earliest evidence consists of script signs on late Uruk tablets (Childe, Fig. 1). Whilst it is generally agreed that the earliest wheeled carts were drawn by oxen, onager bones were found in the chariot graves of the Y Cemetery of Kish, which is of Early Dynastic I

10. *Ibid.*, p. 267.

11. Zeuner, *op. cit.*, p. 329. The work of Childe's on which Zeuner draws is listed in the Bibliography (p. 513): 1951, "The first waggons and carts from the Tigris to the Severn", *Proc. Prehist. Soc. (n.s.)*, 17 (3), pp. 177-194, pls. 8-9.

date. Onagers were buried with the sledge of Queen Shub-ad, whilst the king's grave contained two ox-waggons. These finds are Early Dynastic III. From this and other evidence it is to be inferred that in Mesopotamia the ox was replaced by the swifter onager, though not universally, early in the third millennium B.C. Childe held that this is the source of wheeled vehicles, that they reached the Indus Valley by about 2500 B.C., north Syria – 2200 B.C., Crete – 1900 B.C., Greece – 1550 B.C., south Russia – 1400 B.C., north Italy – 1100 B.C., central and northern Europe – 1000 B.C. and Britain – 500 B.C. This sequence looks indeed convincing, though new finds are apt to modify it".

Mark that wheeled vehicles reached South Russia in 1400 B.C. How then can South Russia send out any kind of chariots to the Near and Middle East, to Europe or to India between 2000 and 1500 B.C.? With its late reception of chariotry, no less than with its late domestication of the horse, South Russia must be ruled out. It cannot figure as a significant centre of early Aryan radiation. Even without the chariot the domesticated horse cannot have gone forth from the Aryans of South Russia in the same antiquity as from those in Turkestān. Indeed, if the horse-representations on the Maikop silver bowl are only of *c.* 2000 B.C., the Aryans of South Russia may themselves have been migrants from Turkestān and any other place that can be considered a seat of Aryanism.

On Piggott's own declarations, there is no reason why North Persia and North Balūchistān should not equally with Turkestān be the Aryan homeland. And, with wheeled vehicles reaching the Indus Valley by about 2500 B.C., there is also no reason why from the regions thereabouts an Aryan wave should not have passed over the Near and Middle East in the early second millennium B.C. At any rate, Piggott's evidence about the domesticated horse gives us a belt of original Aryandom from Anau to Rānā Ghundāī as well as to Sialk in the centuries preceding 3000 B.C.

And on the strength of evidence similar to that which Piggott accepts for Anau, Sialk and Rānā Ghundāī, we may extend the belt at the Anau end. For, at Shah Tepé on the shore of the Caspian Sea in Irān's extreme north, a little to the south-west of Anau, horse-remains from very early times have been claimed. Zeuner[12] mentions the claim and, if we credit it just as Piggott credits the other three, we get a pretty clear answer to our questions about the Aryans apropos of the provenance and chronology of the domesticated horse. Does Zeuner confirm the answer we have based on Piggott? No – and Yes. His treatment of the domesticated horse is a little complicated.

First, he deals expertly with the several types of horse and mentions the two kinds of wild horse that continued into modern times: the tarpan and Przewalski's Mongolian horse.[13] Differing in some respects, they have in common a small build and an upright mane. One of their differences is in colour: the tarpan is mouse-grey with a lighter belly and a dark stripe from the neck to the tail, while Przewalski's horse is yellow-dun with lighter body and dark legs. "The stock which contributed most to the domesticated horse is in all probability the tarpan."[14]

Next, Zeuner asks: When was the horse domesticated? Who were its domesticators and where did its domestication happen?

"From 2000 B.C. onwards the horse-drawn chariot swept across the Western world, a contraption which requires elaborate domestication and special training. The chariot itself, of course, is older. It is therefore reasonable to assume that the horse was domesticated considerably before 2000 B.C."[15]

"The fact that the domesticated horse is almost exclusively of tarpan stock limits the possible area of origin to west and central Europe north of the Alps, eastern Europe and western Asia north of the mountains as far east as Russian Turkestan. That horse domestication did not originate in western or

12. *Ibid.*, p. 316.
13. *Ibid.*, p. 302 f.
14. *Ibid.*, p. 311.
15. *Ibid.*, p. 313.

central Europe is a point on which all workers on the subject agree, partly for chronological reasons and partly because the horse was rare there, most of the country being too densely forested. This restricts the probable area to the Ukrainian and east Russian steppes, Kazakhstan and the steppes of western Asia mainly around Lake Aral and including the plains of Turkestan, Ust-Urt Plateau and Turan... It is probable that agriculture spread at an early date into the plains of Turkestan, as far as they received water from the mountains, for these steppe countries had in places excellent soil... It must, however, be realised that the agriculturally valuable soil is patchily distributed... and the problem of transport must have presented itself at an early date. It is not intended to maintain that animal traction was invented there, merely that it was important. The first beasts to be used would have been cattle.

"Most agricultural areas on the edge of the desert succumbed to desiccation after a millennium or two of crop-raising because, on the one hand, natural water stored in the ground was used up and, on the other, because primitive agriculture destroys the soil and thus invites the desert in.

"Under such conditions transport by means of oxen becomes something of a problem, both for lack of water and fodder. That man should have cast an eye on the horse is natural and it is thus that domestication may have begun.

"The horse gave man greater mobility than he had ever before, and it made possible a *secondary* nomadism, combined with temporary crop-raising. Once this system had been developed, it swept the Western world, except the densely forested areas where its progress was slow...

"The people who brought the horse across the mountains to the Near and Middle East appear to have spoken Indo-Germanic languages. Thus the original centre of the domestication of the horse might briefly be circumscribed as Turkestan. This view is, however, not based on archaeological evidence, but on biological considerations."[16]

16. *Ibid.*, pp. 314-315.

2

Zeuner's development of biological considerations is excellent. And by circumscribing the original centre of horse-taming as Turkestān and noting the Aryan character of those who brought the animal to Mesopotamia and its neighbours, he renders the region round Anau the most likely homeland of the Aryans. Between Anau and Shah Tepé the distance, as we have already remarked, is rather negligible. So the Aryan homeland could, on geographical grounds added to biological ones, contain two of the most ancient sites where the remains of the horse have been claimed. Between Shah Tepé and Sialk the distance, though greater than between Anau and Shah Tepé, is still not much; nor is it really substantial between Rānā Ghundāī and Sialk or between Anau and Rānā Ghundāī. Besides, archaeologists – e.g. Piggott[17] – have found that pottery-styles in prehistoric times link in diverse ways Anau with Sialk, Rānā Ghundāī with Anau, Sialk with Rānā Ghundāī. An additional place in this series of linkings is Hissar which is far neither from Anau nor from Shah Tepé. So it would be nothing unnatural if we expanded the biologically inferred centre of original horse-domestication from Turkestān to North Persia as well as North Balūchistān. Then we cover all the most ancient sites claiming horse-remains. Thus biological considerations prepare perfectly the ground for archaeological evidence.

As for the antiquity to which this evidence may be referred, we shall see how the fourth millennium B.C. fixed by Piggott and others for Anau, Sialk, Shah Tepé and Rānā Ghundāī as sites of horse-domestication is strongly suggested by certain slightly less early "pointers" to the domesticated horse. These "pointers" are listed by Zeuner himself, along with the earlier-dated claims.

But he subjects everything archaeological to criticism, and his general verdict runs: "...archaeological evidence early

17. Piggott, *op. cit.*, pp. 58, 65, 75, 129-130.

enough to shed light on the first stages of horse domestication is completely lacking..."[18] Introducing a detailed account of alleged horse-remains from very ancient sites, he remarks: "Unfortunately, not one of them bears the test of critical examination."[19]

In Zeuner we confront a pair of paradoxes. First, although Turkestān is eminently the place where the horse was originally domesticated, the horse-like remains at Anau and at its neighbour Shah Tepé are not of the horse: they are of the hemione – that is, the onager, the half-ass. Secondly, the domestication was achieved considerably before 2000 B.C., and yet all the early prehistoric sites claimed for the horse have really yielded only the half-ass, the onager, the hemione.

Surely, there is something wrong here in this conflict of archaeology with biology as well as with logic. Let us then glance at the precise terms of Zeuner's criticism.[20]

He begins with the oldest site: Anau. At all the levels Duerst (1906) found the bones of a horse-like animal of the same kind. Duerst describes their relation to the bones of other animals either of a wild or of a domesticated type. We shall concentrate on the significance of this relation at a slightly later stage of our study. Duerst, turning to direct osteological signs, admits in all honesty that exact criteria of domestication such as are present in the skeletons of cattle and sheep are absent from the bones of horses, but he feels justified by all the rest of the evidence in considering not only that here we have the true horse *(Equus caballus)* which he calls *Equus caballus pumpelli* after the name (Pumpelly) of the chief excavator, but also that from the second phase of the lowest level – Ib – this horse is a domesticated one. Zeuner, after touching on the issue of domestication, passes on to the more fundamental issue: Is the equine or equid of Anau at all a true horse? He[21] answers: "Admittedly the majority of archaeo-

18. Zeuner, *op. cit.*, p. 314.
19. *Ibid.*, p. 315.
20. *Ibid.*, pp. 315-318.
21. *Ibid.*, p. 316.

logists, as well as several palaeontologists, have accepted Duerst's identification. Both Hilzheimer and Antonius, however, regarded the Anau equine as a hemione. More recently, Lundholm has conclusively shown that the latter alternative is correct using the first phalanx, a bone of which sufficient specimens for a comparison were available."

But is Lundholm really conclusive? Zeuner himself writes elsewhere[22] in his book when dealing with the onager: "In Turkestan we have an archaeological record from Anau, for the notorious Anau horse is a hemione, as was first established by Hilzheimer." Well, if Hilzheimer (1935) has already established – that is, definitely demonstrated – the Anau horse to be an onager, why is so much weight attached to Lundholm's investigation much later (1949)? Evidently, Hilzheimer's establishing did not prove the case. Why should we take Lundholm's conclusive showing as anything better? The terms used for both the writers are interchangeable: the meaning they carry of finality should be equally suspect.

There is also the possibility that the bones of the onager and of the small tarpan-like horse of primitive times are both present at Anau. They would be difficult to distinguish and then we should have just the situation that Duerst would speak of a horse whereas Hilzheimer and Antonius would speak of a hemione. It would not be surprising too for the "first phalanx" of the hemione to be discovered. But a generalisation from the "sufficient specimens" of it would not cover the whole case. The bones other than the first phalanx could be partly of the true horse no less than of the half-ass.

This is a very concrete possibility because of what Zeuner[23] himself says about Anau's position on the edge of the plains of Turkestān, near Ashkabad at the foot of the mountains of Northern Persia: "This position is significant, since the lowlands of north-western Asia were almost certainly populated by wild horses. It is conceivable that domestication may have begun in such an area."

22. *Ibid.*, p. 371.
23. *Ibid.*, pp. 315-316.

What Zeuner says here may be brought into relation with some statements of his on the onager, and made to illuminate the Anau finds. "It is not generally known that, prior to the introduction of the domesticated horse into Mesopotamia, the half-ass or hemione was domesticated by the ancient Sumerians."[24] The date of its domestication is *c.* 2500 B.C.[25] "With the introduction of the horse into Mesopotamia, early in the second millennium B.C., the onager disappears from the list of animals in the service of man."[26] Among the reasons for the rapid changeover, Zeuner[27] mentions the greater docility of the newcomer and its superior strength. Now, if at the time of the second phase of Anau's lowest level "the lowlands of north-western Asia were almost certainly populated by wild horses" available for domestication, it is hardly likely that the onager should be preferred as a domesticated animal, particularly where the somewhat elaborate process of traction and transport is concerned – the process which Zeuner has described as important among agriculturists like Turkestān's in "areas on the edge of the desert". In short, given the horse in the epoch of Anau Ib, it would undoubtedly render the onager unnecessary as a domesticated animal. At least, the onager would never exclude the horse.

So the crucial question is: Are the bones of the Anau equine a domesticated animal's? If they are, they must be not the onager's but of the small primitive horse or else, together with the onager's, they would definitely be also the horse's. Under no circumstances would the horse be absent. What has Zeuner to declare on the subject of domestication of Anau, whether of the horse or of the onager? When Duerst points out that precise criteria of domestication, as present in the skeletons of cattle and sheep, are absent from the bones of horses, Zeuner[28] comments: "Thus it is in any case not certain

24. *Ibid.*, p. 367.
25. *Ibid.*, pp. 368-369.
26. *Ibid.*, p. 371; also p. 373.
27. *Ibid.*, p. 373.
28. *Ibid.*, p. 316.

whether the equine from Anau was domesticated." But here Zeuner brings out only one aspect of the situation. What may not be certain may yet be extremely probable, be even a near-certainty. And that is how things are at Anau. By Zeuner's own account,[29] the equine bones are associated in the lowest levels with wild animals, but from Ib onwards they occur together with domesticated types. "At the same time, equine bones become more abundant compared with those of other animals..." This is considered by Duerst as evidence that the equine had become tamed or domesticated. Can one logically find fault with Duerst?

Read what Zeuner himself has to say, a little later, on the signs of domestication. There are two passages.[30] First, the pro and con statement: "The statistical argument that large numbers of bones on a site suggest domestication is widely accepted. In this sense, Gromova regards small numbers as evidence of wild status and hunting. Nehring, however, regards the contrary as correct, and Lundholm says that the large number of bones in Baralda Cave (a Tripolye site) indicates that the horse was hunted. This may be true in the case of a cave..."

What is the implication here? Cave-conditions apart, the statistical argument which is widely accepted deserves support. Of course, Zeuner follows up with the wish that "more osteological work" would be done to ensure complete proof; but, short of osteological proof which is confessedly hard to reach, the fact of large numbers of bones on a site is a dependable standard. And it is a standard which broadly Lundholm himself is shown to accept. Zeuner, in the second passage, writes: "...after a careful scrutiny of the Scandinavian material, Lundholm still considers it possible that the battle-axe people knew horse-taming and used the local wild horses for the purpose. He and Degerbol agree that from the Bronze Age onwards the horse is represented by so many bones that it must be regarded as domesticated."

29. *Ibid.*
30. *Ibid.*, pp. 325, 329.

So when, as at Anau, the bones of a particular animal are on the increase in the midst of other *domesticated* animals' bones, the signs for this particular animal's domestication reach almost fulness.

Horse or onager, the Anau equine can for all practical purposes be taken as domesticated. And then, with the horse accepted as present in Turkestān in the Anau-epoch and with the onager admitted to be as good as unnecessary when the horse is there for traction and transport, we have a clear solution. The bones of the Anau equine must refer to the horse, whether exclusively or in association with the onager.

Nor is this all that can be urged in favour of the Anau horse. After telling us that "in the third millennium B.C. the onager was used as a draught animal" by the Sumerians, Zeuner[31] proffers information which almost inhibits us from associating the onager with the horse at Anau. He observes that with "a single exception, a scene from Thebes in Egypt", "outside Mesopotamia the onager does not appear to have been used". Besides Mesopotamian traction, the only use Zeuner in this context mentions for the onager is: "it may have played a part in the breeding of mules right into the Roman period." Surely the Anau-agriculturists were no mule-breeders. And even to breed mules one requires horses to cross with either asses or onagers.

Lastly, the total equation of the Anau equine with the onager may be controverted by a *reductio ad absurdum* with the help of the recent opinion[32] on the equines from the ancient Indus Valley. Lately some bones were found in Area G, Harappā, which are said to belong not to the period proper of the Harappā Culture (2500-1500 B.C.) but to the post-Harappā Civilisation. The earlier find by Sewell and Guha (1931) at Mohenjo-dāro is also reported to have been from an upper level. So one does not know whether it too is part of the Indus Valley Civilisation. But from the scientific account "it is

31. *Ibid.*, pp. 369, 371.

32. *Proceedings of the First All-India Congress of Zoology* (Calcutta, 1959), Part 2, Scientific Papers, pp. 1-14.

evident that the Equid skeletal remains from Area G, Harappā, belong to the true horse, *Equus caballus Linn.*, and not to the onager group; they resemble the modern 'country-bred' horses of India". The writer goes on to include among "the skeletal remains of the true horse" those from an upper level of Mohenjo-dāro. But then what shall we make of Zeuner's pronouncement:[33] "...the few bones found at Mohenjo-Daro, which Sewell (1931) compared with the Anau horse, are likely to belong to the Indian onagers"? Dealing with the Mohenjo-dāro equine, Zeuner has turned its declared resemblance to the Anau equine into a weapon of attack. But the weapon is now seen to be a boomerang.

For, if the Mohenjo-dāro equine, like that from Area G, Harappā, is *Equus caballus*, the Anau bones, in spite of the first phalanx, must be promoted and be labelled as caballine at least in part.

All in all, along various possible lines, whether with Zeuner's own help or otherwise, the case for the domesticated Anau horse – Lundholm notwithstanding – proves very sound indeed.

3

Now we may examine the rest of Zeuner's criticism of prehistoric "horse"-remains. The Sialk find is the next oldest. It comprises two molars assigned by Vaufrey to *Equus caballus pumpelli*, and the Level II that has yielded them has been correlated with the Samara and Halaf phases of Mesopotamia, which are believed to be earlier than 3000 B.C. Zeuner[34] dismisses briefly the equines concerned: "These equines, being identified with the Anau form, have now to be regarded as half-asses also."

What applies to Anau from Mohenjo-dāro applies even more to Sialk. The molars from its Level II have nothing to do with any first phalanx: consequently, by being assigned to the

33. Zeuner, *op. cit.*, p. 371.
34. *Ibid.*, p. 316.

Anau species of "horse", they must be altogether of the true horse.

Even if we did not bring Mohenjo-dāro in, it is amazing how merely from the agreement of Vaufrey's reading of the Sialk molars with Duerst's of the Anau bones the half-ass can be dogmatically asserted for Sialk when there is no first phalanx, as at Anau, to suggest its presence. And why should there be dogmatism here while over Mohenjo-dāro's equines Zeuner is more guarded and, because of their Anau-affinity, speaks just of their being "likely to belong to Indian onagers"? The conclusion for Sialk strikes us as too hasty and facile – based on insufficient premises. Vaufrey's view may well be correct – especially as Sialk lies fairly near Shah Tepé which is the third oldest site of horse-claim and which is almost equally distant from Sialk and Anau. Neither geography nor palaeontology forbids this view.

Now for Shah Tepé. The single fragment of a long spongy bone which is all that Amschler (1940) had taken for a domesticated horse's from the lowest and oldest level is found by Lundholm on investigation to be a portion of a human femur. Lundholm may be right. But what about the next level? It has yielded eleven bones which seem to be of a horse. Zeuner's first remark[35] is: "The investigator again assigns the remains to *E. c. pumpelli*, the Anau 'horse'. This alone might be regarded as sufficient to assign the Shah Tepé form to the half-asses..." We may turn round and retort on the basis of what we have already shown: "This alone might be regarded as sufficient to give a caballine status to the Shah Tepé form." Zeuner's further observation[36] runs: "Level II is recent enough for horse to be present in any case, nevertheless the material could well belong to a hemione form. The jaw contains only teeth that have been ground down to the roots, and the pelvis is assigned to a horse because of its size only. It must be stated, therefore, that there is no evidence for the true horse at Shah Tepé."

35. *Ibid.*
36. *Ibid.*

To the remark – "Level II is recent enough for horse to be present in any case" – let us add an introductory phrase of Zeuner's: "Shah Tepé on the shore of the Caspian Sea, *i.e.* north of the mountains, where wild horses are likely to have occurred." And then let us ask: "If the size of the pelvis favours a horse, why think of a hemione form?" Even an earlier dating than the 2500-1500 B.C. which Zeuner, after Arne the excavator, gives to Level II would not help to suit the size of the pelvis to a half-ass rather than a horse. And, granted the fact that at the place wild horses are likely to have occurred, the half-ass would be put all the more out of court in spite of the date being earlier. To imitate Zeuner: "It must be stated, therefore, that all the available evidence is for the true horse at Shah Tepé."

In our survey of the ancient Middle East the next stage of our analysis is perhaps the most important – apart from the all-round direct implication of the Mohenjo-dāro horse – for the correct approach to the equine bones we have mentioned. Zeuner[37] writes that at Susa in ancient Elam, between Levels I and II, which means the beginning of the third millennium B.C., an engraving on a bone depicts in a diagrammatic fashion a rider on an equine. Zeuner passes judgment on it: "...one must admit that Amschler (1935, 1936) is right in pointing to the short ears and untasselled tail as suggesting a horse and not an onager. On the other hand, Hančar stresses that the engraving is only 33 mm high and that the specific identity of the animal cannot be established." What exactly does Hančar mean? Obviously he cannot mean that the animal may not be an equine at all. One can never mix up any other type with an equine. So he can only mean that we fail to distinguish whether the equine here is a horse or an onager or else a full ass. About the onager, Zeuner[38] writes elsewhere: "its ears are longer than those of the horse but shorter than those of the ass." As the engraved animal is said to have short ears, we may keep the full ass out of the discussion. The

37. *Ibid.*, p. 317.
38. *Ibid.*, p. 368.

difficulty which Hančar appears to suggest is that, although the ears are short, the engraving's mere height of 33 mm prevents us from deciding whether they are shorter than an ass's or shorter than an onager's, whether they belong to an onager or to a horse. But surely there is a proportion between an animal's head and its ears as well as between its head and the rest of its body. To distinguish in general the proportion which is a horse's from that which is an onager's, we do not have to depend on how high the engraving is. It is purely a matter of internal relations. Hančar is raising an irrelevant issue and obscuring the fundamental question. From what Zeuner admits, the internal relations seem definitely to indicate a horse. And if any doubt could still linger, there is the impression of an untasselled tail to settle it. Not the slightest reason exists to deny *Equus caballus* here – and the act of riding proves *Equus caballus* to have been domesticated at Susa at almost 3000 B.C.

In view of this, the other Elamitic illustration which Zeuner mentions immediately after should not be as enigmatic as he suggests. It is "a small bone plate showing nineteen heads of equids with varying profiles, which Amschler regards as representing various types of horses. Antonius, however, is satisfied that these were onagers". If the tamed horse was a newcomer in Elam at the beginning of the third millennium B.C. and that too as a rarity, it is likely to have been an object of curious regard and to have been looked upon in all its available variety. However, we need not pronounce final judgment. And even if these heads are of onagers they can never affect our interpretation of the Susa engraving or support in any way Zeuner's scepticism about it.

Equally mistaken is his hesitation over the earliest evidence for domesticated horse-like animals in Mesopotamia: the Khafaje vase. He writes of the vase: "It comes from a place about fifteen kilometres east of Baghdad and belongs to the Jamdat Nasr period, approximately 3000 B.C. Unfortunately the painting is extremely sketchy. The mane is shown upright, which speaks for the onager or ass rather than the domestic horse, unless these supposed horses had retained the 'wild' type of mane. One might, therefore, discard the Khafaje vase as an early representation of the onager, which was domesticated at Ur, were there not a horse-like tail. It is shown on all three beasts drawing the cart. It is indeed lacking the tuft at the end of the tail (the sign of the onager), and this fact is quoted specifically (e.g. by Hermes, 1936) as demonstrating that the animals are horses. But the tails are shown by a single stroke of the brush, so that details cannot be expected anyway. The specific nature of the Khafaje animals thus remains uncertain."[39]

Here is a piece of faulty reasoning. When several strokes of the brush go to make up the rest of the animal, the single stroke of the tail implies no necessity to avoid details. It is there because details were not required to identify the animal in this part of its body. Let us ask: "Whose tail can be drawn by a single stroke – a horse's or an onager's?" An onager's, having a tuft, must be drawn by more than a single stroke. In an attempt to give a general suggestion, one can draw only a horse's tail in this way. In fact, in a representation[40] of a chariot, from Cyprus round about the fourteenth century B.C., the two equines whom everybody accepts as horses have their tails drawn by single strokes with perhaps a slightly varying pressure of the brush at different points. This technique seems not uncommon for horses, because it suits their tails. Consequently, if the Khafaje animals are equines, as they admittedly are, then they can be nothing except horses.

The upright mane should not stand in the way of this conclusion. Long domestication of the horse-species would lead to a soft mane, but if a wild horse is caught and domesticated it would not acquire a soft mane just by virtue of domestication. The Khafaje vase is old enough for an early stage in the history of domestication, when wild horses newly caught would be tamed and set to use. Even if their progeny were employed, the wild type of mane might continue for

39. *Ibid.*, p. 317.
40. Piggott, *op. cit.*, p. 275, Fig. 13, bottom, right hand.

some generations. We must bear in mind that the early domesticated horses were very near the tarpan or Przewalski's horse, both of whom had upright manes unlike the modern steed's. Besides, a domesticated onager does not necessarily show a more upright mane. There is a picture in Zeuner (p. 372, Fig. 14: 6), the War Panel of the Standard of Ur (*c.* 2500 B.C.), which sets forth onagers drawing chariots. If we look at the first register we shall find the mane of an onager no more upright than that of an Egyptian chariot-drawing horse whose picture from the Tomb of Chaemhet of the eighteenth dynasty (*c.* 1550 B.C.) is reproduced also by Zeuner (p. 321, Fig. 12: 13). Even wild onagers do not always disclose a more upright mane. The scene from the palace of Ashurbanipal (686-626 B.C.) at Nineveh (p. 370, Fig. 14: 4), representing their capture with lassos, has their manes even less upright than that Egyptian horse's.

And here we may mark one of the omissions in Zeuner's account. When referring to Susa, he comments only on the bone-engraving of a rider on an equine. But there is another engraving on a bone from Susa. R. Ghirshman[41] gives a reproduction of it with the title: "Przewalski horse carved in bone." The animal carved may be a tarpan for all we know or a cross, but its mane is just the sort which inclines Zeuner to "discard the Khafaje vase as an early representation of an onager". If the engraving comes from the same period as the equine with rider, the horse is likely to be a domesticated one.

To the same category as Zeuner's Khafaje and Susa animals belong the other Mesopotamian equines reported by him. He[42] writes: "Langdon (1924-34) mentions that on a tablet found about seventeen miles north of Kish the ideogram of the horse appears. The animal is described as living on the mountains. This tablet is dated by Langdon at prior to 3500 B.C., which is certainly too early. The horse is further mentioned in a Babylonian liturgy of the third millennium (Langdon, 1913). This and other evidence is accepted by

41. *Iran* (Pelican Books, Harmondsworth, 1954), p. 35, Fig. 8.
42. Zeuner, *op. cit.*, p. 317.

Hermes as proving that the horse was known in Mesopotamia at that time. It cannot, however, have played an important part in the economy of the people." Over and above the last slightly grudging sentence, Zeuner[43] has an introductory summing-up of the information drawn from Langdon: he finds it equally ambiguous as the Khafaje vase, though he grants that Mesopotamia's acquaintance with northerly countries renders it likely for the Mesopotamians to have heard of the horse and perhaps even occasionally seen it brought in. Our assessment of Zeuner's facts here is exactly the opposite because we go by what Childe and Piggott say about the ideogram-horse: they provide us with the really significant knowledge in this connection.

Childe[44] writes: "It (the horse) is... mentioned in the Jamdet Nasr tablets by the same ideogram 'ass of the mountains', that was employed in classical Babylonian cuneiform." Now, classical Babylonian cuneiform has the clear indication that the true horse is meant; so the ideogram seventeen miles north of Kish and as old as at least 3000 B.C., if Langdon's estimate of 3500 is exaggerative, must be about the same animal. The relevant statement by Piggott we have already quoted. His point is that the Mesopotamian "ass of the mountains", whose horse-character cannot be disputed but which is no native of Mesopotamia, must have hailed from the hilly tracts of Persia and from Turkestān. This point about provenance can hardly be evaded and, if it has to be accepted, Shah Tepé and Sialk and Anau force themselves into the picture before 3000 B.C. and the conclusion of Lundholm, discrediting the claims on their behalf, becomes exceedingly doubtful.

Thus we return inevitably to the suggestion that at Anau, if the horse alone is not there, it is co-present with the onager and that at Sialk the two molars do not, on the available premises, permit their attribution to the hemione instead of the *Equus caballus* and that the pelvis and ten other equine

43. *Ibid.*
44. *New Light on the Most Ancient East* (London, 1934), p. 161.

bones at Shah Tepé are the horse's. Thus also, from Mesopotamia's acquaintance with the horse in *c.* 3000 B.C., we are able to give some sort of precise form to Zeuner's own acknowledgment that the first domesticated horse must be considerably earlier than 2000 B.C.: we can safely put it high up in the fourth millennium B.C.

4

To round off our survey we must hark back to a particular feature in the passage from Piggott bearing on Mesopotamia's first contact with the horse. He has referred to a common geographical province of earliest horse-taming, constituted by Highland Persia, Turkestān and Balūchistān. Balūchistān, to him, means Rāṇā Ghundāī I, to which he refers apropos of the domesticated horse of South Russia in about 2000 B.C. Another of his references[45] runs: "The animal bones were very interesting, comprising the humped ox (*Bos indicus*), domestic sheep (*Ovis vignei*), the ass (*Equus asinus*), and most surprising and important, four teeth of the domesticated horse (*Equus caballus*). Nomadic horse-riding herdsmen using the site as a camping-ground are suggested by the finds in RG I; an infant's skeleton was also found at this level."

H. Peake and H.J. Fleure[46] have attempted to focus the significance of the equine relics of RG I: "...four animal teeth found here have been identified as belonging to the domesticated horse. From the probable dating of later phases at RG this first settlement can hardly be dated later than the earliest part of the third millennium B.C. and is possibly older still, so that these teeth may be the earliest known trace of the domestic horse."

How much "older still" could RG I possibly be is deducible from the materials of Kili Gul Mohammad, not far from Rāṇā Ghundāī, which have come to light since Piggott wrote. And it is meaningful that here also equine remains were

45. Piggott, *op. cit.*, p. 121.
46. *Times and Places* (Oxford, 1956), p. 228.

found scattered through all levels and were labelled by Walter A. Fairservis Jr., on the strength of a figurine, as those of the true horse.* By the way, they mark another *lacuna* in Zeuner's book which overlooks Fairservis' work. Sir Mortimer Wheeler[47] informs us that Carbon-14 tests date KGM to 3500-3100 B.C. Hence Balūchistān in general is nearly on a par with the other oldest sites of horse-claim. And a comparison of RG I with KGM extends the former to at least a part of the same period. D.H. Gordon,[48] speaking of hand-made painted ware with crude geometric designs on an unslipped surface in the second phase of KGM, adds: "This painted ware equates with similar pottery in the Zhob at Rana Ghundai in the earliest level." Also, since much of the pottery of RG I is unpainted and hand-made,[49] like much of the KGM II ware, RG I may synchronise even with the earliest point of KGM II, perhaps 3300 B.C. or earlier. Further, a greater primitiveness of general living is indicated here by the fact that while the KGM I folk were themselves a settlement living in mud-brick houses,[50] none of the 14-feet deposits of RG I disclosed structural remains, though there were frequent layers of ash representing hearths set up by a semi-nomadic people living in impermanent huts or tents.[51] Finally, there is the dating of RG III and II to go by. The third phase of the former – RG IIIc – is itself prior to the start of the Harappā Culture[52] in 2500 B.C. And, according to Piggott,[53] by commonsense calculation the Balūchistān evidence would show that "RG II must have a fair degree of priority over the Harappā Culture, and its date would therefore be well back in the fourth millennium B.C., perhaps contemporary with Jamdet Nasr". As Jamdet Nasr is dated to *c.* 3000 B.C., with an extension beyond it, RG I may

* Letter from Sankalia, dated 1.11.1962.

47. *The Indus Civilisation* (Cambridge, 1960), p. 10.
48. *The Prehistoric Background of Indian Culture* (Bombay, 1958), p. 27.
49. Piggott, *op. cit.*, p. 121.
50. Gordon, *op. cit.*, p. 26.
51. Piggott, *op. cit.*
52. *Ibid.*, p. 142.
53. *Ibid.*, p. 130.

easily be carried further than even the lowest level of Shah Tepé which Zeuner,[54] after Arne, dates to 3000-2500 B.C.

Zeuner's own indication of the antiquity of RG I may be derived from his remark on RG's pottery decorated with humped bulls, which, in Piggott's survey,[55] comes from the second level. Zeuner[56] writes: "At Rana Ghundai in northern Baluchistan, a chalcolithic site, humped bulls are depicted on pottery which can be correlated with Sialk III or Hissar I, and thus with the Al Ubaid period of Mesopotamia, pushing them well back into the fourth millennium B.C." RG I, therefore, can easily equate with KGM's earliest point – 3500 B.C. – if not even predate it.

Yes, Balūchistān's claim, through RG I as well as KGM, for a very early domestic horse is impressive. No doubt, some students of prehistory are reported* to have challenged this claim like all the other ones. But one thing is worth remembering: Lundholm who in 1949 tried to discredit several claims is not quoted by Zeuner or by anybody else against Rānā Ghundāī which Ross excavated in 1946. Robert H. Dyson,[57] who, like Zeuner, sets much store by Lundholm's estimates, lists all the horse-claims, including that for RG I, and then observes: "Most of these equids are identified as asses or onagers, the taxonomy used being inconsistent. Lundholm (1949), reviewing those remains identified as true horse, *Equus caballus Linn.*, at Anau, Sialk, and Shah Tepé, shows conclusively that they belong to the onager group and not to the true horse." What is to be marked here is not only Lundholm's omission of the equine of RG I but also Dyson's own use of the word "most" rather than "all" when he refers to the identification of the excavated equids as asses or onagers.

54. Zeuner, *op. cit.*, p. 316.
55. Piggott, *op. cit.*, p. 121.
56. Zeuner, *op. cit.*, p. 239.
* Sankalia's letter dated 1.11.1962.
57. "Archaeology and the Domestication of Animals in the Old World", *American Anthropology* (Chicago), Vol. 55, No. 5, Part I, pp. 666-667.

Thus RG I seems to enjoy a privileged position. And if the arguments against the horse-nature of the equines connected with the Middle East are, by our computation, pretty weak, the "horse" of RG I must be considered indisputable.

However, Zeuner[58] strikes here also a critical note: "The earliest horse remains so far reported [from India and Pakistan] come from Rana Ghundai in northern Baluchistan (Ross, 1946). In Level I (Piggott's terminology, 1950), the date of which is regarded as earlier than 3000 B.C., four teeth of the 'domestic horse' have been found together with ass. This identification cannot be accepted as reliable unless it is carefully checked. The ass, being an African animal, cannot be right in this early period. The remains attributed to this species more probably belong to the hemione, which survives in north-west India to the present day. The four teeth are not sufficient to make a definite pronouncement. They may well belong to hemiones, too, and to recognize them as domesticated is, on the experience gained everywhere else, impossible. It appears, therefore, as if only hemiones existed at Rana Ghundai, and that they were hunted."

Two points may be pressed against Zeuner. Although it is possible for the hemione's bones to be mistaken for either the ass's or the horse's, the mistake is likely to be very rare at one and the same site. In the period when all the three might be domesticated, there is no precedent for it provided in Zeuner's book. Even in the pre-domestication period, the hemione at one and the same site has never been erroneously considered as both the ass and the horse. And at Rānā Ghundāī we have an additional fact which differentiates the case of substituting the hemione for the ass from that of substituting the hemione for the horse. The time of RG I is too early, as Zeuner tells us, for an African animal like the ass to be in Balūchistān. So we are on fairly firm ground in "hemionising" the ass at this site. But the horse is not impossible or improbable here at earlier than 3000 B.C. And so the teeth

58. Zeuner, *op. cit.*, p. 332.

which were originally found not to go structurally with the "ass"-finds would appear very much to be of *Equus caballus*, however primitive.

Zeuner himself strikes us as being none too confident about their "hemionisation". For, in his general summary,[59] he not only brings himself to notice what he still dubs "debatable pictorial representations", "including the rider from Susa and the Khafaje cart (giving it the benefit of the doubt), indicating that horse domestication was known" between 3000 and 2500 B.C. He also remarks: "The bones from Rana Ghundai I are dated even earlier, but domestication cannot be proved." This means that the RG teeth may be of a horse, even though an undomesticated one. However, even the reservation here is indirectly offset by Zeuner's very next sentence: "It is possible, and for theoretical reasons probable, that the original domestication of the horse had taken place by this time, and probably in areas north of the Persian mountains, *i.e.* mainly in Turkestan."

So we come full circle. Anau and, with it, Sialk and Shah Tepé once more swim into our ken, although the emphasis falls explicitly on Susa and Khafaje and most on Rānā Ghundāī. And well may this be so; for, Piggott[60] indicates that the evidence of RG I does not lack continuation. He says about a find at a site in the Zhob valley related to RG: "one clay figurine from Periano Ghundai seems to represent a horse, and is interesting in connection with the find of horses' teeth in RG I at the type site." This figurine he assigns to the RG III phase which begins some centuries before 2400 B.C.

There is also the figurine from Kili Gul Mohammad, adjudged by Fairservis to be of a horse. And both the figurines remind us of Zeuner's phrase:[61] "clay figurines usually represent domestic types."

Thus we reach, *via* Zeuner and in spite of all the hurdles he sets up, the same picture as Piggott's statements traced for us.

59. *Ibid.*, p. 337.
60. Piggott, *op. cit.*, p. 126.
61. Zeuner, *op. cit.*, p. 325.

The domesticated horse, the sign *par excellence* of the Aryan, is not only a characteristic of the earliest cultures oi North Balūchistān but also a characteristic almost as early there as anywhere else in the Asiatic world which is its original home. The natural conclusion should be that the Aryan was present in the population of North Balūchistān at Rānā Ghundāī and Kili Gul Mohammad in the same prehistoric period practically as at Anau in Turkestān and at the North-Persian Sialk as well as Shah Tepé.

Only one more question faces us: Does the belt of original horse-taming Aryanism, running through these five sites, extend from RG and KGM into the Indus region where Indian tradition places the Vedic Aryans not as invaders in the post-Harappā epoch but as remote ancients who had no memory of arriving there from outside?

5

The Indus Valley, as we have seen, had the true horse a little after *c.* 1500 B.C. It is thought to belong not to the Indus Civilisation, the Harappā Culture, which ended then and whose beginning was in *c.* 2500 B.C. But, even if the *Equus caballus* from an upper level of Mohenjo-dāro and from Area G at Harappā is really of some other civilisation we should not jump to the conclusion that it was brought from outside India or that the Harappā Culture was unacquainted with the true horse.

A.D. Pusalker[62] speaks of the model of an animal, found in an early stratum of Mohenjo-dāro, which E.J.H. Mackay took as the representation of a horse. Childe[63] tells us that at the same site "model saddles occur": they point to knowledge and use of the horse. Piggott[64] writes of a Harappān site in Sind: "what looks like a little clay model of a pack-saddle has been found at Jhukar in Sind, probably of the Harappā

62. In *The Vedic Age* (London, 1952), p. 194.
63. *New Light on the Most Ancient East*, p. 210.
64. Piggott, *op. cit.*, p. 175.

period." And in the same context he opines that in trade during this period "pack-horses may well have been used".

Again, at Lothal, which is a site of the same civilisation in Saurāshtra and whose commencement is by Carbon-14 tests as early as *c.* 2000 B.C., Sankalia[65] marks in its early phase a terracotta figurine of an equine with a thick short unmistakably horselike tail and the whole head very much like that of *Equus caballus.* In a footnote (96) Sankalia reports that Zeuner suggested to him the onager and that later Zeuner and B. Subbarao specially went to see the onagers in their natural habitat nearby, the Rann of Cutch. Zeuner, in his book,[66] records what he saw, but there is no reference to the Lothal figurine just as there is none to the figurines of Rānā Ghundāī and Kili Gul Mohammad. We may presume that Sankalia's own impression stands uncontroverted.

So the Harappā Culture, not only in the Indus Valley but also elsewhere in India, appears to have used the horse. And, as there is some uncertainty whether the equine bones of an upper Mohenjo-dāro level come from the Indus Valley Civilisation itself or not, we may justifiably refer them to this civilisation in the light of all the signs mentioned above. Further, the horse from Area G, Harappā, may not have been an import into the Indus Valley of an animal foreign to it but a continuation of its fauna.

Even without the signs above-mentioned we should be able to postulate the horse for the Harappā Culture. For, we have many proofs of this culture's contacts with Balūchistān which is its next-door neighbour. According to Piggott,[67] "bitumen, alabaster, and probably steatite seem likely to have been obtained from Baluchistan..." Wheeler,[68] dealing in general with the more than sixty sites that have produced significant elements of the Harappā Culture, refers to those

65. *Indian Archaeology Today* (Bombay, 1962), p. 61 and fn 95; for the Carbon-14 tests, letter dated 21-3-1963.

66. Zeuner, *op. cit.*, pp. 372-373.

67. Piggott, *op. cit.*, p. 174.

68. *The Indus Civilization*, p. 2.

immediately westward of the Indus Valley, *i.e.* in Balūchistān: "To the west, the hills include innumerable cognate village-cultures (earlier, contemporary and later) which on occasion descend also to the plains..." Wheeler[69] mentions too the Harappān outpost of "Sutkāgen-dor, near the coast of the Arabian Sea, 300 miles west of Karachi". All over Balūchistān and beyond it to Makrān the Indus Valley Civilisation travelled in one way or another. Piggott[70] declares: "There is good evidence that trade exchanges did take place, and goods and even people found their way from the Balūchistān hills to the Indus plain." With Rānā Ghundāī itself Piggott[71] traces the Harappā Culture's relationship. Among the types of Harappā pottery, "one is particularly noteworthy, which consists of a platter on a raised foot, usually referred to as an 'Offering-stand'. The appearance of sherds of this type of vessel on a site marks the presence of the Harappā Civilization as surely as 'Samian' pottery betokens Roman occupation in Europe. These offering-stands derive from the pedestalled bowls known, for instance, in the Zhob Valley in the Rana Ghundai II phase..." "The decorated pottery of the Harappā Culture gives one an immediate clue to its likely origins, for it is a black-on-red ware, the designs being painted on a deep red, lustrous slip. This strongly suggests that its connexions lie with the North Baluchistan wares, such as those of the Rana Ghundai III phase at Periano Ghundai and other sites." Even in the matter of the characteristic "stamp-seals" of the Harappā Culture which point to antecedents outside of Balūchistān, the only two specimens found in the latter country belong to areas of RG culture. One is from Dabar Kot, south of Loralai, whose upper layers formed actually a Harappā occupation. The other is probably from Periano Ghundāī.

With all this relationship with Balūchistān as a whole and with RG in particular, we may certainly expect horse-knowl-

69. *Ibid.*
70. Piggott, *op. cit.*, p. 114.
71. *Ibid.*, pp. 192-193, 193, 128, 185.

edge and horse-use to be spread over the Indus-region even before 2500 B.C. And what clinches our expectation is that we can go still further than close neighbourly interchange between RG and the Harappā Culture. We have evidence that the culture of RG was actually established in the Indus-region precedent to the typical Indus Valley Civilisation.

Piggott[72] writes: "...the small amount of material available from the recent (1946) excavations of Harappā shows that the first town on that site overlies a settlement of people using pottery which appears to belong to the North Baluchistan group, in that phase of development seen in the IIIc phase at Rana Ghundai." Gordon,[73] who designates the RG and related pottery as Loralai ware, writes that from – 32 feet at Mohenjo-dāro, which gives almost the earliest period of the city, sherds of polychrome ware were recovered, having a series of ovals with a vertical line down the centre of each, a motif so far found only in the bichrome Loralai III ware at Sur Jungal. So we have in the Indus-region before and during 2500 B.C. a culture which knew the domesticated horse.

The Aryans, typified by this animal, must have been in remote antiquity in the Indus-region. May we not take them to be those whose high-priests composed the *Ṛgvedic* hymns which indicate that region as the early centre of Aryan civilisation? Even the scholars who date the Ṛgveda to *c.* 1500 B.C. admit that it contains no hint of being the composition of immigrants at that time or at any other. And by external means its age, as Pusalker[74] reminds us, "is not known with even an approximate degree of certainty". Consequently, we are free to make it precede the Harappā Culture in North-west India.

This does not mean that the Harappā Culture was a wholly Aryan product. It could be a part derivative and a part deviation – a development of *Ṛgvedism* on the one hand and on the other an assimilation of Balūch and Sumero-Irānian as

72. *Ibid.*, p. 142.
73. Gordon, *op. cit.*, p. 59.
74. Pusalker, *op. cit.*, p. 194.

well as perhaps Central-Asian elements – a manifold composite natural in the region concerned if *Ṛgvedism* proper had moved to the Kuru-Pañchala area east of the land of the seven rivers, *Sapta-Sindhu,* after leaving its mark in this land and even further west in the midst of influences from Irān through Balūchistān and from Mesopotamia through Irān and from Turkestān through the Afghān territory.

To make Aryanism the background and semi-basis of the Harappā Culture does not also call for an eminent presence of the supposed Aryan races in this culture's population. Aryanism is essentially a cultural entity and not a racial one. And even racially it must not be traced to an entirely "Nordic" stock. S.K. Chatterji[75] gives us the information: "The Aryan speakers... are believed to have represented a cultural union of two distinct racial stocks, the tall, blonde, long-headed, straight-nosed Nordics, and the comparatively short and dark and short-headed Alpines..." Now, Wheeler[76] has written about the few skulls from the Indus Valley Civilisation thoroughly analysed and described: "three were defined as Proto-Australoid, six as Mediterranean, one as the Mongolian branch of the Alpine stock, and four probably as Alpine." Hence we cannot rule out even a racial Aryan constituent of this civilisation. Indeed, Pusalker[77] states: "As to the existence of the Aryans in the Indus Valley at so early a period as the age of the Indus culture, it is held by some, on the evidence of skeletal material, that the Aryans formed part of the diverse population of those days."

Even if the recent anthropological survey of all the Harappā skeletons were to diminish the Alpine percentage to almost nothing, the background and semi-basis of the Indus Culture in Aryanism would not be disproved. The movement of the Vedic Aryans towards Kurukshetra away from the

75. In *Interrelations of Cultures* (Unesco, Paris, 1953), p. 170.

76. Wheeler, *op. cit.,* p. 56.

77. Pusalker, *op. cit.,* p. 194. cf. Datta, *Rigvedic Culture of the Prehistoric Indus,* Foreword, p. XXV; N.M. Chaudhuri, "The Pamirian Alpines in the Indus Valley in Chalcolithic Times", *Calcutta Review,* June, 1945.

Punjāb after their early cultural efflorescence would explain their racial exiguity in the Indus-region from *c*. 2500 to *c*. 1500 B.C. After the end of the Harappā Culture there may have been a reflux to the old seat. Perhaps the end, to a considerable extent, was due to such a reflux – a reflux which may have overflowed the Indus-region and its neighbourhoods and constituted the *Maryani* Aryans who ruled the Mitanni people on the Upper Euphrates and one of whose kings – Matiuazza, son of Dusratta – invoked in *c*. 1380 B.C. in his treaty with the Hittites the Vedic gods as witness: Mitrā-Varunā, Indra, Nāsatya.

Such an overflow need not rule out a westward movement of Aryan tribes from Turkestān, North Irān and even South Russia in more or less the same period. It may itself have set off that movement, or that movement may have set it off. And a part of that movement may have been a new influx of Aryans from Turkestān and Irān into Afghānistān, Balūchistān and the Indus-region and further inland.

No doubt, this picture complicates things a good deal in place of the more plain popular account of an Aryan exodus from outside India to various parts of the Middle and Near East and Europe, with one stream pouring into India in *c*. 1500 B.C. But historical truth has nothing to do with simplicity as such. And even the current view is not really as simple as the popular version. It posits two waves of Aryan exodus, one starting round about 2000 B.C. and the other round about 1000 B.C., the latter no less than the former bringing Aryans into India. The function of history is to cover all the available facts and not bother whether the result is simple or complex. Were the fact of the Aryans' characteristic domesticated animal to demand a complication of things, we should not shirk to answer the call.

Only one question here is historically legitimate: If the Aryans were already there in the Indus-region no less than in its neighbourhoods before the Harappā Culture, have we any decisive signs of them other than the domesticated horse?

The question brings in a host of issues that lie outside the range of our paper. One answer, however, may be made in the form of a counter-question: Have we any decisive signs of the Aryan invasion of India in *c.* 1500 B.C., which is reported in all our history books? Wheeler,[78] referring to it as an archaeologist, says: "it is best to admit that no proto-Aryan material has yet been identified in India." Pusalker,[79] looking at the claims of proto-Aryanism staked out for various potteries, sums up: "There is no... positive or conclusive evidence to connect Vedic Aryans with the excavated cultures subsequent to those of the Indus Valley... So far archaeological excavation has yielded nothing of the nature of sacrificial implements or other ritual paraphernalia that can definitely be called Aryan and associated with the Vedic-Aryans..." Do we then require to make much of any lack of decisive Vedic-Aryan traces in still remoter antiquity?

After all, the one point which is always attended to whenever there is talk of the Aryans is whether the evidence includes the domesticated horse. If the evidence excludes it, the Aryans are excluded. It is not perhaps impossible that the domesticated horse may have existed without the Aryans. But the converse is never true, so far as historical knowledge goes. And from the extremely intimate, recurrent and universal association of the Aryans with this animal we may practically assume for the earliest period: No Aryans, no domesticated horse. And, if that is so, the Aryan homeland was a broad territory taking in not only Turkestān, parts of Persia and all North Balūchistān but also North-Western India in the fourth millennium B.C.

Stress may be laid especially on North-Western India because there we may expect the earliest development of horse-chariotry. Balūchistān is too hilly for it. The Indus-region is ideal for it. And, as we learn from Childe that next to Mesopotamia of *c.* 3500 B.C. the oldest known area of wheeled vehicles is the Indus Valley from the beginning of the Harappā Culture in 2500 B.C., we may logically conjecture a

78. *Early India and Pakistan* (Bombay, 1959), p. 126.
79. In *The Cultural Heritage of India* (Calcutta, 1958), Vol. I, p. xlvi.

passage of the art of chariotry from Mesopotamia to the Indus-region, in hitherto unknown ways, through the period 3500-2500 B.C. to make its presence felt, together with that of horses, in the hymns of the *Ṛgveda*.

Our logical conjecture gets a very suggestive support from Harappān stamp seals. About the writing on them Fairservis Jr. remarks:[80] "It appears to be hieroglyphic or ideographic in form. Human, animal and floral figurines are recognizable, multiple dashes probably represent numbers, while such objects as wheels, bows and arrows, and trees very likely represent themselves." Now, if we look at the wheels in the illustrations[81] provided by Fairservis we find them with six spokes. No doubt, the clay-models of cars and chariots recovered have solid wheels. But the stamp seals' testimony is also undeniable. Those models, therefore, are not a full index of vehicular detail. Their wheels are solid not because Harappā never made spokes but because spoked wheels were rarer or simply because solid ones were easier to model.

Spoked wheels, however, are a puzzle in the context of vehicles in the ancient world of 2500 B.C. Except for one debated representation of a chariot on a Tell Halaf painted pot of extreme antiquity, there is no evidence in early Mesopotamia, the inventor of wheeled vehicles, that spoked wheels existed.[82] Although two-wheeled vehicles originated in Sumer, the wheels not only in Early Dynastic times but also in the times of the Royal Tombs of Ur (*c.* 2500 B.C.) were solid.[83] Only in the beginning of the second millennium B.C. did Asia Minor know the use of spoked wheels and the horse-drawn chariot moving upon them.[84] "Such chariots," says Piggott,[85] "also make their first appearance in the Aegean countries, significantly associated with Indo-European speakers soon

80. "The Ancient East", *Natural History* (New York), November 1958, p. 507.
81. *Ibid.*, p. 505.
82. Piggott, *op. cit.*, p. 274.
83. *Ibid.*
84. *Ibid.*
85. *Ibid.*

after this time..." How, then, shall we explain the spoked wheels of the Harappā Culture nearly six centuries before they appeared anywhere else in the world?

They imply a notable development of metal tools. And a couple of pointers to this development have been found. A.L. Basham[86] writes: "In one respect the Harappa people were technically in advance of their contemporaries – they had devised a saw with undulating teeth, which allowed the dust to escape freely from the cut, and much simplified the carpenter's task. From this we may assume that they had particular skill in carpentry." Then there is the twisted copper or bronze drill discovered by S.R. Rao at Lothal. Sankalia[87] records the find and comments: "Its occurrence at so early a date is of great moment in the history of civilization."

The general impression of mediocrity, created by much of the existing work, especially in metal of the Harappā Culture, must be due to self-imposed limitations, a conservatism of mind. As Piggott[88] says: "The dead hand of conservatism in design, rather than in technique, lies heavy on all the Harappā products. Complex technical processes were known, well understood, and admirably organized for production, but the output suffered from standardization and an almost puritanical utilitarianism." The Harappāns' metallurgy was advanced enough to turn out complex works whenever they wanted them.

But how did it reach such a stage? As spoked wheels are not known anywhere outside India at that period, we have to search for some clue to their background in India itself. There is no archaeological clue. The sole possible clue is literary: the *Ṛgveda*. And, if according to the horse-evidence part of the Aryan homeland lay in the Indus-region as well as North Balūchistān in the pre-Harappān age, the *Ṛgvedic* mention of horse-chariots could indicate an explanatory background, provided those chariots moved on spoked wheels. A.A.

86. *The Wonder that was India* (New York, 1954), p. 21.
87. Sankalia, *op. cit.*, p. 61.
88. Piggott, *op. cit.*, p. 200.

Macdonell and A.B. Keith,[89] describing the *Ṛgvedic* chariot, state: "The wheel consisted of a rim (*Pavi*), a felly (*Pradhi*), spokes (*Ara*) and a nave (*Nabhya*)." There are many references to spokes.[90] "Sometimes", say Macdonell and Keith,[91] "a solid wheel was used." This fact links the *Ṛgveda* to the clay-models of the Indus Valley Civilisation, while the spokes account for the wheels on the stamp seals.

The development between 3500 and 2500 B.C. of the craft of chariot-making, which these seals demand but which is underivable from the land of chariot-invention, Mesopotamia, is no longer a mystery. We can legitimately see it reflected in the most ancient mass of Indo-Aryan literature.

6

Now we have a practically complete picture of original Aryandom including not only the characteristic animal, the horse, but also the characteristic chariot drawn by that animal.

The most significant centre of this Aryandom was the Indus-region from about the middle of the fourth millennium B.C., with perhaps an extension into the third. From there it carried on some cultural exchanges with lesser seats of Aryanism in Balūchistān, Irān and Turkestān, before it moved further east and the Indus Valley was left to the growth of the half Vedic and half non-Vedic Harappā Culture.

Judging from the evidence of *Ṛgvedic* Aryandom's outpost in Balūchistān, we may say that as provinces of horse-taming the seats of Aryanism in Turkestān and Irān are a little older than the Indus-region. But the degree of cultural progress displayed by *Ṛgvedic* Aryandom tends to give this region equally ancient antecedents. Part of that progress lies in the manufacture of the spoked wheels of the horse-chariot. And perhaps from the horses themselves of the *Ṛgveda* we may draw a hint of their domestication going beyond the

89. *A Vedic Index of Names and Subjects* (Delhi, 1958), Vol. II, p. 201.
90. *Ṛgveda*, I.32, 15; 141, 9; V.13, 6; 58, 5; VIII.20, 14; 77, 3; X.78, 4.
91. Macdonell & Keith, *op. cit.*, p. 201.

archaeological age denoted by Rānā Ghundāī or Kili Gul Mohammad, the age we have allotted also to the *Ṛgvedic* Aryans of the Indus-region. Zeuner[92] writes: "Ridgeway (1905) derived from the *Ṛgveda* descriptions of these early Aryan horses which suggest that they were chestnut-coloured on the head and back, and dun below. The chestnut colour is not primitive, whilst the lighter belly may be so regarded. Nothing can therefore be said about their provenance." Even if their provenance be uncertain, the non-primitive chestnut colour may afford us a glimpse of long domestication and progressive breeding in the period before *c.* 3500 B.C., so that the antiquity of the horse-taming Aryans of the Indus-region and of Balūchistān may be considered as great as that of their kinsmen in Turkestān and Irān.

92. Zeuner, *op. cit.*, pp. 332-333.

RĀMA, RĀVANA, LANKĀ

LEGITIMATE RECONSTRUCTIONS AND DUBIOUS SPECULATIONS

1

In connection with Vālmīki's epic and Dr. H.D. Sankalia's discussion,[1] which were the subject of a review-article by Angad in the January and February *Mother India* (1976), a few more points may be made. One or two would be in further clarification of Sri Aurobindo's outlook on Rāma's historicity and Avatārhood.

What the reviewer has said so far goes a long way to modify the view taken by Sankalia that Sri Aurobindo totally denies the existence of the Vālmīkian Rāma as a historical person. The correct situation that emerges is simply that Sri Aurobindo is not sure of the particulars of the story Vālmīki tells in the *Rāmāyaṇa* and of the particular "name and form", as it were, of its hero. Sri Aurobindo has no doubt of an Avatār's reality behind it all and of some great event whose central character was that Avatār – call him by any name and see him in any form.

An additional touch may be given to this vision by references to Sri Aurobindo's letters. Sri Aurobindo says that in the scheme of Avatārhood showing the chief evolutionary stages established by successive Divine Incarnations the stage of "the sattwic civilised human being who governs his life by the reason, the finer emotions, morality, or at least moral ideals, such as truth, obedience, co-operation and harmony, the sense of domestic and public order"[2] has to be fixed by someone, and he sees "no one but Rama who can fill the place" of "the Avatar of the sattwic Human".[3] This statement

1. *Rāmāyaṇa: Myth or Reality?* (People's Publishing House, New Delhi, 1973).
2. *Letters on Yoga*, Sri Aurobindo Birth Centenary Library, Pondicherry, 1972, Vol. 22, p. 415.
3. *Ibid.*, p. 417.

invests with a basic actuality the psychological fundamentals and the episodic essentials of the Vālmīki-narration of Rāma's life and work. Even the particular "name and form" acquire a core of historicity.

In another place Sri Aurobindo alludes to the topic of Atlantis and mentions the highly developed but Asuric or Rākshasic (ego-aggrandising) civilisation the Atlantis legend portrays. Then he tells us that in India too such a civilisation has figured in legend as having existed at some point of humanity's career. According to him, Rāvana's Lankā, as depicted by Vālmīki, images the Indian counterpart of Atlantis. This declaration not only indicates, for Sri Aurobindo, a supporting reality behind Vālmīki's picture of Lankā. It also implies, for him, the utter improbability of the locale of Lankā such as Sankalia[4] urges: an isle within a lake or marsh in forests inhabited by crude aborigines near Jabalpur, the home of a Goṇḍ Rāvana on the Chhota Nagpur plateau. The evolutionary transition Sri Aurobindo spotlights as the work of the Avatār of the sattwic Human who is central to the *Rāmāyaṇa* is surely not confined to a passage from the primitive Goṇḍ-psychology to the Aryan mentality? In fact he[5] lists two types of "anarchic forces" to be replaced: "the Animal mind and the powers of the vital Ego making its own satisfaction the rule of life, in other words, the Vanaras and the Rakshasa." Sankalia's Goṇḍs could be Vānaras, but only Rāvana with his luxurious and powerful Lankā beyond the southern sea can exemplify the Titan vitalism from which a movement to a condition of enlightened conscience and inner self-disciplinary Law was effected. Indeed, with an eye to the future, predominantly "it was Rama's business to make the world safe for the ideal of the sattwic human being by destroying the sovereignty of Ravana, the Rakshasa menace."[6]

4. Sankalia, *op. cit.*, pp. 49, 62.
5. *Letters on Yoga*, SABCL Vol. 22, p. 415.
6. *Ibid.*, p. 416.

2

Whether we should choose old Ceylon (present-day Sri Lankā) as the seat of an opulent "Atlantean" culture whose memory lingered in Indian tradition as handed down by Vālmīki is a matter one may debate. But one should seriously pause before accepting the opinion Sankalia[7] voices: "In Ceylon itself the *Rāmāyaṇa* – Rāma's story – is not so popular, though some places are associated with Ashokavana (where Sītā was kept by Rāvana).... Lastly, in Ceylon (or Sri Lankā) itself, there are no monuments which answer to the description of Lankā in Sundarakanda of the *Rāmāyaṇa.*"

Some years back K.V.S. Vas, a close student of affairs Ceylonese, wrote an article, *Buddhism in Ceylon.*[8] In the course of it he tells us:

"Sangham literature of the first, second and third Tamil Sangham periods, corroborated indirectly by internal evidences available in the Pali chronicles themselves, would go to show beyond reasonable doubt that Hinduism and Hindu civilisation were at their peak in Ceylon, centuries before Buddha was born at Kapilavastu and that Ceylon, contrary to what the Mahavamsa and other Pali chronicles would make us believe, was not inhabited by a semi-naked uncivilised tribe but had remained the focal point of a great civilisation which endured the passage of many centuries.

"Rāvana, the epic king of Lankā, who is believed to have ruled over the island some four thousand to five thousand years ago, was a staunch devotee of Koneswara and his father-in-law, Maya, is said to have built the ancient temple at Tiruketeswaram at Mannar district in North Ceylon.... According to tradition, Sri Rāma who is said to have built a Siva temple at Rāmeshwaram, is believed to have worshipped Lord Shiva at Tiruketaswaram on his way back to India from Lankā with his beloved wife Sītā....

7. Sankalia, *op. cit.*, pp. 51-52.
8. *The Hindu*, Madras, May 12, 1957.

"Whether one believes the story of the *Rāmāyaṇa* or not, belief is still there in Ceylon as to the rule of Rāvana in Ceylon and there is a temple to Vibhishana at the ancient town of Kalyani, now called Kelaniya. There are a number of places which are associated with Rāvana....

"Coming to the period of Buddha himself, the Mahavamsa and such other ancient chronicles mention two Naga strongholds in the sixth century B.C., one at Nagadipa ...in North Ceylon and the other at Kalyani... on the West coast of Ceylon near Colombo. Kalyani, reputed to have been the capital of the epic king Rāvana, was the centre of Hindu civilisation in the past.... Of the Naga kingdom of Mani-Palavam which is identified with Nagadipa, a tiny island off Jaffna today, only a very small slice of a once powerful kingdom remained. A large portion of the kingdom should have been submerged almost at the same time as the Western Naga kingdom of Kalyani during the reign of Kelani Tissa in about 250 B.C. The great deluge which the Ceylonese chroniclers mentioned as having occurred during the time of Kelani Tissa wrought irreparable damage to the landscape of Lankā as had done the much earlier one during the reign of Rāvana which engulfed his fortress, 25 palaces and 400,000 streets situated between Mannar and Tuticorin. An idea of the damage done by the deluge to the powerful Naga kingdom may be had from the account given in the *Rajavaliya* which states among other things that the two deluges caused by the wickedness of Rāvana and Kelani Tissa destroyed eleven-twelfths of the island of Lankā and that only one-twelfth of Lankā remained after these two deluges.

"Whatever may be the truth or historical value of these stories, the existence of powerful Naga kingdoms in Ceylon many centuries before Buddhism was introduced, the high state of civilisation of the people of the island in the pre-Buddhist era and the practice of Hinduism before Buddhism was introduced – all these go to show that Ceylon was after all not an uncivilised island, as Sinhalese chroniclers would have us believe, before Mahinda brought the gospel of the Buddha.

These tales also indicate that it was the hand of a cruel fate intervening in the shape of a deluge, petty quarrels, etc., that had destroyed the Naga dynasty and given place to a new race and a new faith."

What is of special interest here is that Vālmīki's Lankā, which represents Sri Aurobindo's Indian "Atlantis", is said to have suffered, like its Western counterpart, a natural disaster which sank its glory under water. A touch of credibility is lent to the legend by the evidence of actual marine destruction occurring even in historic times in Ceylon. The temple at Koneswaram, associated with both Rāvana and Rāma, does lie sunk today below the waves and, as Vas tells us, "the excavations done by the well-known undersea photographer Mr. Mike Wilson and Mr. Aubrey Clarke, the explorer, have shown that the ancient temple is still there under the sea mostly intact."

3

It may not be possible to establish beyond question the identity of Vālmīki's Lankā with Ceylon. But neither can the opposite case be positively proved. One instance of controversy that our reviewer has picked out underlines both the futility and the irrelevance of the type of argument it illustrates. Sankalia[9] points to the *Rāmāyaṇa*'s mention of sala trees being used by the Vānaras against the Rākshasas and observes that "a study of botanical literature showed that the sala – *Shorea robusta* grew in the Chhota Nagpur plateau only and nowhere else". Our reviewer faults this botanical literature by citing the presence of *Shorea robusta* in the Dehra Dun Valley. This must play down the importance Sankalia attaches to items of such sort as constituting geographical indices to the location of Lankā. A further fact quoted by our reviewer from A.D. Pusalker[10] knocks these items clean out of the

9. Sankalia, *op. cit.*, p. 50.

10. "Location of Lanka", *Journal of the Oriental Institute,* Vol. XV, Nos. 3-4, March-June 1966, p. 340.

field. The *Rāmāyaṇa* (III.33.13,21; IV.40.14,18; VI.4.75; 22.55), in its account of the area where Lankā is located, refers to sandalwood trees, coconut trees, etc., which cannot ever be associated with the Chhota Nagpur plateau but strongly suggest the South. Vālmīki, bringing in various botanical features, was letting his imagination run as it liked without any thought of providing scholars with geographical directions.

A passage to which Sankalia himself refers appears to bear out Vālmīki's attitude. He[11] writes: "The sea was filled up [by the Vānaras] with all kinds of trees – sala, asvakarva, tala, tilaka, kutaja, arjuna, bilva, saptavarva, kamikara, asoka (6-15-15-20).... One may ask, 'From where did they bring all these trees?' Some (many) do not grow at all in the vicinity or for that matter in South India!" It is obvious that the jumble of trees suits no locality in particular, whether South India or the Chhota Nagpur plateau, and that the poet's botany has nothing to do with geography.

Rather, we should make a fine point by saying that the "sala"-instance is non-determinative because of *Shorea robusta* occurring a second time in a context in which its possible determinative character is annulled. One context cancels out another. Whenever such a conflict of contexts is there, Vālmīki's botany and geography cease to be related and he is indulging in imaginative creativity more than exercising "the eye upon the object". Botany would be a finger-post to geography only when a survey of the poem yields a clear-cut, univocal, uncontradicted vision.

In pursuance of his anti-Ceylon brief, Sankalia[12] tells us: "Lankā or Lakka is a Mundari [Goṇḍi] word, and so also Rāvana." This bit of ethnographic and linguistic information is said[13] to confirm the location of Lankā in the Chhota Nagpur region. But the source of a word is really neither here nor there in the discussion. The river name "Gangā" has been

11. Sankalia, *loc. cit.*
12. *Ibid.*, p. 7.
13. *Ibid.*, p. 50.

claimed to be in all likelihood a Muṇḍā derivate.[14] Must the Ganges be located exclusively among the habitats of Goṇḍ tribes? At any rate, Ceylon, which is far indeed from Jabalpur, is yet designated "Lankā". And, like "Gangā", it is so much part and parcel of the Sanskritist consciousness that its supposed origin has no meaning left for any conclusion. As far back as we can go in time, we find this fact. Sankalia[15] has himself quoted what seems the earliest available mention of the term. Referring to Tamil Sangham literature which dates to "a period between the first century B.C. and sixth century A.D.", he writes: "...Dr. Vaidyanath, Reader in Dravidian linguistics, Deccan College, kindly informs me that in *Purananaru* occur words like *iraman* (verse 378, line 18) and *ilankai* (verse 378, line 6) which stand for Rāma and Lankā respectively. According to him both these are loan words from Sanskrit in Tamil."

Apropos of this information one may submit that if in 100 B.C.-600 A.D. the name "Lankā" crops up in South-Indian literature it must, in the first place, point to Ceylon and not Chhota Nagpur and, in the second place, show that Ceylon was called Lankā at quite an earlier date than the one which Sankalia[16] inexplicably notes when he says: "The name Lankā is not known earlier than inscriptions of the 10th century A.D." He[17] bases his statement on *The Early History of Ceylon* (1947) by G.C. Mendis; but surely, even apart from the Purananaru, there are the Pali Chronicles, the *Dīpavaṁśa* and *Mahāvaṁśa*, belonging to the 4th and the 6th centuries A.D. respectively, about which B.M. Barua[18] writes: "The Pali Chronicles apply the names Lankā, Sīhala and Tambapaṇṇi to one and the same country and island of Ceylon." Further, with "Lankā" borrowed by southern literature from Sanskrit,

14. *The Vedic Age*, edited by R.C. Majumdar and A.D. Pusalker (London, 1952), p. 154.

15. Sankalia, *op. cit.*, pp. 55, 70.

16. *Ibid.*, p. 51.

17. *Ibid.*, p. 69.

18. *Aśoka and His Inscriptions* (New Age Publishers, Calcutta, 1946), Part I, p. 336.

it is hardly credible that, as Sankalia[19] opines, Ceylon has accepted to be termed "Lankā" because in Austro-Asiatic languages like Goṇḍi the word "means 'an island', 'a high elevated place'". The most likely reason is the identification of the *Rāmāyaṇa*'s Lankā with Ceylon.

4

Sankalia is at pains to rule out South India from the epic. The Critical Edition of the *Rāmāyaṇa* has retained the reading "Godāvari" as genuine,[20] but, as the river Godāvari is south of the Vindhyas which for Sankalia is the utmost southern limit of the stage of the poem's drama, he[21] refers us to "Hiralal and others" who tell us of "a small river Godāvari" which was north of the Vindhyas and which "has now disappeared". And, when in the Kishkindhākāṇḍa this shadowy Godāvari cannot be pressed into service because the Godāvari mentioned there is placed south of the Narmadā which is itself south of the Vindhyas and cannot be equated to any small namesake of a river that has disappeared, Sankalia[22] remarks that "the most remarkable thing" is "the fact that the river Narmadā which flows south of the Vindhyas, almost across the heart of India, is not once mentioned except in the much later interpolated sargas in Kishkindhākāṇḍa, wherein Sugriva gives instructions to the Vānara chiefs how and where to seek Sītā". True, the Narmadā occurs only in this place, but may it not have been unnecessary elsewhere? It may not have been sufficiently southern for Vālmīki's purposes, whereas the Godāvari, if it is not the river of "Hiralal and others", was just right for the required southward orientation. Besides, what proof is there that the sargas to which Sankalia refers are "later" and "interpolated"? One cannot dismiss them for being inconvenient to a certain

19. Sankalia, *op. cit.*, p. 51.
20. Pusalker, *op. cit.*, p. 336.
21. Sankalia, *op. cit.*, p. 48.
22. *Ibid.*

theory. And indeed they are the acme of inconvenience, for they list not only the Narmadā and the Godāvari but also the countries of the Andhras, Puṇḍras, Cholas, Pāṇḍyas, Keralas and the region of the Tāmraparni river – an ensemble painting an undeniable picture of the South.

This ensemble, which is ascribed to a late interpolation, can be easily given its *terminus ad quem*, its latest necessary time limit. For, here is a collocation of countries remarkably resembling the series of southern territories provided by Aśoka's Rock Edict II. The sole difference, as Barua[23] notes, is: "we have the Puṇḍras instead of Aśoka's Pārimdas, and the Keralas in place of Aśoka's Satiyaputras and Keralaputras." The general succession is too obviously the same to allow us to dwell on minor differences. It is as if Aśoka had the *Rāmāyaṇa* at the back of his mind or the *Rāmāyaṇa* echoed Aśoka. The unmistakable correspondence is the sign of related epochs. Aśoka, as presently dated, promulgated his Rock Edicts in *c.* 256 B.C. So the criticised sargas need not be later than the middle of the third century B.C. And, as Aśoka's own declared addition to the empire he inherited is only the province of Kalinga, his string of southern territories was continuing a geographical fact of a fairly earlier time. To that very time the sargas can be attributed.

Perhaps we should speak of "times", and hazard a guess at the earliest period. The immediate collocation of Andhras and Puṇḍras occurs first in the Aitareya Brahmana (VII.18), a very ancient scripture, though there it is followed by a mention of Savaras, Pulindas and Mutibas. What is particularly to be marked is that the Andhra-Puṇḍra pair is put in the Vindhyan jungles, unlike in later books where the country of the Puṇḍras corresponds to Bengal and Bihar. The *Rāmāyaṇa*'s ensemble appears to be a sort of palimpsest, in which more than one age may be traced. But an impression of considerable antiquity is conveyed from its deepest layer. A very old account seems to have been worked upon. And even

23. Barua, *op. cit.*, p. 76.

the latest working could be substantially pre-Aśokan.

To return to our discussion. As against the absence of the Narmadā in one sole place of the poem, we may counter-argue: "If there is nothing more southern than that Vindhya and if Kishkindhā is not to its south, how is it that the Vānara army marching southward from Kishkindhā does not encounter the Vindhya and how is it that Rāma returning from Lankā to Ayodhyā does not see the Vindhya before passing over Kishkindhā? The Vindhya is absent from both the accounts (VI.4, 70-71, 92-94 and VI.123) bearing on the region to the south of Kishkindhā."

These two accounts, let us stress, are not in the suspect Kishkindhākāṇḍa. They are in Book VI, the Yuddhakāṇḍa. And in Book V, the Sundarakāṇḍa (63.8-10), we are explicitly told: "Lankā is situated on the southern bank of the southern ocean." Book III, the Aranyakāṇḍa (47.10 and 46.25), makes Rāvana speak of Lankā: "Beyond the ocean stands my beautiful capital Lankā" – "That great city in the midst of the ocean, Lankā."

A general indication southward and therefore on the way to a southern Lankā is met with also in the Aranyakāṇḍa (11.51). The topic now is the hermitage of the Rishi Agastya. There is an old tradition that Agastya led the first colony of Aryans into the Podiyal Hills. Scholars of Sankalia's school discredit it, but in this kāṇḍa Rāma, mentioning to Lakshmana the route to Agastya's hermitage, says:

> Pippalīnām cha pakvānām vanādasmādupāgataḥ.
> Gandho'yam pavanotkṣiptaḥ sahasā katukodayaḥ.

This is to be translated: "The smell wafted by the winds from the pippali forests bearing ripened fruits is very pungent." The reference to the pippali forests is suggestive, for it is in Malabar that these forests of pepper stand. If one has to pass by, or in sight of, them in order to reach the hermitage of Agastya, one has surely to travel to South India? And we may note that, unlike sala-trees which relate to vegetation in

Central India, pippali trees are nowhere in the poem jumbled with any vegetation sweeping us away from the geographical direction in which they seem here to point – namely, southward.

We have no particular precision here in placing the hermitage, but the general indication is definitive in support of its southern location. The Kishkindhākāṇḍa, in one (41) of the allegedly interpolated sargas, bears out the old tradition of the Podiyal Hills by locating Agastya on the top of Malaya near the river Tāmraparni. Hence that kāṇḍa itself gets supported once more by a passage against which no charge of interpolation can be levelled. In any case, we may safely assert that the *Rāmāyaṇa* directs us southward and does not stop short with Central India for its Lankā.*

Even if all the allusions in the epic to South India occurred nowhere except in the Kishkindhākāṇḍa, our judgment on this part of the poem would depend on a certain decision of ours: we have first to make up our minds on what would qualify as interpolation. Did Vālmīki intend Lankā to be far to the south of the Vindhya or not? Sankalia claims that the original *Rāmāyaṇa* was concerned only with a Goṇḍ Rāvana from the Chhota Nagpur plateau abducting Sītā and being attacked and defeated by Rāma and that Vālmīki turned this nucleus into a heroic poem – that is to say, the poem which has grandiose descriptions of Lankā and embodies other great flights of imagination. In other words, Vālmīki's *Rāmāyaṇa* takes us far south of the Vindhya down to the southern sea and beyond it to Lankā. In that case many of the so-called interpolations are Vālmīki's and several are by other hands after him and all of them are introduced into a modest poetic work before his time, consisting of ballads. To the eyes of readers like Sankalia, there are clear signs of that work in Vālmīki's *Rāmāyaṇa* and in subsequent inflations. But here arises a most crucial literary point.

* The line of argument followed in this paragraph and in part of the preceding is based on pp. 69-70 of the remarkable book on linguistics, *Dravidian Theories* by R. Swaminatha Aiyar (The Madras Law Journal Office, 1975).

If Vālmīki was the great poet and consummate artist he is universally held to be, it is unthinkable that he should leave clear signs of a Goṇḍ Rāvana from Central India within the Rākshasa Rāvana who is king of magnificent Lankā and the gigantic villain of the epic story whose godlike hero is Rāma – a story full of "adventure and daring" as well as of "high ethical and philosophical principles", as Sankalia[24] says. Vālmīki would certainly have removed such contradictions of his theme if they had ever existed. He may have enlarged and extra-supernaturalised a theme originally treated on a less splendid and less multi-significant scale. But he could never have allowed traces of an altogether different motif and treatment. Whatever signs such as Sankalia banks on must be gaucheries injected later in the course of the inflation the *Rāmāyaṇa* underwent in lesser hands through the centuries. The original or *Ur Rāmāyaṇa* must have been Vālmīkian and conjured up a southern "Atlantean" island of Lankā whose remnant is most probably modern Ceylon.

The actual interpolations are, on the one side, those passages that blow up beyond the rich yet inevitable poetic word the lofty natural-*cum*-supernatural conceptions of Vālmīki and, on the other side, the passages that go against these conceptions and reduce the theme to restricted issues and terms of mundane probability and suggest an episode about which Sankalia[25] can say: "There is nothing unnatural about it – either the persons or the places."

To get hold of the true nucleus of Vālmīki's story we must not resort to the image of a quite human king of a moderate dominion fighting and killing an aboriginal woman-stealer in a primitive marshland, all within a small area between Ayodhyā and the Vindhya mountains. We must create the vision of extraordinary embodiments of divine and diabolical forces pitted against each other and ranging across the whole subcontinent which represented for them the wide earth at a critical psychological stage of human development. We have

24. Sankalia, *op. cit.*, p. 62.
25. *Ibid.*, p. 63.

to distinguish between the supernatural agencies behind and the natural instruments in front, but we must not cut down the grand size of those instruments, the size without which they would not be the instruments of such agencies. Neither must we limit too severely the scale of their activities and the measure of their organised life-expression, nor, again, deny totally the occasional influx of supernature into nature in a period of the remote past when man's consciousness was not as outwardly faced and fixed as now. Rāvana's ten necks and twenty arms (III.30.8) we should consider symbolic of the transmundane Titanic vitalism he incarnated, but we must not underestimate the power of the two human hands which he used for his visible action: at the back of them we must keep our sense of those numerous necks and heads and arms. It is to help us do so and yet focus our attention on the visibly human that Vālmīki has lines (III.50.12-13) enabling Sankalia to say: "Though he has 20 arms he fought with two hands only." The visibly human is even more frankly expressed by saying that Rāvana "had only two ears and one head" (V.20. 27). This proves that Vālmīki conceived Rāvana as a man among men, however endowed he might be with more-than-human strength and power: it does not prove that the Rākshasa Rāvana is wholly a myth foisted by Vālmīki on a Goṇḍ original. To be able to extricate a human Rāvana from the heroic poem is not to identify him as an aboriginal tribesman: it is simply to realise that Vālmīki knew and recognised the human exterior to the Rākshasic actuality within.

5

As regards the chronology of the *Rāmāyaṇa,* there are two issues involved. The first is the date of the events reported as if historical. The second is the date of the *Ur* version, which for us is Vālmīki's epic poem. In Sankalia's view,[26] we have no certainty for the first issue: "If we place any reliance on the

26. *Rāmāyaṇa: Myth or Reality?*, p. 61.

dynastic history as reconstructed from the Purāṇas by Pargiter and Pusalker or from the co-ordination of the Vedic and Purāṇic data by Pradhan, Bhargava and others, then the foundation of Ayodhyā and other sites in U.P. and Bihar might be placed around *c.* 1700 B.C. and the birth of Rāma in the Ikshvāku dynasty about 1500 B.C. But this is pure speculation. Unless Ayodhyā is excavated and a reliable time-table obtained it is not profitable to say anything about its antiquity."

On the *Ur Rāmāyaṇa,* which for Sankalia is a group of ballads anterior to Vālmīki's time, his upper limit is marked by the reference to "ayasa" in the poem. Sankalia[27] declares: "...ayasa in the *Rāmāyaṇa* definitely means iron and not copper. Otherwise we would not have been told in the Ayodhyākāṇḍa, after the scene when Kaikeyi insisted on Sītā's donning *valkala* and *cīra* and removing her silk sari, that someone said the heart of Rāma's mother seemed to be made of iron. For iron *(ayasa)* here like stone is hard, and not soft like copper." With "ayasa" understood as iron, Sankalia's chronology is easily fixed: "...in our present knowledge, it is not possible to date the first introduction of iron in Northern India, and particularly in Uttar Pradesh and Bihar, before 800 B.C. This might be the time when the *Rāmāyaṇa* was first composed."

We are afraid the conclusions in both issues are intrinsically shaky. If we go by the Purāṇic chronology we shoot far beyond 1500 B.C. for Rāma. For the central date there is of the alleged Kaliyuga: 3102 B.C. This date marks the death of Kṛṣṇa, the abdication of Yudhiṣṭhira and the coronation of his nephew Parikshit. We are at the tail-end of the age of the Bharata War. Rāma should be centuries earlier. We may not credit the Purāṇic computation, but we have to keep a fair distance between the Bharata War and the events of the *Rāmāyaṇa.* Pusalker,[28] trying to co-ordinate Purāṇic data with

27. Sankalia, *op. cit.,* pp. 60-61.

28. *The Vedic Age,* edited by R.C. Majumdar and A.D. Pusalker (London, 1951), p. 269.

modern historical affirmation, dates the Bharata War to *c.* 1400 B.C.

One of the intervals the Purāṇas put between the birth of Parikshit during the War and the coronation of Mahapadma Nanda is 1015 years. Adjudging it reasonable and working back from F.E. Pargiter's 382 B.C. for Nanda, Pusalker reaches 1397 B.C. for the War. Nanda, in R.K. Mookerji's more modern historical scheme,[29] comes at 364 B.C. So the War would occur in 1379 B.C. There is not much of a difference. And Rāma, receding into still remoter antiquity, would have his return to Ayodhyā more or less where Pusalker[30] sets it: 1950 B.C., that is, 571 years earlier. If we favour the longer instead of the shortest interval the Purāṇas permit, this event would stand at (364+1500+571=) 2435 B.C.

Coming to "ayasa", we may point out that copper is not the sole alternative to iron. The word is as old as the *Ṛgveda* and, as we may gather from *The Vedic Index of Names and Subjects* by A.A. Macdonnel and A.B. Keith,[31] the most likely sense there seems to be "bronze". We may note that the Latin counterpart of the word – namely, ạes – always connotes "bronze" and that the typical quality of bronze comes out in Horace's famous line about his own poetry: "Exegi monumentum aere perennius" – "I have built a monument more durable than bronze." The same sense strikes us in Sri Aurobindo's phrase[32] about King Aswapati:

> He made great dreams a mould for coming things
> And cast his deeds like bronze to front the years.

Bronze is a strong hard metal and would fit excellently the *Rāmāyaṇa*'s statement on Kaikeyi's heart. Hence the *Ur Rāmāyaṇa* could easily be much earlier than 800 B.C. Tradi-

29. *The Age of Imperial Unity*, edited by R.C. Majumdar and A.D. Pusalker (Bharatiya Vidya Bhavan, Bombay, 1952), p. 37.

30. Pusalker, *op. cit.*, p. 294.

31. John Murray and Co., London, 1912, Vol. I, pp. 31-32.

32. *Savitri: A Legend and a Symbol* (Cent. Ed., 1970), p. 45.

tional history[33] makes Vālmīki, who was called Prachetasa, a contemporary of Rāma and therefore his poem as old as 1950 or 2435 B.C.

There are some other chronological clues, submitted by Sankalia, to several later ages for various parts of the epic. In the passage we have just dealt with, as in a number of places elsewhere, Sītā's "silk sari" is mentioned. Sankalia[34] informs us that Chinese silk was introduced into India in the period from the 1st century B.C. to the first century A.D. If Kauṭilya's *Arthaśāstra* could be dated to *c.* 324-300 B.C. and if the *sūtra* referring to silk *(Chinapatta)* and to China *(Chinabhumi)* is not a later interpolation, Sītā's silk sari can be as early as that time. But surely archaeology has something more to say? On May 12, 1966, in answer to a query of mine, Sankalia was good enough to write to me about his finds at Nevasa, District Ahmednagar: "Silk was found in a copper necklace along with one string of cotton. C-14 for this is about 1100 B.C. This has been confirmed by Shri A. Gulati, an expert on the subject. But he thinks that the silk may not be of Chinese origin." In an article, "The Dawn of Civilisation in Maharashtra", in the *Sunday Standard,* Madras (January 4, 1976, p. 7, col. 3), Sankalia refers to the same silk of Nevasa. There it is said to be "as early as 1200 B.C.".

Sankalia makes much also of the ring Rāma gave to Hanumāna for Sītā. The ring is said to have been inscribed with Rāma's name. Sankalia[35] writes: "...an archaeologist would inquire: how did Hanumān acquire a ring bearing the letters 'Rāma'? For as far as we know, all the earlier rings in India, from about 2500 B.C. to the first century B.C., are all simple round wires of copper, bronze, or terracotta (those of gold seem to have disappeared). No ring, except the one from Harappā, has a bezel, i.e. a flat broad space on which the name can be inscribed. So all these early rings are without any name. Signet-rings, i.e. rings bearing the wearer's name,

33. *The Vedic Age*, p. 293.
34. Sankalia, *op. cit.*, pp. 57, 70-71 (note 31).
35. *Ibid.*, p. 56.

usually of a king, were first introduced by the Indo-Greeks who ruled in North-Western India, at times up to Kausambi, in the latter part of the second century and early part of the first century B.C. This being the origin of the signet finger-ring in India, its use in the *Rāmāyaṇa* and even Shakuntalā by Vālmīki and Kālidāsa respectively should be normally a century or two later."

Our immediate retort could be: "Rāma's ring, being of a royal personage, was surely of gold. If all gold rings have disappeared, how can we assert that they had no bezels?" Royal signet-rings were common to early civilisations. For instance, signet-rings of Queen Hatshepsut and King Tuthmosis III of Egypt, both of whom flourished in *c.* 1500-1450 B.C., were found in the tombs excavated at Jericho by J. Garstang.[36] The absence of such rings in our discoveries of early Indian remains may not really constitute negative evidence. All we can truly infer is that bezels were not in general vogue in much of early India. However, from Sankalia's own information a retort on a more positive level can arise: "If a bezelled ring, providing space for lettering, is as old in India as *c.* 2500 B.C., why should we wait till the Indo-Greeks of *c.* 150-50 B.C. for a reference to a signet-ring in the *Rāmāyaṇa*?" Nor is the suggestion here of the time of the Harappā Culture the only one in the *Rāmāyaṇa*. Sankalia,[37] basing himself on the poem's text, tells us about Lankā: "Inside, the city *(puri)* was divided like a chessboard by roads *(suvibhaktam patha)*..." Now, in his masterly survey, *The Prehistory and Protohistory of India and Pakistan,*[38] he lists among "the typical Harappān features" "a city... laid like a chess-board, with arterial roads and lanes..." The chessboard pattern of city-planning was neglected in India after the end of the Harappā Culture. It is thought-provoking that Lankā should have been endowed with it by Vālmīki. And it is

36. *The Story of Jericho* (London, 1940), pp. 113-25.

37. Sankalia, *op. cit.*, p. 5.

38. Deccan College Postgraduate and Research Institute, Poona, 1974, p. 347, col. 2.

curious that, like this pattern, the pattern of the bezelled ring – so far at least as common usage was concerned – was also neglected in India between *c.* 1500 (the end of the Harappā Culture, by Sankalia's own estimate[39]) and the advent of the Indo-Greeks in the latter part of the second century B.C. Thus both Rāvana and Rāma appear to have, in different ways, a typical touch of the Harappān epoch.

It is tempting to put the *Ur Rāmāyaṇa* in the period 2500-1500 B.C. – just the period suggested by the Purāṇic tradition co-ordinated with the modern dating of Mahapadma Nanda. We may also remember Vas's word which we quoted earlier:[40] "Rāvana, the epic king of Lankā who is believed to have ruled over the island some four thousand to five thousand years ago..." They carry us to the earlier of the two dates we have reached by counting backwards from Nanda's coronation: 2435 B.C.

At any rate we should be justified in suspending assent to the sundry chronological inferences Sankalia draws from topics in the poem. The problem of chronology, in both its aspects, is a rather complicated one. And, from what we have before us, it is not possible to refuse considerable antiquity to the poem's events as well as to its composition. We should also refrain from doubting, with an eye focused on the idea of a petty fight in a forest near Jabalpur, the general and fundamental historicity at the base of the vast vision Vālmīki poetises of a momentous confrontation between great imperial embodiments of the godlike and the demonic, with a *grand finale* of war in ancient Ceylon.

Postscript

According to Sankalia, Rāma's status as an avatār is rather late in India. He[41] says that, "though Vishnu worship became popular under the Early Guptas (*c.* A.D. 350), as yet Rāma was

39. *Ibid.*, p. 280, col. 2.
40. *Mother India*, March 1976, p. 196.
41. Sankalia, *op. cit.*, p. 53.

not worshipped as a god or as Vishnu." He[42] adds: "The early Cholas, the successors of the Pallavas, do not yet seem to have taken to Rāma worship, but it was not far now... Rāma worship is of a considerably late date and in South India not earlier than the 10th century A.D."

Here we may bring to notice a very knowledgeable article by V.R. Mani, "Deification of Rama", in *The Hindu* of March 13, 1966 (p. III of Magazine Section, cols. 1 and 2). After stating the current stand, Mani writes:

"A careful examination of the available evidence, literary and archaeological, would, however, demonstrate that the divinity of Rama was recognised as early as the early centuries of the Christian era and that there was a well-developed cult centering round him.

"Kalidasa's mention of Rama as Hari *(Ramabhidano Hari)* in the *Raghuvaṁśa* and the narration [Canto XI] in the same work of the promise of Vishnu to be born as a son of Dasaratha for the destruction of Ravana clearly indicate that during the Gupta period Rama was conceived of as a god. The *Ahananuru* and *Purananuru*, the ancient Tamil Sangham classics, make reference to Rama but it is in the *Silappadikaram* [before 7th century A.D.] that we come across an explicit mention of his avatarhood; it is said in this work that the feet that measured the universe in the Vamanavatara walked in forests in the Ramavatara indicating the contemporary recognition of Rama as an incarnation and a god. Many an early Alvar and Nayanmar, Vaishnava and Saiva devotional hymnists, refers in their compositions to several incidents in the life of Rama while Kulasekharalvar has rendered the Ramayana in twenty verses.

"An inscription in the Adivaraha cave temple at Mahabalipuram, incised in florid Pallava Grantha characters and hence assignable to the seventh-eighth centuries, enumerates in order all the incarnations including that of Rama.

"The decline of the Pallavas and the rise of the Cholas in

42. *Ibid.*, p. 54.

the latter half of the ninth century appear to have synchronised with a new impetus given to the worship ot Rama in the Tamil country. For it is during this period that we come across numerous epigraphical references testifying to the popularity and extent of the Rama cult. An inscription from Pulalur in the Chingleput District, dated in the thirty-fourth year of Chola Parantaka, refers to a shrine of Sri Raghava in the temple of Tiruvayoddhi at Pulvelur in Eyirkottam.

"An early Rajakesari inscription from Alangudi in the Thanjavur District records the gift of land for offerings to Raghavaperumal at Irumbulai in Simhavishnu Chaturvedemangalam. A Parakesari record from Uttiramerur in the Chingleput District speaks of a gift of land to Tiruvayodhyai Perumandagal, evidently Rama. An inscription of Rajaraja I, from Ammangudi in the Thanjavur District, refers to the reconstruction (indicating thereby that the temple was anterior to the period of that king) of a shrine under the name Tiruvayoddhi to Ramadevapperumal and consecration of the image of the deity therein besides an endowment of land for offerings, worship and lamps to the god. A very early epigraph of the Pandya ruler Maranjadaiyan Varaguna II mentions a gift to Raghavapperumandadigal.

"The picture presented by these copious epigraphical references is supplemented and corroborated by the happily extant metal images of Rama assignable to different phases of the early Chola period. The idols under worship in the temples at Paruthiyur and Tirucherai, both in the Thanjavur District, and the image from Vadakkuppanaoyur in the same district which is at present on display in the National Art Gallery, Madras, are the most remarkable examples of the deity rendered in metal...."

No doubt, we observe, as Mani is not hesitant to admit, "the absence of any reference to Rama in Patanjali's *Mahabhashya*, in the lexicon of Amarasimha in his scheme of gods and in several early inscriptions which speak of other incarnations." These *lacunae* are strange, but the evidence Mani has marshalled is enough to counteract the hasty inference that there was no Rāmāite sect in early times.

The allusion which Mani has cited from Kālidāsa has a point beyond the one he has in mind. Kālidāsa is mostly taken to have flourished under the third of the Imperial Guptas, Chandragupta II, usually dated to 375-414 A.D. But a persistent tradition places him in the 1st century B.C. in the reign of a king named Vikramāditya, by whom or in whose honour the Vikrama Era of 57 B.C. was founded. One of our best historians, R.C. Majumdar,[43] withholds final judgment. He says that the only thing certain is that Kālidāsa "must have flourished after Agnimitra (*c.* 150 B.C.), who is the hero of one of his dramas", and most probably before 450 A.D. since "competent scholars" hold that "some verses in the Mandasor inscription of A.D. 475 indicate knowledge of Kalidasa's works". About the usual dating of Kālidāsa, namely, "the end of the fourth century A.D.", Majumdar states: "we must admit that the evidence adduced in support of it is neither definite, nor direct and decisive." So the Rāma cult could easily be much more ancient than even Mani claims.

To the question why we do not hear of it in contexts like Patañjali and Amarasimha, we may oppose the query: "Although Megasthenes, the Greek ambassador to the Indian king 'Sandrocottus' who has been taken as Aśoka's grandfather Chandragupta Maurya, attests to a wide-spread cult of Vasudeva Kṛṣṇa, why does Aśoka breathe no word about it in his numerous inscriptions where he mentions several religious practices and denominations?" There are always certain anomalies in the mention and non-mention of things. We have to take all relevant items in a totality and then come to a conclusion.

The sanest conclusion here is that the worship of Rāma is fairly old, as the idea of Rāma's avatārhood is as old as Vālmīki's *Rāmāyaṇa*. But perhaps the cult was for a long time more private than public. Also we must realise that the

43. In the section on Kālidāsa in *The Classical Age*, edited by R.C. Majumdar and A.D. Pusalker (Bharatiya Vidya Bhavan, Bombay, 1954), p. 303.

common chronological hunt is in regard to Rāma as one of Vishnu's incarnations; but D.C. Sircar[44] rightly asks us to remember "in connection with the *Avatāra* a theory that the deification and worship of the incarnations are earlier than their identifications with Vishnu".

44. In the section on Vaishnavism in the same book, p. 415.

THE SEARCH FOR SOMA

A BOOK-REVIEW WITH COMMENTS ON ITS THEME

The Fortifying Fungus[1]

R. Gordon Wasson: *Soma, the Divine Mushroom of Immortality*, 381 pp. New York: Harcourt Brace and World. $200.00.

The price is sensational, the production – print, paper, and the stunning colour plates alike – impeccable. And the variety of the ground covered daunting. The subject? The fly-agaric (what the Germans call the *Fliegenpilz*), that lovely but somewhat sinister fungus which enlivens the woods of northern Europe in autumn and for which the British have no familiar name. The novelty of the book is that it identifies the Soma of the Vedic hymns with this beautiful but toxic mushroom.

The identity of the plant Soma has baffled all students of the subject from the earliest post-Vedic literature until today. The problem is this: the Vedic Indians and the pre-Zoroastrian Iranians worshipped a plant called *soma* (Avestan *Haoma*) which was at the same time a god. It was intoxicating, gave strength in battle as well as widening of consciousness. It was golden-red in appearance, grew on high mountains, its stalks were crushed to extract the intoxicating juice, but there is no reference to roots or leaves, blossom or seed. What is extraordinary, however, is that in both India and Iran the identity of the plant was very soon forgotten, and substitutes had to be used in its place; the earliest substitutes seem to have been creepers of one sort or another, grasses maybe, but never a mushroom. The efforts of scholars, both ancient and modern, to identify the plant have been meticulously catalogued by Dr. Wendy O'Flaherty in Part Two of *Soma, the Divine Mushroom of Immortality*.

Among the moderns the favourite has been the swallow-

1. With grateful acknowledgments to *The Times Literary Supplement*, 22.5.1969, p. 562, cols. 3-5.

wort (*sarcostemma brevistigma*) but there are plenty of other suggestions more or less plausible. Hitherto no one has thought of a mushroom except Aldous Huxley, whose experience under mescalin caused him to muse not so much on peyote, a cactus, the active principle of which is mescalin, as on hallucinogenous mushrooms in use in Mexico. This idea has now been taken up with enthusiasm by Mr. Wasson, a retired banker and a mycologist.

Soma, he thinks, was a mushroom, and not only a mushroom but the fly-agaric. This amiable fungus, he thinks, was consumed by the Vedic (and Iranian) priesthood both (as the Veda explicitly says) in the form of juice pressed out of the stalks and in the form of urine issuing from the Soma-intoxicated hierophant. His argument on behalf of the latter mode of ingestion has a certain cogency, although the evidence is rather thin, though he seeks to substantiate it from all Asia and beyond and from every period of history. In so doing he has invariably consulted the best experts available to him in the enormous field he covers. Thus, he investigates in great detail the Chinese *ling chi*, the "divine mushroom of immortality", and he submits that this is an alliterative reflection of the Indian Soma, maybe.

He further maintains that the Manichees, whose mycophilia was scorned by the great Augustine and indeed seems to have been excessive, inherited this taste from their Iranian religious forbears and their cult of Haoma. If so, it is strange that the Iranian Zoroastrians, who continued the Haoma cult, had long since forgotten what the Haoma plant was. And this indeed is the main argument against the mushroom theory: if Soma-Haoma was the fly-agaric, and if in the course of the Indo-Iranian migration from the north to hotter climes it had become at first difficult and then impossible to find, why were the substitutes themselves never mushrooms but always creepers of one sort or another?

Mr. Wasson's mushroom thesis rests on two pillars: the fly-agaric corresponds more nearly to the descriptions of Soma-Haoma in the Veda and Avesta than does any other plant so far suggested, and, until the Russian authorities clamped down on them, certain Siberian tribes used to use fly-agaric as a religious intoxicant. Did not the Indo-Iranians in their southern migration do the same? The implausibility of this has already been pointed out. There are, however, further difficulties; for it is generally known that the fly-agaric has a most unpleasant taste and causes vomiting, while it is only pleasantly intoxicating if it is first dried and then rehydrated. There is no evidence that the early Indo-Iranians did this. Intriguing though the hypothesis is, it still leaves the identity of the Soma plant wide open.

However, *Soma, the Divine Mushroom of Immortality* is a joy to look at, a pleasure to read, and a mine of curious information not always relevant to the subject at hand. Few people, for instance, know that reindeer have a passion for both the fly-agaric and human urine, whereas the gluttony of the Manichees for this mushroom had hitherto been overlooked. Interesting too is Mr. Wasson's separation of the human race into mycophils and mycophobes. Among the latter the Anglo-Saxons are far in the lead, as the paucity of their mycological vocabulary all too plainly shows.

It was, however, a brilliant hunch to seek the solution of the Soma problem among the mushrooms. But must it be the fly-agaric? The stock epithet of Soma in the Rig-Veda is *hari*, and this appears originally to have meant "reddish-brown verging on yellow" or "golden" (Compare Persian *zarr*, "gold", with its Avestan and other cognates): it is for instance used for foxes in the Ṛgveda as well as for the sun. In Sanskrit the cognate *harita* later comes to mean "yellow" or "yellowish green", whereas in Persian its correlative *zar-d* settles down firmly in the sense of "yellow". The fly-agaric, on the other hand, is, before it starts to decay, brilliantly red; and if this was indeed Soma, it is a little difficult to see how it could later have been firmly identified with the moon.

Would Mr. Wasson be prepared to consider some other fungus? To throw out a casual suggestion, could it not be the girolle chanterelle which, when young, has the colour and shape of the moon and, when past its prime, is reddish-brown, rather the colour of the fox? In this connexion, it is perhaps worth noting that the Czechs call the girolle *liska*, the ordinary meaning of which is "fox". Can the juice of this mushroom, if suitably treated, produce intoxication of any kind? Probably not, but perhaps Mr. Wasson might consider casting his net wider in his fascinating fungoid world.

Comment

It is legitimate for scholars to seek the identity of the marvellous Soma of the *Ṛgveda*. Their efforts claim justification from the fact that an actual plant was used in rituals of the times succeeding those of the ancient scripture which had made Soma famous. But, as the reviewer of Mr. Wasson's book clearly tells us, the plant in question was acknowledged to be a substitute. The fundamental fact, as pointed out by the reviewer, is: nobody could tell, even in antiquity, what plant the original Soma had been. Surely, therefore, it is legitimate for one to counter the scholars by asking: "Was the *Ṛgvedic* Soma ever a plant at all?"

This question is supported by the reviewer's words: "...the Vedic Indians and the pre-Zoroastrian Iranians worshipped a plant called *soma* (Avestan *Haoma*) which was at the same time a god." There is also the information to be derived from the reviewer that even in later times Soma was more than a mere plant; it was "firmly identified with the moon". A sense of the deific, the numinous, in the "high-lights", so to speak, of Nature is evident here, taking us beyond a mere earth-plant and indicating much more than the reviewer's inference that the original plant must have had not only the colour but also the shape of the moon. An esoteric tradition seems to have persisted from the *Ṛgvedic* time into a later period, a lingering remembrance of the usages natural to an age of spiritual symbolism. The Sun and the Moon are obvious symbols of Divine Knowledge and Divine Delight. Identification of the God Soma with the moon argues for more than a plant's colour and shape – more even than for the urge of Nature-worship. It harks back to the psychology of the cult of "Mysteries" – the ancient mind's resort to a set of symbols which, to the adept, signified realities and realisations of the inner mystical or Yogic life while to the commoner it stood for external objects and forces and a religious ritual, a sacrifice at which professional priests officiated.

The unearthliness of the *Ṛgveda*'s Soma is hinted even by the account of it as if it were a plant of the earth. The reviewer writes: "It was golden-red in appearance, grew on high mountains, its stalks were crushed to extract the intoxicating juice, but there is no reference to roots or leaves, blossom or seed." The lack noted in the last two phrases is puzzling indeed for an earthly plant. The growing on high mountains is extremely suggestive too – and when we find, in *Ṛgveda* X. 34.1, Soma described as coming especially from the mountain named Mujavant the suggestion acquires extra concreteness, for no mountain of that name has ever been identified. Zimmer[2] tried to equate it with one of the lower hills on the south-west of Kashmir, but, as Hildebrandt[3] has asserted, the equation lacks evidence. We can conjecture a connection with a people designated as Mujavants in the Atharvaveda (V.22) and the Yajurveda Samhitas (*e.g.* Taittiriya Samhita, 1.8.6.2) and considered as dwelling far away and typifying distant folk. Such a connection can only convey a vague remoteness for the provenance of Soma, agreeing with the total blur in the minds of both the Indians and the Irānians about the identity of the scriptural plant.

What clinches the unearthliness of Soma is the manner in which the supposed "sieve" purifying it, *pavitra,* as the *Ṛgveda* (*e.g.* I.28.9) terms it – is spoken of. We have to take into account two points about it.

First, its "material". No doubt, it is said to be made of a ram's or sheep's wool (IX.75.4). But we have to weigh Sri

2. *Altindisches Leben,* 29.
3. *Vedische Mythologie,* I, 65.

Aurobindo's gloss:[4] "The strainer in which the Soma is purified is made of the fleece of the ewe. Indra is the Ram [I.10.2; 51.1; 52.1; VIII.2.40; 87.12]; the Ewe must therefore be an energy of Indra, probably the divinised sense-mind, *indriyam*." Such a psycho-spiritual view is natural if we look at what the Aitareya Upanishad has to say. To quote Sri Aurobindo[5] again: "In the Aitareya Upanishad Soma, as the lunar deity, is born from the sense-mind in the universal Purusha and, when man is produced, expresses himself again as sense-mentality in the human being. For delight is the *raison d'être* of sensation, or, we may say, sensation is an attempt to translate the secret delight of existence into the terms of physical consciousness. But in that consciousness, – often figured as *adri*, the hill, stone, or dense substance, – divine light and divine delight are both of them concealed and confined, and have to be released or extracted. Ananda [the divine principle of Bliss] is retained as *rasa*, the sap, the essence, in sense-objects and sense-experiences, in the plants and growths of the earth-nature, and among these growths the mystic Soma-plant symbolises that element behind all sense-activities and their enjoyments which yields the divine essence. It has to be distilled and, once distilled, purified and intensified until it has grown luminous, full of radiance, full of swiftness, full of energy, *gomat, āṣu, yuvāku*. It becomes the chief food of the gods who, called to the Soma-oblation, take their share of the enjoyment and in the strength of that ecstasy increase in man, exalt him to his highest possibilities, make him capable of the supreme experiences. Those who do not give the delight in them as an offering to the divine Powers, preferring to reserve themselves for the sense and the lower life, are adorers not of the gods, but of the Panis, lords of the sense-consciousness, traffickers in its limited activities, they who press not the mystic wine, give not the purified offering, raise not the sacred chant."

4. *The Secret of the Veda* (Centenary Edition), p. 541, fn. 2.
5. *Ibid.*, pp. 249-50.

It is because of the spiritual nature of Soma that it is "called sometimes *amṛta,* the Greek ambrosia, as if it were itself the substance of immortality". And this nature stands out in *Ṛgveda* IX.83.2, where the true sense of *pavitra* emerges beyond a doubt. In the course of commenting on that hymn, Sri Aurobindo writes:[6] "This strong and fiery wine has to be purified and the strainer for its purifying has been spread out wide to receive it in the seat of heaven, *tapoṣpavitraṁ vitataṁ divaspade;* its threads or fibres are all of pure light and stand out like rays, *śocanto asya tantavo vyasthiran.* Through these fibres the wine has to come streaming. The image evidently refers to the purified mental and emotional consciousness, the conscious heart, *cetas,* whose thoughts and emotions are the threads or fibres. Dyau or Heaven is the pure mental principle not subjected to the reactions of the nerves and the body. In the seat of Heaven, – the pure mental being as distinguished from the vital and physical consciousness, – the thoughts and emotions become pure rays of true perception and happy psychical vibration instead of the troubled and obscured mental, emotional and sensational reactions that we now possess. Instead of being contracted and quivering things defending themselves from pain and excess of the shocks of experience they stand out free, strong and bright, happily extended to receive and turn into divine ecstasy all possible contacts of universal existence. Therefore it is *divaspade,* in the seat of Heaven, that the Soma-strainer is spread out to receive the Soma."

Surely such a strainer cannot be the sieve for the juice of any actual plant. True, the hymn in question "begins with an imagery which closely follows the physical facts of the purifying of the wine and its pouring into the jar".[7] But even here we get hints that what appears like a wine used in an external sacrifice is a symbol of a deity who is the supernal wine of Bliss and Immortality. Soma "is pressed out by the

6. *Ibid.,* pp. 344-5.
7. *Ibid.,* p. 343.

pressing-stone (*adri, grāvan*) which has a close symbolic connection with the thunderbolt, the formed electric force of Indra also called *adri*. The Vedic hymns speak of the luminous thunders of this stone as they speak of the light and sound of Indra's weapon. Once pressed out as the delight of existence Soma has to be purified through a strainer (*pavitra*) and through the strainer he streams in his purity into the wine bowl (*camū*) in which he is brought to the sacrifice, or he is kept in jars (*kalaśa*) for Indra's drinking. Or, sometimes, the symbol of the bowl or the jar is neglected and Soma is simply described as flowing in a river of delight to the seat of the Gods, to the home of Immortality. That these things are symbols is very clear in most of the hymns of the ninth Mandala which are all devoted to the God Soma. Here, for instance, the physical system of the human being is imaged as the jar of the Soma-wine..."[8]

Sri Aurobindo[9] continues: "But it is not every human system that can hold, sustain and enjoy the potent and often violent ecstasy of that divine delight. *Ataptatanūr na tad āmo aṣnute*, he who is raw and his body not heated does not taste or enjoy that; *śṛtāsa id vahantas tat samāśata*, only those who have been baked in the fire bear and entirely enjoy that. The wine of the divine Life.... cannot be held in the system unprepared for it by strong endurance of the utmost fires of life and suffering and experience. The raw earthen vessel not baked to consistency in the fire of the kiln cannot hold the Soma-wine; it breaks and spills the precious liquid. So the physical system of the man who drinks this strong wine of Ananda must by suffering and conquering all the torturing heats of life have been prepared for the secret and fiery heats of the Soma; otherwise his conscious being will not be able to hold it; it will spill and lose it as soon as or even before it is tasted or it will break down mentally and physically under the touch." Sri Aurobindo[10] also elucidates the Godhead of Soma

8. *Ibid.*, pp. 342-3.
9. *Ibid.*, p. 344.
10. *Ibid.*, pp. 345-6.

in IX.83: "*Arūrucad uṣasaḥ pṛśnir agriyaḥ*, the supreme dappled One, he makes the dawns to shine: *ukṣā bibharti bhuvanāni vājayuḥ*, he, the Bull, bears the worlds, seeking the plenitude. The word *pṛśniḥ*, dappled, is used both of the Bull, the supreme Male, and of the Cow, the female Energy; like all words of colour, *śveta, śukra, hari, harit, kṛṣṇa, hiraṇyaya*, in the Veda it is symbolic; colour, *varṇa*, has always denoted quality, temperament, etc., in the language of the Mystics. The dappled Bull is the Deva in the variety of his manifestation, many-hued. Soma is that first supreme dappled Bull, generator of the world of the becoming, for from the Ananda, from the all-blissful One they all proceed; delight is the parent of the variety of existences.... He makes the Dawns shine out, – the dawns of illumination, mothers of the radiant herds of the sun; and he seeks the plenitude, that is to say the fullness of being, force, consciousness, the plenty of the godhead which is the condition of the divine delight."

To complete the picture we may cull from Sri Aurobindo a few more passages about the same hymn. Now the last two verses (4 and 5) are under comment. They begin with the mention of "Gandharva". The name is additional testimony to the unearthly status of Soma. It first occurs in the *Ṛgveda* in I.22.14. In the well-known translation of Ralph T.H. Griffith, which seeks no esoteric sense, we have the sufficiently esoteric pointer[11] in a note to the phrase "the Gandharva's steadfast place": "Though in later times the Gandharvas are regarded as a class, in the Ṛgveda more than one Gandharva is seldom mentioned. He is commonly designated as 'the heavenly Gandharva', whose habitation is the sky, and whose especial duty is to guard the heavenly Soma, which the Gods obtain through his permission." In the hymn under comment, Griffith[12] proposes the Sun as the Gandharva, while in hymn 85.12 his note[13] says: "here Soma, the Moon." But his

11. *The Hymns of the Ṛgveda*, translated with a Popular Commentary (The Chowkhamba Sanskrit Series Office, Varanasi, 1971), Vol. I, p. 26, note to line 14.

12. *Ibid.*, p. 338, note to line 4. 13. *Ibid.*, p. 342, note to line 12.

translation[14] of the relevant phrase in 83.4, where so far only Soma has been mentioned, indicates the same meaning: "Gandharva verily protects his dwelling-place; Wondrous, he guards the generations of the Gods." In any case we are clearly directed towards Heaven and not Earth for Soma's original status. Sri Aurobindo's comment on the two concluding verses runs[15]:

"Soma is the Gandharva, the Lord of the hosts of delight, and guards the true seat of the Deva, the level or plane of the Ananda; *gandharva itthā padam asya rakṣati*. He is the Supreme, standing out from all other beings and over them, other than they and wonderful, *adbhutaḥ*, and as the supreme and transcendent, present in the worlds but exceeding them, he protects in those worlds the births of the gods, *pāti devānāṁ janimāni adbhutaḥ*. The 'births of the gods' is a common phrase in the Veda by which is meant the manifestation of the divine principles in the cosmos and especially the formation of the godhead in its manifold forms in the human being. In the last verse [3] the Rishi spoke of the Deva as the divine child preparing for birth, involved in the world, in the human consciousness. Here he speaks of Him as the transcendent guarding the world of the Ananda formed in man and the forms of the godhead born in him by the divine knowledge against the attacks of the enemies, the powers of division, the powers of undelight (*dviṣaḥ, arātīḥ*), against the undivine hosts with their formations of a dark and false creative knowledge, Avidya, illusion (*adevīr māyāḥ*).

"For he seizes these invading enemies in the net of the inner consciousness; he is the master of a profounder and truer setting of world-truth and world-experience than that which is formed by the senses and the superficial mind. It is by this inner setting that he seizes the powers of falsehood, obscurity and division and subjects them to the law of truth, light and unity; *gṛbhṇāti ripuṁ nidhayā nidhāpatiḥ*. Men there-

14. *Ibid.*, p. 339.
15. *Ibid.*, pp. 346-8.

fore protected by the lord of the Ananda governing this inner nature are able to accord their thoughts and actions with the inner truth and light and are no longer made to stumble by the forces of the outer crookedness; they walk straight, they become entirely perfect in their works and by this truth of inner working and outer action are able to taste the entire sweetness of existence, the honey, the delight that is the food of the soul. *Sukṛttamā madhuno bhakṣam āśata.*

"Soma manifests here as the offering, the divine food, the wine of delight and immortality, *haviḥ*, and as the Deva, lord of that divine offering (*haviṣmaḥ*), above as the vast and divine seat, the superconscient bliss and truth, *bṛhat*, from which the wine descends to us. As the wine of delight he flows about and enters into this great march of the sacrifice which is the progress of man from the physical to the superconscient. He enters into it and encompasses it wearing the cloud of the heavenly ether, *nabhas*, the mental principle, as his robe and veil. *Havir haviṣmo mahi sadma daivyam, nabho vasānaḥ pari yāsi adhvaram.* The divine delight comes to us wearing the luminous-cloudy veil of the forms of mental experience.

"In that march or sacrificial ascent the all-blissful Deva becomes the King of all our activities, master of our divinised nature and its energies and with the enlightened conscious heart as his chariot ascends into the plenitude of the infinite and immortal state. Like a Sun or a fire, as Surya, as Agni, engirt with a thousand blazing energies he conquers the vast regions of the inspired truth, the superconscient knowledge; *rājā pavitraratho vājam āruhaḥ, sahasrabhṛṣṭir jayasi śravo bṛhat.* The image is that of a victorious king, sunlike in force and glory, conquering a wide territory. It is the immortality that he wins for man in the vast Truth-Consciousness, *śravas*, upon which is founded the immortal state. It is his own true seat, *itthā padam asya*, that the God concealed in man conquers ascending out of the darkness and the twilight through the glories of the Dawn into the solar plenitudes."

Having made out the case that the *Ṛgveda* is not merely religious ritualism directed at deified nature-forces but a spiritual cult aiming at the human soul's realisation of the Supreme Being by an inner Yogic process of deepening, widening and heightening the consciousness and that it has both an esoteric and an exoteric side and that its true understanding comes by a symbolic vision of it, we have still to ask: "If there are two sides, have we not to assume an actual plant whose juice represents the occult experience of the Divine Delight? Was there not a physically drinkable wine as a symbol of the Wine of Immortality with which the aspiring soul was filled when it invoked, under the particular name of Soma, the one Existent to whom the seers give different names (I.164.46), the timeless Unknowable beyond the mind (I.170.1), the Unmoving and Infinite which is the single mightiness of the Gods (III.55.1), the transcendent and universal Deva, 'the Father of things who appears here as the Son in the human soul',[16] 'the Blissful One to whom the movement of the Gods ascends, manifest as at once the Male and the Female, *vṛṣan dhenu*'?"[17]

We can only answer: "There are hymns like IX.83 where the physical interpretation is impossible. There are no hymns where this interpretation alone stands forth. There are double-aspected hymns where, in spite of physical appearances, the spiritual-symbolic interpretation can be maintained. Therefore all the hymns are capable of such an interpretation and the sole logical course is to give it to them. Thus nowhere in the *Ṛgveda* can an actual plant be taken as intended." But this need not imply that no plant existed in the *Ṛgveda*'s day by the name of Soma. Just as the fire, the clarified butter which was put into it, the cow, the horse, the wealth, the hills, the rivers existed as physical counterparts to their psycho-spiritual originals and served as symbols for the processes of the inner Yogic life, so too an actual plant whose juice was pressed out must have been present for the exoteric sense to have some bearing here as everywhere else. However, it would be a mistake to look for a sort of point-to-point

16. *Ibid.*, pp. 341-2.
17. *Ibid.*, p. 342.

correspondence with the divine *amṛta* which was meant by Soma. We should not bother to search for some extraordinary herb whose extract, as Mr. Wasson's reviewer puts it, "was intoxicating, gave strength in battle as well as a widening of consciousness". The *Ṛgveda* (X.85.3,47)[18] very clearly forbids any quest for point-to-point correspondence:

> One thinks, when they have brayed the plant, that he hath drunk the Soma's juice;
> Of him whom Brahmans truly know as Soma no one ever tastes.

> Soma, secured by sheltering rules, guarded by hymns in Bṛhati,*
> Thou standest listening to the stones; none tastes of thee who dwells on earth.

Some sort of winy liquid was obtained, but it was not more unusual or in a class by itself than were all the other physical analogues of inner realities. The only thing we can affirm with certainty is that it differed from common "spirituous" drinks. The *Ṛgveda* calls these drinks Sura as distinguished from Soma and sometimes frowns upon them (*e.g.*, VII.86.6) and twice (VIII.2.22; 21.14) regards them as causing broils. It is possible that its actual Soma was more or less like the creepers or grasses later epochs employed as substitutes. Perhaps those creepers or grasses were not really substitutes but believed to be so because the *Ṛgvedic* symbolism and esotericism were forgotten and the high qualities ascribed to Soma were taken literally to belong to an earthly plant.

18. Griffith, *op. cit.*, Vol. II, p. 501.
* That is, hymns in that metre.

THE TIME OF KĀLIDĀSA

1

A wit may wise-crack that it is natural for Kālidāsa, the poet for all time, to have still no time of his own. Indeed the age in which he lived has been differently dated, but the wise-cracking is a little beside the mark in that it suggests a large number of datings. The controversy at present would seem to toss the poet mainly between two ages.

A wide-spread and persistent tradition places him in the reign of a Vikramāditya of Ujjayinī, reputed to have been a patron of learning, a paragon of liberality, a destroyer of the Śakas and the founder of the era of 57 B.C. Most historians deny the very existence of this Vikramāditya and so the placing of Kālidāsa in his reign has struck them as highly fanciful. But they have been impressed enough by tradition to grant Kālidāsa, as patron and contemporary, some Vikramāditya or other who was connected with Ujjayinī.[1] And they have found further encouragement in the poet's purposive alteration in the name of the hero of a drama from Purūravus to Vikrama by styling the work *Vikramorvaśīyam*[2] – an alteration as if to bring in the name of his patron at even the cost of breaking a rule of Pāṇini that the suffix *īya* is to be added only to Dvanda compounds.[3] Since competent scholars hold some verses in the Mandasor inscription dated by them to 473 A.D. to indicate knowledge of Kālidāsa's works which must require at least a quarter century to become famous, the lower limit of his age is supposed to be *c.* 450 A.D.[4] This makes the major choice, for his patron and contemporary, fall on the third Gupta emperor, Chandragupta II Vikramāditya, whom our historians put in 376-414 A.D.[5]

Evidently the central point to resolve in the Kālidāsa-controversy is the identity of this Vikramāditya. Is there any

1. R.C. Majumdar in *The Classical Age*, 1954, p. 302.
2. *Ibid.*
3. H.R. Agrawala, *A Short History of Sanskrit Literature*, p. 79.
4. *The Classical Age*, p. 303.
5. *Ibid.*, pp. 18, 303.

definite reason for us to accept from tradition the name "Vikramāditya" of a great ruler, yet reject its association with 57 B.C. and refuse to put Kālidāsa around this date? Are we compelled by anything decisive to pass by the figure cherished in India by the popular mind with an admiration next only to that for Rāma and Kṛṣṇa, and to fasten on a different king who bore as a title the same name?

The most elaborate defence of this figure is R.B. Pandey's *Vikramāditya of Ujjayinī*,[6] with a Foreword by R.C. Majumdar who, with A.D. Pusalker, has championed his cause the most in our day. All matter relevant to the Vikramāditya-tradition has been collected by Pandey with praiseworthy scholarship and given detailed consideration. But the essential issue boils down to meeting four arguments mustered by modern historians against this tradition. First, we have no positive date in the form of inscriptions or coins throwing light on the existence of a Vikramāditya of the first century B.C. Secondly, the Era called Vikrama was not associated with his name during its early career and the first mention of it is in the Dhiniki inscription of Jaikādeva dated in the Vikramasaṁvat 794.* Thirdly, the post-Christ astronomers of India do not use and mention the Vikrama Era in their work; they seem to attach no importance to it and date their compositions in the Śaka Era. Fourthly, the Vikramāditya-tradition occurs only in mediaeval times and the most important pre-mediaeval Indian documents – the Purāṇas – which preserve an outline or skeleton of history in their dynastic lists – ignore Vikramāditya although they pass beyond 57 B.C. and touch on kings up to the Gupta Age which begins in 320 A.D. by the present computation.

Pandey[7] confronts the first argument thus: "Even great figures like Chandragupta Maurya, Mahāpadma, Ajātaśatru,

6. Banaras, Shatadala Prakashana, 1951.

* Bhandarkar, *List of Inscriptions of Northern India*, No. 17. Curiously, Pandey does not mention this inscription: he starts (p. 4) with the Dholpur inscription of Chanda-mahāsena dated in the Vikram-kāla 898.

7. Pandey, *op. cit.*, p. v.

Bimbisāra, etc. have bequeathed no so-called positive date for the reconstruction of their history. Yet nobody questions their historicity." In his Foreword Majumdar[8] says: "So many historical figures of ancient India, who were unknown, even to popular tradition, have suddenly emerged into our view by the chance discovery of a single inscription. The examples of Gautamīputra, Samudragupta and his successors, Khāravela, Pravarasena, Dharmapāla, Devapāla, Bhoja (Pratihāra) and many others, whose very names were unknown a century ago, should warn us not to put too much weight on negative evidence."

What Pandey and Majumdar write should certainly prevent dogmatism and induce an open mind. But the weak point about Pandey's statement is that, unlike Vikramāditya, figures like Chandragupta Maurya, Mahāpadma, Ajātaśatru and Bimbisāra are the subject of references in pre-mediaeval early documents, while the weak point about Majumdar's is that at least in the case of Gautamīputra, Samudragupta and his successors we have, besides inscriptions or coins directly bearing on them, epigraphic or numismatic records which put them in a definite historical sequence and so make them part of a large body of connected knowledge: Vikramāditya lacks even an indirect support in epigraphy or numismatics because no predecessor or successor of his is indicated in any inscription or coin, and epigraphy and numismatics attest no sequence of historical events in which, even if we have no direct positive data about him, we may legitimately conjecture him to be a link. Thus the answer to the first argument, though sufficient on the surface, is not quite satisfactory on a deeper scrutiny.

The second argument is sought to be countered by a double answer, a sort of pincer movement. In the first place, the non-association of Vikramāditya's name with the Vikrama Era during the early centuries after 57 B.C. is not something peculiar to this Era. Pandey[9] writes: "The Śaka Era is called so

8. *Ibid.*, p. i.
9 *Ibid.*, preface, p. v.

in the 500th year of its currency; before that it was referred to as mere Varsha. The case of even the Gupta Era is not different. Out of fifty references (Bhandarkar's list in *Epigraphia Indica*) to it up to G.E. 221, ten refer to it as Varsha, thirty-seven call it mere Saṁvat and only three designate it as Gupta Kāla." In the second place, the non-association of Vikramāditya's name is explicable, in contrast to the case of the word "Śaka" in connection with the Era of 78 A.D., by the conclusion of scholars that the Eras which are called Kṛta and Mālava and which in inscriptions precede on the whole the Vikrama Era are identical with the latter. The Era of 57 B.C. was not named the Vikrama simply because, whenever it did not go undesignated, it was named the Mālava before it and the Kṛta still earlier: all that we should do is to show the three epithets as possessing a common core of meaning and give a reason why they occurred in the order in which we find them.

Pandey sums up an amount of research by scholars and tells us about some inscriptions made in Mālwā and neighbouring areas. "At Mandasor (ancient Daśapur)," he writes,[10] "two epigraphs[11] dated 493 and 589, Mālava era, refer to an era current in the Mālava Republic. In these epigraphs, there occurs a significant phrase 'Mālava-ganasthitī'. Scholars have interpreted it differently. Keilhorn[12] took the term 'gaṇa' in the sense of 'gaṇanā' or 'counting of years'. That the term 'gaṇa' might have some other meaning was not thought of by scholars and they were doubtful regarding the existence of republics in ancient India. Later researchers, however, revealed that there were republican states in ancient India, and the interpretation offered by Kielhorn was challenged and even rejected. K.P. Jayaswal[13] interpreted the phrase 'Mālava-gaṇ-sthitī' as 'an era founded to commemorate the republican constitution of the Mālavas'. Dr. A.S. Altekar[14] would

10. *Ibid.*, p. 36.
11. Fleet, *Gupta Inscriptions*, No. 18.
12. *Indian Antiquary*, Vol. XIV, p. 326.
13. *The Journal of the Bihar and Orissa Research Society*, 1930.
14. *Epigraphia Indica*, Vol. XXVI.

prefer to translate the phrase 'Mālavānām gaṇa-sthityā' as 'according to the era current in the Mālava Republic' and 'according to the usage of the Mālava Republic'. The first translation of Dr. Altekar is easy and natural; his second one is also acceptable unless it means that the Mālavas had nothing to do with the foundation of the era, as it was maintained by D.B. Bhandarkar."[15]

Pandey[16] continues: "Some recent discoveries have revealed that the Mālava era was called Kṛta era in its early centuries. The Nandsa sacrificial pillar inscriptions (very ably edited by Dr. A.S. Altekar) disclose that the Mālava people, in the Mālava-vishaya (the territories of the Mālava republic, which was shifted according to their habitation), were using the Kṛta era." Pandey[17] writes also: "Fleet accepted that the Mālava era... was co-eval with the Vikrama era and was also identical with it..." The decided opinion of Dr. Altekar is that the Kṛta, the Mālava and the Vikrama eras are identical... In associating Vikramāditya with the Mālava republic we have to explain only one fact. According to the Jain tradition he belonged to the Gardabhilla family. In the opinion of the present writer the Gardabhillas were one of the sections of the Mālavas. That the Mālavas were divided into sections and groups is proved by the Nandsa inscriptions, according to which the Mālava section, which was responsible for the sacrifices, was called Sogi. Thus the Gardabhilla, Sogi, etc., were the various groups among the Mālavas. Therefore, Gardabhilla, the family name of Vikramāditya, is no bar to his identification with Mālava-gaṇa-mukhya (a leader of the Mālavas' republic). Similarly his being called a Rāja or his ruling after his father need not present a difficulty. We know from the Nandsa sacrificial pillar inscriptions that among the Mālavas of south-eastern Rājputāna sometimes chieftainship continued for two or three generations together in the same family. That the title "Rāja" was borne by republican leaders

15. *Bhandarkar Commemoration Volume*, p. 191.
16. Pandey, *op. cit.*, pp. 36-7.
17. *Ibid.*, pp. 36, 37-38.

in ancient India is a well-known fact.[18] Besides, there are some literary evidences which connect Vikramāditya with the Mālavas and their republic.

The reason why the same Era was first called Kṛta, then Mālava and finally Vikrama is set forth by Pandey:[19] "Vikramāditya... was the leader of a republic (gaṇa-mukhya) and not an absolute monarch. Though he was mainly instrumental in the foundation of an era, he could not claim the sole credit for it. In a republican type of state the gaṇa is more important than the individual leader, however influential he might be. Great achievements, like success in war, were shared by the entire gaṇa (republic), as there was a fear of dissension, in case one single individual aspired to claim them. Under the circumstances, the era was to be named after the Mālava-gaṇa (of which Vikramāditya was the leader). The era was started to commemorate the Victory of the Mālava Republic against the barbarous Śakas whose expulsion from India freed the country from foreign invasion and inaugurated an era of peace and prosperity, which, figuratively, might be regarded as Kṛtayuga (Golden Age). So the era was significantly called as Kṛta.... India, free from foreign invasion, enjoyed peace and prosperity for 135 years from 57 B.C. (when the era was founded) to 78 A.D. At the end of this period the Śakas again started their invasions... The Mālava people were defeated... They continued their struggle... but owing to the disintegration of their power they were not able to restore their lost territories and prestige. This rendered a rude shock to their dream of the Kṛtayuga. The name Kṛta was dropped from the era. But, as the Mālava-gaṇa was alive, the era was still remembered as to commemorate the firm foundation of the Mālava republic in 57 B.C. when the Śakas were defeated. It came to be called the Mālava era... When the Gupta power was rising in the first half of the fourth century A.D. the Mālavas were still a powerful republic... The Gupta empire engulfed them and spread over Malwa, Rajputana and

18. *Arthaśāstra*, XI.I.6.

19. Pandey, *op. cit.*, pp. 5-8.

Central India... But the ideal of freedom, for which the Mālavas stood, still possessed the mind of people in Mālwā and Rājputāna... The era of the Mālavas outlived Gupta imperialism and continued in the name of the Mālava-gaṇa, the Mālava people and the Mālava lords. By the eighth and ninth centuries A.D. absolute monarchy with all its implications became an established institution in India. The very conception of a republican state passed beyond the horizon or the mind of the Indians. In the last decade of the ninth century the Mālava-gaṇa was entirely merged into the luminous personality of Vikramāditya, whose memory was still enshrined in the popular mind, and the era was called after him. Vikramāditya himself came to be regarded as a king and the era was sometimes called the era of the king Vikrama or Vikramāditya."

In support of his notion of a Mālava victory over the Śakas in 57 B.C., Pandey[20] appeals not only to epigraphs but also to certain Mālava coins. A pioneer archaeologist, Carlleyle, discovered and secured from others a large number of small coins in Uniyar, a tributary jagir of the Jaipur State, at a town called Nagar. What he regarded as the earliest coins bore in ancient Brāhmi characters the phrases: "Mālavānāṁ-jayaḥ", "Mālava-gaṇasya jayaḥ" and "Jayaḥ Mālavānām". Pandey comments: "The clear meaning of these legends is 'the Victory of the Mālavas' or 'the Victory of the Mālava republic'. The later coins have legends in blurred Brāhmi characters." Sir Alexander Cunningham dated the coins "from, perhaps, B.C. 250 to A.D. 250". Pandey notes: "Rapson and Smith slightly differ from Cunningham and in their opinion the age of the coins cannot be pushed back earlier than 150 B.C. The latest limit of the earliest coins was fixed by Allan at 100 B.C. ....It can be admitted, however, that on a palaeographical basis no exact date can be assigned to these coins; we can, at the best, determine the sequence and the approximate period. In the development of characters a

20. *Ibid.*, pp. 40-41.

margin of fifty years cannot be eliminated. Fortunately the legends on the coins are very helpful in the present case. The legends evidently point to the fact that the first issue of the coins was promulgated to commemorate the victory of the Mālavas over some very dangerous enemies. This victory must have been a signal and very important one, because its memory was perpetuated for many centuries to come, as it is evidenced by the coins. Now the question is: Who were the enemies of the Mālavas and what is the date of their defeat by the Mālavas? In search of an answer, our thought at once goes to the 'Constitution of the Mālava Republic' in 57 B.C. Taking into consideration the localities where the coins and epigraphs are found, it becomes almost a certainty that the same event was celebrated by the foundation of an era and by promulgating 'the Victory Type of Coins'."

What should be our estimate of Pandey's explanation about the coins and epigraphs, as well as of the defence made, on the analogy chiefly of the Śaka Era, for the non-association of Vikramāditya's name with the Era ascribed to him? Historians, with whom Pandey breaks a lance in favour of the Indian tradition about Vikramāditya while agreeing with them in the rest of their historical scheme and chronology, are not likely to be much impressed. If, with them,[21] we put the Sātavāhana king Gautamīputra Sātakarṇi in 124 A.D. and the Mahākshatrapas Nahapāna, Chashṭana and Rudradāman in about the same period, we have ample evidence, both epigraphic and numismatic, of Śaka rulers soon after 78 A.D. Further, if, with them,[22] we begin the Imperial Gupta dynasty in 320 A.D., we have again the Śakas mentioned in the Allāhābād Pillar inscription of Samudragupta and, a little later, a proof of their extirpation by Chandragupta II who annexed completely their provinces to his empire. What is more, we have numerous coins of the Śaka rulers themselves,[23] belonging to the family of Chashṭana and Rudra-

21. *The Age of Imperial Unity*, 1951, pp. 180-83.
22. *The Classical Age*, pp. 4, 10, 19.
23. *The Age of Imperial Unity*, pp. 183-190.

dāman, all dated in the years of an era in continuation of the years 52 and 72 respectively of Chashṭana's Andhau inscription[24] and Rudradāman's Junāgarh epigraph.[25] No pointer to the traditional Vikramāditya can be found in the years when the era of 57 B.C. is unassociated with his name. The lateness of its association is thus not exactly on a par with that of the association of 78 A.D. with the name "Śaka": much less is it on a par with that of the association of 320 A.D. with the name "Gupta". As in the matter of the absence of positive data, here too the comparison holds on the surface but suffers when examined more deeply.

Pandey's explanation of why the same Era was successively called Kṛta Mālava and Vikrama on epigraphs is not inherently implausible, yet there is nothing compulsive about it. After all, the name Kṛta occurs first in the Nanda inscription in the last quarter of the third century A.D., and the phrase "Mālavānām gaṇa-sthityā" in the Mandasor inscription of year 493 and the phrase "Mālava-gaṇa-sthitī" in the Mandasor inscription of year 589 need not be read as referring to the foundation of the Mālava Republic: Altekar's readings, as quoted by Pandey himself, of "mālavānām gaṇa-sthityā" are "according to the era current in the Mālava republic" and "according to the usage of the Mālava republic." Sircar[26] speaks of the era "handed down by the Mālava Republic" and of the year "counted in accordance with the custom established by the Mālava Republic" though he does not deny the possibility of reading "from the foundation of" in place of "in accordance with the custom established by". He believes, as we shall see a little later, the era to be of a foreign origin and to have nothing to do with a victory over the Śakas in the first century B.C. According to him,[27] the word Kṛta may be the name of an illustrious Mālava leader who secured the independence of his tribe from foreign yoke at a later date and

24. *Ibid.*, p. 183.
25. *Ibid.*, p. 184.
26. "The Vikram Saṁvat" in *The Vikrama Commemoration Volume*, 1948, p. 582.
27. *The Age of Imperial Unity*, pp. 163-64.

thus got his name associated with his tribe's era. The fight with the Śakas of Western India who were the allies of the Mālavas' enemies, the Uttamabhadras of the Ajmer region, can be traced, in Sircar's view,[28] as early as the beginning of the second century A.D., but the question of freedom and prosperity returning to the country does not arise till some time before the Nandsa inscriptions of A.D. 226 – freedom and prosperity "owing to the brilliant achievements of a Mālava chief whose name has not been fully deciphered. The reference seems to be to the success of the Mālava people chiefly against the Śakas". 57 B.C. is thus shorn of the significance seen into it by Pandey. Nothing precisely is proved against Pandey, but his vision is shown to be not imperative.

In the matter of the coins, Sircar[29] says: "Some of the Mālava coins may be assigned to the first century B.C., but most of them are later." He does not feel forced to connect them with any victory over the Śakas in 57 B.C. As we have already seen, Sircar puts their success against the Śakas much later. Besides, the issuing of Victory coins is not confined to the Mālavas and has served various occasions for various tribes and need not be joined to an exceptional event like founding an era. Sircar[30] records: "Coins of the tribal republic of the Ārjunāyanas bear the legend *ārjunāyanānāṁ jayaḥ* in the Brāhmi script of about the closing decades of the first century B.C." Then there is the case of the Yaudheyas, another tribal republic, some of whose coins which may be assigned to the third and fourth centuries A.D. carry the legend: *yaudheya-gaṇasya jayaḥ*.[31] In the matter of the coins, although nothing definite is quite established against Pandey, he is again deprived of the convincingness at which he aims.

What really operates to his extreme detriment is one fact arising from his acquiescence in a historical scheme and

28. *Ibid.*, p. 164.
29. *Ibid.*, p. 165.
30. *Ibid.*, p. 163.
31. *Ibid.*, p. 167.

chronology identical with that of his opponents except in the Vikramāditya-issue. His position well-nigh dissolves the moment he takes with them the extirpation of the Śakas by Chandragupta II to be at about the end of the fourth century A.D. D.R. Bhandarkar[32] was the first to emphasise the significance of this Gupta king in the Vikramāditya-controversy. It is established history that Chandragupta II took the title Vikramāditya; again, by his extirpation of the Śakas he could be termed Śakāri just as the traditional Vikramāditya is: finally, he is known to have made Ujjayinī a secondary capital after his victory over the Śakas. It is difficult to carry the Vikramāditya of mediaeval tradition to the first century B.C., consider him the "mukhya" of the Mālava Republic against the Śakas, look on him as the founder of the Era of 57 B.C. and dismiss the claim instituted by Sircar[33] for the anti-traditionalists: "Chandragupta II gradually became famous in Indian tradition and folklore as Vikramāditya Śakāri, the Lord of Ujjayinī. Thus in the early mediaeval period 'the lord of Mālava' *par excellence* was no other than Vikramāditya (Chandragupta II) and it was then quite natural to identify the Mālaveśa with whom the Kṛta era came to be associated after the extirpation of the Mālavagaṇa with the great Vikramāditya of tradition."

Pandey attempts to neutralise the claim for Chandragupta II. When he[34] pleads that just because this Chandragupta was an actual Śakāri he need not have been the sole one, we have not much of an argument for the legendary Śakāri's existence. Nor is there much of an argument when we are told by him[35] that since Chandragupta II got known as Vikramāditya only by taking a title whereas the traditional king had Vikramāditya as his own proper name they cannot be the same and that the assumption of the title "Vikramāditya" in the fourth century A.D. presupposes the existence of the proper name

32. *The Journal of the Bombay Branch of Royal Asiatic Society*, 1900, p. 398.
33. *The Vikrama Commemoration Volume*, p. 584.
34. Pandey, *op. cit.*, pp. 62-63.
35. *Ibid.*, pp. 63-64.

Vikramāditya in earlier times which set an example to be followed by later kings. Proper names of one age have indeed been used as titles in a later time, but a generalisation is not possible. We may as well argue that the titles of the other Gupta kings – Mahendrāditya, Prakramāditya, Bālāditya, Kramāditya, Chandrāditya – prove that some famous emperors of the past bore them as personal names. Why not argue also that the traditional Vikramāditya's titles[36] – Vishamaśīla, Sāhasānka, Śakāri – imply that they were the proper names of previous kings? Although remarking[37] that presumably in imitation of the legendary hero the third Gupta assumed the title Vikramāditya which was probably adopted by his father too, Majumdar is evidently not particular that the traditional king of Ujjayinī should have Vikramāditya as his personal name. Discussing the word Kṛta, he[38] states: "This word has not yet been satisfactorily explained. Some regard it as a technical astronomical term, while others think that it was the name of a king who founded the era. If the latter view be held, it goes a great way in supporting the Jain tradition, for we may easily hold that this was the king who assumed the title Vikramāditya as many others did in later times."

What would appear likely to the modern historian is that, as the quotation from Sircar implies, Chandragupta passed into tradition not under his own name but under his title and, when his title got associated like a proper name with the Kṛta-Mālava Era of 57 B.C., the myth arose of a Vikramāditya having existed at Ujjayinī in the first century before Christ and having freed the Mālava province from the Śakas. The very late birth of the Vikramāditya-tradition tends to incline us to this hypothesis.

Against the "lateness" of the tradition Pandey[39] brings up two points. One is apropos of the *Gāthāsaptaśatī*, a Prākṛt anthology of romantic verses composed by one Hāla. It

36. *Ibid.*, p. 63.
37. *The Classical Age*, p. 19.
38. *The Age of Imperial Unity*, p. 157.
39. Pandey, *op. cit.*, pp. 11-22.

contains the verse: "The heroine, through her feet, satisfied at the pleasure of being massaged and spreading lac on your hands, teaches you lessons on the life of Vikramāditya." The commentator Gadādhara explains the cryptic expressions thus: "In the context of Vikramāditya 'saṁvāhana' (massaging) means 'saṁvādhana' (crushing of enemies) and 'lakkhaṁ' (red dye) means a 'lac of coins'. Vikramāditya, being satisfied at the defeat of his enemies by his subordinate, gives away a lac of coins in his hand." Pandey says that Hāla, the author of this hint at Vikramāditya's conquests and liberalities, must be the Sātavāhana king Hāla who is dated by our historians in the closing years of the first century A.D. The identification is based on the introductory verse 13 of Bāṇa's *Harṣa-Charita,* a book of the seventh century A.D. where Sātavāhana is spoken of as having composed a Kośa of songs, and also on some other late sources calling Hāla Sātavāhana a great patron of Prākṛt literature and a great poet. If the identification is correct, the fame of a Vikramāditya is shown to have been prevalent as early as a century and a half after 57 B.C. and little reason remains to doubt the existence of the king of Ujjayinī cherished by tradition.

Bhandarkar,[40] however, agrees with Weber[41] that there are no grounds to suppose that this Kośa is Hāla's *Saptaśatī*: on what he calls internal evidence he assigns Hāla of the *Saptaśatī* to the commencement of the sixth century A.D. He draws attention to the reference to Kṛṣṇa and Rādhikā contained in verse I.89 and the reference to a week-day, Tuesday (Mangalavāra) in III.61. "The earliest mention of Rādhikā that I have been able to trace," he observes, "is in the *Pañcha-tantra* I (*Bom. Sk. Series* No. IV), p. 38, which was compiled in the fifth century after Christ. Similarly the practice of citing the week-day in dates or for any other general purposes came into vogue in the ninth century, though the earliest instance of its use is found in the Eraṇa inscription of Buddhagupta dated A.D. 484 (*Journal of the Royal Asiatic Society*, 1912,

40. *R.G. Bhandarkar Commemoration Volume,* 1917, pp. 198-9.
41. *Ueber das Saptaśatakaṁ des Hāla,* pp. 2-4.

pp. 1044-45)." Pandey retorts: "A reference to Rādhikā in the *Pañcha-tantra* of the fifth century does not necessarily mean that it was the first reference of its kind. A reference to Rādhikā in the fifth century only means that her concept was already a popular one before that time, and it must have taken centuries to develop it to warrant its use by a story-writer. Under the circumstances, it is not impossible that the cult of Rādha was current in the first century A.D.... Concerning the use of a week-day in the *Gāthā* Dr. Bhandarkar himself admits that its earliest use is found in Buddhagupta's inscriptions of 484 A.D. In a much older inscription of Śaka Kshatrapa Rudradāman dated Śaka 52 (=130 A.D.) a week-day (Thursday) is mentioned. Hence the mention of Rādhikā and a week-day in the *Gāthāsaptaśatī* does not drag down its date to the sixth century to suit the theory of Dr. Bhandarkar that Vikramāditya, the founder of the Vikrama Saṁvat, was the Gupta king, Chandragupta II Vikramāditya."

This is well said. But the *Saptaśatī* employs only the name Vikramāditya: there is no indication of Ujjayinī or the era connected with that name or anything relating to the first century B.C. Consequently we remain uncertain whether the traditional figure of the Gupta king is intended. No clue is present to lead us through Hāla to Hāla Sātavāhana of the closing years of the first century A.D. The *Saptaśatī* is quite indecisive by itself. And, as an actual Vikramāditya was there in 376-414 A.D., the balance would tilt in favour of putting Hāla not before that time.

The second point urged by Pandey is in relation to three Sanskrit works of the eleventh century A.D. – (1) the *Bṛhatkathāmañjarī* of Kshemendra, (2) the *Kathāsaritasāgara* of Somadeva and (3) the *Śloka-saṁgraha* of Buddha-svāmi – which contains tales about the Mālava Vikramāditya but which are self-avowed to be based on a much earlier work, the *Bṛhatkathā* of Guṇāḍhya, originally written in Paiśāchi and rendered into Sanskrit before the eighth century A.D. Pandey writes: "There is a difference of opinion among scholars regarding the date of Guṇāḍhya, but it cannot be brought down after the first or second century A.D." Now, if the three later works founded on the *Bṛhatkathā* are properly examined and compared, says Pandey, "it is possible to reconstruct the contents of the original *Bṛhatkathā* and it can be claimed with certitude that the *Bṛhatkathā* dealt with the life of Vikramāditya exhaustively... Thus the existence of Vikramāditya before the first century A.D. is indicated by the *Bṛhatkathā*."

Unfortunately, Pandey's opinion on Guṇāḍhya's date is not as well informed as one may wish. Majumdar[42] tells us about the *Bṛhatkathā*: "Its date is not later than A.D. 500, though some place it much earlier, – even in the first century A.D. This is, however, quite conjectural."

Also an unfortunate thing here is that the *Kathāsaritasāgara* has also a story about Vikramāditya of Pāṭaliputra. Pandey tries to turn this story to account by saying: "Somadeva mentions him separately and there was absolutely no confusion in his mind regarding the independent existence of two Vikramādityas, one of Ujjayinī and the other of Pāṭaliputra. This fact is fatal to the theory that attempts to identify Chandragupta II Vikramāditya with Vikramāditya of Ujjayinī." However, in order to safeguard the "antiquity" of the Vikramāditya of Ujjayinī, he declares the story to be one of the interpolations received by Guṇāḍhya's *Bṛhatkathā* some centuries after its composition, "interpolations which were current in the time of Somadeva". This declaration throws serious doubt also on the authenticity of the tales about the Vikramāditya of Ujjayinī in all the works drawing upon Guṇāḍhya. Those very tales, like the story about the Vikramāditya of Pāṭaliputra, may well have been interpolations after the time of Chandragupta II in the fourth and fifth centuries A.D. A certain particular in those tales is highly suggestive of their interpolated character. As there were more than one Vikramāditya among the Guptas we may expect a mixture of influences from their history, and it is very striking that the name of the Ujjayinī Vikramāditya's father in both the *Bṛhat-*

42. *The Classical Age*, p. 314.

kathāmañjarī and the *Kathāsaritasāgara* should be Mahendrāditya,[43] the very name borne by Skandagupta Vikramāditya's father Kumāragupta.[44]

Of course, Somadeva can still be said to have acknowledged the existence of two separate Vikramādityas. But the acknowledgment does not render the Vikramāditya of Ujjayinī less a legend and more a reality. Once Śakāri Chandragupta II passed into legend under this title and got associated with the Kṛta-Mālava Era and was transposed to the first century B.C., there would naturally be two Vikramādityas.

Pandey cannot be deemed to have succeeded in disproving the lateness of the Vikramāditya-tradition. Really the strongest attack by him[45] on Bhandarkar's theory lies in pointing out that all through the Gupta period, even after Chandragupta II had become ruler of Mālwā, the Mālavas and their neighbours used the Mālava Era and that this Era was preserved in spite of the rival Gupta Era and, as shown by the Kanaswa inscription[46] of Sivagaṇa in Kota State of the Mālava year 795 and the Gyaraspur inscription[47] in the State of the Mālava year 936, survived the Gupta empire. "It really passes beyond comprehension," writes Pandey, "how the title 'Vikramāditya' of Chandragupta II or of any other Gupta king came to be associated with the Mālava era."

The mystery deepens for him[48] yet more because "Ujjayinī was, at the best, their provincial headquarter" and they "were essentially the lords of Pāṭaliputra" just as the great Moghul emperors who had "their provincial headquarters and temporary residence at Agra, Lahore, Ajmer and Shrinagar" were "still called 'the lords of Delhi' and not of those provincial capitals".

43. Pandey, *op. cit.*, pp. 15, 21.
44. *The Classical Age*, p. 23.
45. Pandey, *op. cit.*, pp. 64-65.
46. *The Indian Antiquary*, Vol. XIX, p. 59.
47. *The Archaeological Survey Report*, Vol. X, Plate II.
48. Pandey, *op. cit.*, p. 65.

A rejoinder to Pandey can be framed on the following lines: "We know that after the termination of the Imperial Guptas a dynasty whom our historians dub the Later Guptas[49] were ruling over Mālwā up to about 750 A.D. They are not known to have used either the Gupta or the Mālava Era. But it is during their time that the Era of 57 B.C. began to be termed Vikrama: the Dhiniki inscription's Vikrama year 704 is equal to 737 A.D. Although they did not claim to be directly connected with the Imperial Guptas, the memory of the most illustrious Gupta – Chandragupta Vikramāditya – may have revived under the constant presence of the reigning name 'Gupta' in the province. Then the Mālava Era may have begun to get Guptafied and assumed the name Vikrama with the disappearance of the republican constitution so that, though the name Mālava cropped up now and then just as the name Kṛta had done previously when the Mālava Era had already got on its way, the rule henceforth was the use of the Vikrama Era both in Mālwā and outside. The point about Ujjayinī having been only a provincial capital is not very relevant. The Mālavas knew Chandragupta II in relation to their own chief city and when this city got the special honour of being a secondary royal centre for him they would be particularly inclined to consider him who had destroyed the Śakas the lord of Ujjayinī".

Sircar[50] has a persuasive passage on the Mālava Era getting Guptafied: "There seems to have been a long-drawn struggle between the Mālavas using the Kṛta era and the Kārdamakas (Western satraps) using the Śaka era, in the third and fourth centuries A.D. But both the powers had soon to submit to the Guptas. While, however, the Śaka house was extirpated by the conquerors, the Aulikaras, apparently a Mālava dynasty, flourished at Daśapura (modern Mandasor, formerly in the realm of the Kārdamakas) under the vassalage of the Gupta emperors. It was probably the Aulikaras, especially the

49. *The Classical Age*, pp. 73-75, 128.
50. *The Age of Imperial Unity*, pp. 114-15.

mighty Aulikara king Yaśodharman (A.D. 532), who were responsible for the name Mālava being applied to a wide region of Central and Western India, including the old *janapadas* of Avanti (district round Ujjayinī) and Ākara or Daśārna (district round Vidiśā). It may be noted that the kings, even when they were subordinate to the Guptas, used the Kṛta era (then also called the era of the Mālava people or their republic) in preference to the era of the Guptas. The favour shown to the Mālava family of the Aulikaras and to the Mālava era in contradiction to the attempt of Chandragupta II Vikramāditya, and probably also of his father Samudragupta Vikramāditya, to extirpate both the Śakas and their era might have contributed to the growth of the Śakāri Vikramāditya saga attributing the foundation of the era of 58 B.C. to Rājā Vikrama."

Sircar's passage and what we have said cannot be regarded as final, for, we may be told: "If the traditional Vikramāditya has behind him Chandragupta II who bore the title Vikramāditya and was a Śakāri and made Ujjayinī a secondary capital, why did tradition create a figure differing in several respects from him, why did it whisk him away to 57 B.C., consider him principally the king of Ujjayinī and give him, as the Jain tradition has it, a Gardabhilla family? Surely the Gupta associations could have been retained if the Mālavas honoured Chandragupta II for extirpating the Śakas and encouraging the Mālava Era in preference to the Śaka Era. The differences persisting, despite these factors which would make for complete similarity, imply a real earlier Vikramāditya whose personality and circumstances must have refused to be gainsaid."

There is certainly some force in this objection. But if the differences suggest a real earlier personage, the resemblances must suggest derivation of the legendary figure from Chandragupta II – and as the resemblances are undeniably in the more central matters they should seriously reduce the relevance of the differences.

That the Vikramāditya legend was influenced by a

memory of Gupta greatness cannot be disputed by any scholar who concurs with the present historical disposition of the Guptas. Even Majumdar writes in general: "There is no doubt that the legend owes much of its vitality and inspiration to the lives and achievements of the Gupta Emperors, no less than three of whom actually assumed the title Vikramāditya." And again about Chandragupta II in particular: "It is... likely that some of the traditions associated with Vikramāditya, especially his liberality and patronage of learning, owed their origin to this historic king." Somehow the differences from this most famous of the three Gupta Vikramādityas may be thought to have arisen owing to the extreme national propensity of the Mālavas as well as to the association of Chandragupta II with an ancient date like 57 B.C. What is more, the important resemblances are with an attested historical being: the differences direct us to a being about whom we have no comparable testimony. So Sircar's passage and what we have said, though wanting in finality, must be accorded preference and taken as adequate in the midst of the general uncertainty on some matters on both sides and in view of the irrefutable existence of a Śakāri Vikramāditya of Ujjayinī among the Guptas. History and logic compel us to put the traditional Vikramāditya aside, however strongly we may feel about the differences between him and his Gupta namesake.

With him his alleged protégé Kālidāsa also will have to leave the first century B.C.

2

Sircar's own view[51] on the origin of the Era ultimately known as the Vikrama is more cogent than Pandey's in the context of the current chronology. "The earliest documents of the indigenous kings of India," he writes, "bear no trace of the use of any era. Many of them contain no date at all. But some

51. *The Vikrama Commemoration Volume,* pp. 557-72.

of the official records of the independent rulers as well as those belonging to their officials and subordinates and persons residing in their dominions are dated. The date is, however, always expressed in the reckoning of the king's regnal years." The Edicts of Aśoka (*c.* 272-32 B.C.), the Besnagar inscription (*c.* beginning of first century B.C.) in which King Kautsīputra Bhāgabhadra is mentioned, the Pabhosa inscription of the time of Ūdaka (*c.* end of first century B.C.), the Nasik inscription of Gautamīputra Sātakarṇi (*c.* 106-30 A. D.), the Hathigumphā inscription of Khāravela (*c.* end of first century B.C.), the Nāgār-Junikonda inscription of Śāntamūla II (*c.* 270-85 A.D.) are some of the examples that can be brought forth to support Sircar.

As for some Indian eras with their epochs falling before the 4th century B.C. – the Kaliyuga Era of 3102 B.C., the Śri Harsha Era of 457 B.C. and the Parinirvāṇa Eras of the Buddhists and the Jains – Sircar has no difficulty in showing in the context of the current chronology that none of them were in use among kings in ancient India. Fleet[52] demonstrated that before the astronomer Āryabhaṭṭa, who is dated in the fourth quarter of the 5th century A.D., nobody used the Kaliyuga Era. According to our knowledge, the first king to use it was Pulakeśin II of the Aihole inscription (634 A.D.), who defeated that contemporary of Hiuen Tsang, Harsha of Kanauj. Indian epigraphy is unaware of any use of the Śri Harsha Era of 457 B.C., mentioned by Alberuni; it also looks, like the Kaliyuga Era, as if invented only by Indian astronomers for the purposes of their calculations. The Buddhist Parinirvāṇa Era was limited within the Buddhist church and it never figured as a popular era in ancient India: besides there was no uniform Era, for the epoch had a large number of variants in different parts of the world. The absence of any use of the reckoning in even the inscriptions of Aśoka, the greatest Buddhist king, proves that it was unknown in early Indian times. "The Jain ecclesiastical reckoning," remarks

52. *Journal of the Royal Asiatic Society*, 1911, p. 479.

Sircar, "has even less claim than the Buddhist one to be taken as anything like a regular era in the early history of India." Then Sircar adds: "The absence of any trace of the use of an era in the dated records of the early indigenous kings of India is to be taken with the fact that the earliest use of the regular era in India is noticed in the epigraphic and numismatic records of foreigners. The two facts together would doubtless point to the extraneous origin of the custom of dating records according to the years of an era. It seems very probable that the use of an era in royal as well as private records was introduced and popularised in India by kings belonging to non-Indian extraction such as the Scytho-Parthians and the Kushāns..."

Sircar continues: "The evidence of paleography and the attested facts of early Indian history suggest that the epoch of the Kanishka era, i.e., the first regnal year of Kanishka, has to be assigned to a period later than the epoch of the Scytho-Parthian reckoning.... It is interesting to note that the earliest extant historical eras of India, viz., the Vikrama and Śaka Saṁvats of 58 B.C. and 78 A.D. respectively, have epochs falling exactly in the Scytho-Parthian and Kushān periods of Indian history... between the 2nd century B.C. and the 3rd century A.D.... It is only natural to think that the Vikrama and Śaka reckonings may after all be the same as the two foreign eras known from epigraphs... The identification of the Scytho-Parthian era with the Vikrama Saṁvat is... supported at least by one evidence. The Takht-Bāhī inscription... is dated in the year 103 of this era and in the 26th regnal year of Gondopharnes. It is interesting to note that a Parthian king named Gondopharnes, called king of India in some versions, is represented in an old Christian tradition as a contemporary of Saint Thomas, the apostle (one of the 12 disciples of Jesus Christ, 4 B.C.-29 or 33 A.D.) who flourished in the 1st century A.D.[53] It will be seen that, if year 103 of the Takht-Bāhī inscription be referred to the Vikrama Saṁvat, the reign of

53. Smith, *The Early History of India*, 4th ed., pp. 245-50, 260-62.

Gondopharnes falls exactly in the same epoch, *i.e.*, in the period 21-46 A.D."

Sircar's view is not quite safe from criticism. To begin with: the testimony of the Takht-Bāhī inscription can hardly be considered clinching. Saint Thomas would be contemporaneous with Gondopharnes if the latter were reigning at any time after 29 or 33 A.D. The year 103 of the era observed by him could easily fall a little before or a little after 58-57 B.C. without his missing the supposed visit of the Christian apostle. And there is nothing improbable in two eras - one Scytho-Parthian, the other Indian - having been founded within the same few years. We know, for instance, that Diodotus the Bactrian and Arsaces the Parthian revolted within the same few years against Greek rule and that the latter's era starts from 248 B.C.[54] and that, as Sircar[55] himself grants, the former might also have initiated an era at more or less the same time.

Further, it is hard to understand why an era observed by the Mālavas as the Kṛta Era should be called by that name if the era were Scytho-Parthian. Of all the possible explanations of the name, the one that would suit Sircar most is that it is the Indianised form of a foreign name. But he[56] has to admit: "Kṛta as the personal name of a king is no doubt known to Indian folklore; but the name is not found among the known Scytho-Parthian kings...." It is also hard to understand why a Scytho-Parthian era accepted by the Mālavas from their alleged conquerors should be styled, as Sircar[57] tells us, "the era handed down by the Mālava Republic," "the year counted in accordance with the custom established by (or, from the foundation of) the Mālava Republic", "the date (*pūrva*) of the Mālavas" or the era "that speaks of the glory of the Mālava dynasty". The natural suggestion is that the Era had originally to do with the Mālava Republic or the Mālavas in general

54. Smith, *Classical Dictionary, s.v.* Arsaces.
55. Sircar, *op. cit.*, p. 566.
56. *Ibid.*, p. 585.
57. *Ibid.*, pp. 582, 83.

and not with the Scytho-Parthians. Finally, the Scytho-Parthians are said by Sircar[58] to have dominated over the Panjāb in the first century B.C. and the first century A.D.; but what proof is there that the Mālavas had their home in the Panjāb in this century? We know of them in the Panjāb in the time of Alexander in the 4th century B.C., long before the Scytho-Parthians were heard of. The earliest mention of the Kṛta Era is in the Nandsa inscription dated year 282 of that era and found in Udaipur State, Rājputānā. The coins found in the Jaipur State show the Mālavas to be in Rājputānā already in the first century B.C. So it is pure conjecture on Sircar's part[59] to declare: "Thus it appears that the Mālava tribe carried the Kṛta i.e., the Scytho-Parthian era to Rājputānā and Mālawā from their original home in the Panjāb."

Yes, Sircar's view is dubious at several points. But, if we accept the current chronology which places Chandragupta Vikramāditya in 376-414 A.D., it is very probable that he was the original of the legends about the Śakāri Vikramāditya of Ujjayinī, and, if we accept the identity of not only the Kṛta with the Mālava Era but also of both these with the Vikrama Era, Sircar's view is logically more appealing on the whole than the one championed by Pandey and we may imagine the Mālavas to have just come to Rājputānā from the Panjāb in the latter half of the first century B.C. with a foreign era.

Now we face Pandey's[60] answer to the third argument – the omission, implying the unimportance, of the Vikrama Era in the astronomical works. He says that it is capable of an easy explanation. The explanation is: "Though the Śakas were repelled in their first attempt at invading India, they renewed their invasion in about 78 A.D. They conquered Avanti and made Ujjayinī their capital. We also know from the Jain work *Prabhāvaka-charita* that they started the Śaka era in 78 A.D. In those days Ujjayinī was a great seat of learning and a centre of astronomical researches. Astronomers, like other erudites,

58. *Ibid.*, p. 585.
59. *Ibid.*, p. 583.
60. Pandey, *op. cit.*, pp. 8-9.

flocked to this city even under the Śakas. The Mālavas were dislodged from Avanti and pushed towards the north-east and the city of Ujjayinī was compelled to discontinue the era founded by the Mālavas and was forced to adopt the era started by the Śakas. During the long period of about three hundred years, when the Śakas were ruling Avanti and Saurāshtra, the Mālava era had hardly any chance of revival at Ujjayinī. The astronomers used the official Śaka era. In the beginning they did so under compulsion. Later on it became fashionable and habitual. Further, some sanctity was attached to the Śaka era when it came to be associated with Śālivāhana which made it more popular than before. The Guptas conquered and ruled over Avanti for about a century and a half. The official era of the Guptas was their own. But the astronomers who had become conservative at this time and were psychologically reconciled to the Śaka-Śālivāhana era, persisted in its use and would not adopt the Gupta era. When the power of the Guptas disappeared, the Mālava era was still current, but the astronomers would not change the mode of their dating. Such was the case not only in central India and the Deccan where the Śaka era became widely current and popular, but also in northern India where the Vikrama era assumed its present name and became universal. Astronomers and astrologers date their compositions in the Śaka era as late as the nineteenth century A.D. It was mainly due to their reconciliation to the Śaka-Śālivāhana era and partly due to the lack of proper political perspective in them."

Pandey's statement is fairly credible when it tells us that the passing of Avanti into Śaka hands and the fall of Ujjayinī to the Śakas forced the astronomers of Mālava and neighbouring places to eschew the era of 57 B.C. and adopt that of 78 A.D. It is also pretty plausible when it tells us that the Śaka Era became fashionable and that the astronomers got used to it and would not drop it in spite of all compulsion having been removed. They may be charged with "lack of proper political perspective" and one may speak of their getting reconciled to the Śaka Era because it came to be associated with and sanctified by the name of Śālivāhana. But the association with Śālivāhana cannot ever be spoken of as preceding the time of the Guptas. The current chronology makes the Guptas start in 321 A.D. The name of Śālivāhana occurs in the thirteenth century. How can it popularise the Śaka Era before the Guptas conquered and ruled over Avanti? How can astronomers get psychologically reconciled to a Śaka-Śālivāhana Era during or soon after the time of the Guptas? A strange historical oversight is here, contradicting Pandey's own earlier remark that the Śaka Era is referred to namelessly as mere Varsha up to its 500th year. It weakens the total impact of Pandey's passage. However, even without it, the passage would not compensate the inadequacy of the answers to the profounder implications of the previous arguments or suggest in any way the existence of Vikramāditya. It merely neutralises the idea that the omission by the astronomers to use the Vikrama Era shows their unawareness of any such momentous figure as Vikramāditya and therefore his non-historicity.

The fourth argument – the omission of Vikramāditya by the Purāṇas – is more difficult to get over. If Vikramāditya was a great king and if the Purāṇas bring the dynastic lists and other historical matters up to at least 320 A.D., the age of the Guptas, it is incomprehensible how this great king's name should appear nowhere in them. Pandey[61] believes a good answer can run thus: "It can be submitted that the existence of a ruler cannot be denied simply because he is not mentioned in the Purāṇas. It is a well-known fact that the Purāṇas do not include a large number of republican states, which existed in ancient India, in their dynastic history, but the history of these states is revealed by the Buddhist and Jain sources. Thus the omission in the Purāṇas is not a conclusive proof of the non-existence of a state, a people, or a person. The Purāṇas, however, fortunately, throw light on the history of Vikramāditya. While dealing with the history of the Āndhras,

61. *Ibid.*, pp. 22-25.

the Purāṇas state that 'taking their own off-shoots there will be six contemporary dynasties of the Āndhras' which will be listed as follows:

(1) The Āndhra-bhṛtyas
(2) The ten Ābhiras
(3) The seven (ten) Gardabhilas (Gardabhins)
(4) The ten Śakas
(5) The eight Yavanas
(6) The fourteen Tukhāras, thirteen Muruṇḍas and eighteen Maunas.

It is evident from the Jain tradition* that Vikramāditya belonged to the family of the Gardabhilas. When the Purāṇas refer to the Gardabhila family, they are obviously not oblivious of the existence of Vikramāditya.

"Besides the categorical reference to the family of Vikramāditya in the Purāṇas, we have specific reference to him also in them. The Bhavishya-purāṇa mentions him twice... Another mention of Vikramāditya is found in the Kumārikā-Khaṇḍa of the Skanda-purāṇa where it is said that he flourished three thousand years after the beginning of the Kali age.

"The date of the Bhavishya-purāṇa is controversial. According to Pargiter it was composed during the reign of Yajñaśri, an Āndhra King, in the second century A.D. In this case it is good evidence for the historicity of Vikramāditya in the first century B.C. But many scholars dispute the date assigned by Pargiter and are of the opinion that it has received a number of interpolations in course of time. Even accepting the view that the Bhavishya-purāṇa underwent changes, it can be emphasised that the tradition of Vikramāditya was known to the later editors of the Purāṇas, though they were sometimes confused in their memories of the past events."

Pandey's answer is unconvincing. About the Skanda and

* The *Prabhāvaka-charita*.

Bhavishya Purāṇas, Haraprasad Sastri,[62] in what Pusalker[63] calls the most satisfactory grouping on a thorough and critical examination of the contents of the Purāṇas, says: "The original matter in these Purāṇas has been lost out of recognition on account of various revisions of a drastic nature." Hence the references to Vikramāditya in them cannot be regarded as original matter unless we can find a real reason why he is ignored in the more authentic Purāṇas. If we take these references as genuine, to say at the same time that he is ignored in those other Purāṇas because many republican states are not included in them is not logical: a different cause of the omission is wanted. Much more illogical does the excuse about republican states become when it is actually said that the Gardabhīla family of Vikramāditya is noticed where we find the omission of the name of even Khāravela who was not the leader of a republican state but an absolute monarch and a very powerful one at that. Evidently a different cause is operative.

In addition, the very claim of a "categorical reference to the family of Vikramāditya" is vitiated by an important fact which is forgotten by Pandey and gets blurred in the form in which he has quoted the Purāṇic enumeration of the "six contemporary dynasties". One would imagine that the Gardabhīlas and the rest were contemporary with a part of the great Āndhra-Sātavāhanas who began with Simuka and ended with Pulumavi III. But the fact is that if the great Āndhra-Sātavāhanas are dated as in the modern chronological scheme where they start a little before the Christian Era and terminate about two and a quarter centuries after it, we cannot get any Gardabhīla in the 1st century B.C., the supposed time of Vikramāditya. For, the Purāṇas talk of the "six contemporary dynasties" as existing at the *termination* of the great Āndhra-Sātavāhanas with Pulumavi III. Pargiter[64]

62. *Journal of the Behar and Orissa Research Society*, XIV, pp. 330-37.
63. *Studies in the Epics and Purāṇas of India* (1955), pp. xlix-l.
64. *The Dynasties of the Kali Age*, p. xv.

writes regarding the chronological summary in the Matsya, Vāyu and Brahmaṇḍa Purāṇas that it "brings the reckoning down definitely... to the end of the Āndhras and uses the vague term *Āndhr-ānt-ādyās* in referring to future kings." Pargiter's own translation[65] of the relevant passage is: "When the kingdom of the Āndhras has come to an end, there will be kings belonging to the lineage of their servants: 7 Āndhras and 10 Ābhira kings, also 7 Gardabhins (or Gardabhīlas), 18 Śakas. There will be 8 Yavanas, 14 Tusāras, 13 Muruṇḍas, 11 Maunas." He observes that the numbers differ in the Purāṇas and even the names have variants, but he nowhere informs us that these "future" kings did not follow *in the wake* of the dynasty closing with Pulumavi III. So the Gardabhīlas have to be commenced a little after the end of the reign of Pulumavi III in 227 A.D.[66] – that is, over two and a half centuries later than 57 B.C. How, then, can the Purāṇas be declared to have a categorical reference to Vikramāditya's family and to suggest his existence in the first century B.C.?

The argument against Vikramāditya from the Purāṇas remains untackled by Pandey. To render his declaration valid and also give a chance to the mention in the Skanda and Bhavishya Purāṇas to be authentic, he must surrender the historical pattern and chronological chart of modern historians which he wholly accepts save for the inclusion he makes of the traditional Vikramāditya. The chronology followed by the Purāṇic tradition puts the *Mahābhārata* War in 3138 B.C., 36 years before the Kali Yuga of 3102 B.C. With this point of departure Pulumavi III will never reign in 210-227 A.D., nor will the Imperial Guptas come to the throne in 320 A.D. If out of the several versions of the period (1015, 1050, 1500 years) given by the Purāṇas as intervening between the *Mahābhārata* War and Mahāpadma Nanda's coronation, we take the longest and then understand correctly the statement about the intervals between this War and the beginning and the end of the Āndhras, we shall reach at the time of Alexander's

65. *Ibid.*, p. 72.
66. *The Age of Imperial Unity*, p. 206.

invasion the Imperial Guptas so that the "Sandrocottus" of the Classical historians would be not Chandragupta Maurya but Chandragupta I, the founder of the Imperial Guptas, and the Gupta Era of 320 A.D. would be not an Era marking the beginning of the Imperial Guptas but, as Alberuni[67] has said, an Era founded to celebrate the ending of the "wicked and powerful" Guptas. The Purāṇic scheme may look fantastic, at least at first sight, and call for a drastic readjustment of some historical data, but nothing short of it will here help out Pandey, Majumdar, Pusalker and others who wish to reinstate the traditional Vikramāditya.

For, with this scheme, the Gardabhīlas will fall in the period before the Christian Era and they would be mentioned in general without bringing in Vikramāditya by name because the chief Purāṇas actually close at the time of the beginning of the Guptas and cannot therefore know of any great ruler of 57 B.C. The Purāṇas' antecedence to Vikramāditya and not any omission of republican states will be accountable for the omission of his name as also for the omission of the name of a mighty conqueror like Khāravela who lived some centuries after Alexander's time though before the Christian Era. This will make the mention of Vikramāditya by the Skanda and Bhavishya Purāṇas non-contradictory of the testimony of the better-preserved and less interpolated Purāṇas, and consequently the mention can be looked upon as authentic instead of as thrust in during the mediaeval period: we shall at least be left free to think the mention a piece of historial news entered any time before India's middle ages.

The Purāṇic scheme, by shifting the long line of the Sātavāhanas to the centuries before and after 500 B.C. will naturally put around the same date the Śakas Nahapāna, Chashṭana and Rudradāman who were contemporaries of Gautamīputra Sātakarṇi. Then there will be true sense in what Pandey[68] feels his way towards, apropos Āmarāja's statement that Varāhamihira the astronomer died in 509 Śaka: "It is

67. Sachau, *Alberuni's India* (1914), II, p. 7.
68. Pandey, *op. cit.*, p. 74.

advisable to inquire whether the Śaka Era used by Āmarāja in the case of Varāhamihira is the same as the one founded in 78 A.D. or some other Śaka Era, which was known in the astronomical school of Varāhamihira and which was most probably referred to by Āmarāja." In this connection the following verses of Varāhamihira are very useful:

> I shall tell you, according to the theory of Vṛddha Garga,/the course of the Seven Seers by whom the northern region is as it were protected.../The Seven Rishis were in Maghā when King Yudhishṭhira ruled the earth,/And the period of that King is 2526 years before the Śaka Era....[69]

From the last line of the second verse quoted above, it is evident that the difference of time between the starting of the Yudhishṭhira Era and the foundation of the Śaka Era referred to here was one of 2526 years. After this, there follows a slip on Pandey's part, for he takes the Yudhishṭhira Era to be 3101 B.C., the Kali Yuga counted from the completion of its first year, whereas the introduction of the Saptarishis ("Munis" in Varāhamihira's phrase) reminds us of Bühler's fixing[70] of the Kāshmiri Saptarishi Era in 3076 B.C. and brings to our recollection the death of Yudhishṭhira in the same year according to the *Mahābhārata*[71] – *i.e.*, 25 years after 3101 B.C. which is the first year of the Kali Yuga and in which Yudhishṭira is spoken of in the epic as hearing of Kṛṣṇa's death, abdicating in favour of Parīkshit and setting out on a country-wide pilgrimage. The Purāṇas[72] relate the same story except that they are silent about Yudhishṭhira's death. If 3076 B.C. is understood to be the starting-point of the Yudhishṭhira Era we get (3076-2526=) 550 B.C. as the Śaka Era meant by

69. English translation by Kern in Cunningham's *Book of Indian Eras* (Calcutta, 1883), p. 9.

70. *The Indian Antiquary*, Vol. VI (1877), pp. 264-268 .

71. *Mahāprasthānika Parvan, Adhyāya*, I.

72. Pargiter, *The Dynasties of the Kali Age*, p. 75.

Varāhamihira. Pandey[73] himself at another place in his book writes: "The Śaka Era used by Varāhamihira and Āmarāja was most probably one which was founded in 550 B.C." Taking 550 B.C. and not 78 A.D. which would yield, as in Kalhaṇa's famous but fantastic interpretation, 2448 B.C. as the time of Yudhishṭhira as well as of the *Mahābhārata* War, we have a Śaka Era exactly suiting the Purāṇic scheme in which the Śakas Nahapāna, Chashṭana and Rudradāman occur round about 500 B.C.

The death of Varāhamihira will then be in (550-509=) 41 B.C. and he will have been, as in the Vikramāditya-tradition, a contemporary of that king of Ujjayinī, one of the "nine gems" set by this tradition in his reign. Such a dating of Varāhamihira's death will remove the wonder why Āryabhaṭṭa never mentions the Vikrama Era and even Varāhamihira does not while mentioning the Śaka Era: Āryabhaṭṭa as a predecessor of Varāhamihira must have lived before 57 B.C., and the omission by Varāhamihira must be due to his writing both his *Pañchasiddhāntikā* and *Bṛhatsaṁhitā* before 57 B.C. Further, the extirpation of the Śakas of Chashṭana-Rudradāman's family by Chandragupta II will go to some centuries prior to the Christian Era and we shall be left uncompelled to consider 78 A.D. as connected with the flourishing of these Śakas but can accept the tradition that Śālivāhana founded an Era at this date on defeating the Śakas who had come up again after their previous defeat by Vikramāditya in 57 B.C. when they had invaded India a second time in the second century B.C. Knowing, though not naming, Śālivāhana to be the founder of the Era of 78 A.D. the post-Christ Indian astronomers would really be expected to adopt this Era owing to its sanctification by association with a national hero's name. The Vikrama Era, by being anterior to the Śālivāhana Era, would fall a little into the shade in the most natural manner.

The greatest advantage which the Purāṇic scheme confers on the protagonists of the traditional Vikramāditya is the

73. Pandey, *op. cit.*, p. 204.

removal of Chandragupta II Vikramāditya, a legitimate *Śakāri* and lord of Ujjayinī, from 376-414 A.D. to the third century B.C. With the path cleared of him, we can validly consider the traditional Vikramāditya of 57 B.C. as the inspirer of the legends current in mediaeval India. Without the Purāṇic scheme we shall never get to him over so tremendous a hurdle. Once the Gupta is out of the way we can contemplate with some ease the fairly long non-association of the name Vikrama with the Era of 57 B.C. and draw a perfect parallel to the fairly long non-association of the word Śaka with the Era of 78 A.D. For, with the Śakas of the Chashṭana-Rudradāman family ending in the 3rd century B.C. and the later Śakas ending in 78 A.D., we have no evidence of Śakas in the period from 78 A.D. to the time when the first mention of "Śaka" occurs in relation to this date. The situation thus is on all fours with the situation with regard to the Era of 57 B.C. There are no depth-dissimilarities to outweigh the surface-similarities. The second argument of the opponents of the traditional Vikramāditya will be met just as cogently as the third and the fourth arguments.

The whole explanation by Pandey of how the same Era was known first as Kṛta, then as Mālava and lastly as Vikrama will become in itself more plausible. But it is not really necessary any more than it is necessary to explain why the association of "Śaka" with the other Era came so late on the scene. In fact the Purāṇic chronology may require the non-identity of the Vikrama Era with the Kṛta-Mālava. The identity of the Kṛta with the Mālava is directly established by the Mandasor inscription of Naravarman dated 461[74] and the Nagari inscription of some Vaiśyas dated year 481,[75] but no such proof is there for identifying the Vikrama with both the Kṛta and the Mālava. The Kṛta-Mālava may need to be taken far beyond 57 B.C., if the Mandasor inscription of Bandhuvarman[76] dated 493 of the Mālava Era cannot find anybody

74. Sircar, *Select Inscriptions*, p. 377.
75. Bhandarkar, *List of Inscriptions of Northern India*, No. 5.
76. Sircar, *op. cit.*, p. 295.

except a Kumāragupta of the Imperial Gupta line to answer to the name "Kumāra" mentioned by it as that of the reigning monarch.[77] This will demand a drastic readjustment of further historical data. But such a readjustment cannot be shirked by those who desire to historicise the traditional Vikramāditya.

The sole anti-traditional argument that will remain not fully countered will be the first one. As it is the weakest of all, it cannot stand against tradition of the sort that has clustered round the name Vikramāditya of the reputed founder of the Era of 57 B.C. Especially striking is the tradition transmitted by the Jain work *Prabhāvaka-charita* about which Pandey[78] says: "The library of the *Pātanasaṁgha* contains its earliest manuscript, which is assigned to the fourteenth century Vikrama Era. Evidently, the work was written late but the author states that his writings were mostly based upon earlier works, traditions maintained by widely read sages' historical and biographical lore. It imitates the *Sthavirāvali-charita* of Hemachandrasūri and contains biographies of eminent Śvetāmbara Jain saints, scholars, their patrons and kings, who flourished during the period between the first century and the thirteenth century Vikrama Era. Some of the most important rulers who adorn the pages of this work are Vikramāditya, Harshavardhana, Āmarāja, Bhojadeva, Bhimadeva, Siddharāja, Kumārapāla. These are the well-known rulers of ancient India and the inclusion of their lives in the *Prabhāvaka-charita* amply justifies its historical character. The work contains the biography of one of the most notable Jain saints, Kālakasūri, which narrates the Śaka invasion of India and the reconquest of Ujjayinī by Vikramāditya and the foundation of his era."

Studying the story which develops from Kālaka's seeking the help of the Śakas against Gardabhīla, the ruler of Avanti who had insulted and injured him, Rapson[79] opines: "The story can neither be proved nor disproved; but it may be said in its favour that its historical setting is not inconsistent with

77. *The Classical Age*, pp. 68, 69, 72, 75.
78. Pandey, *op. cit.*, p. 28.
79. *The Cambridge History of India*, Vol. I, p. 532.

what we know of the political circumstances of Ujjayinī at this period." F. Egerton[80] strikes a more assertive note: "I am not aware that there is any definite and positive reason for rejecting the Jainistic chronicles completely... It seems on the whole at least possible, and perhaps probable that there really was a king named Vikramāditya who reigned in Mālava and founded the era of 58-57 B.C." Sten Konow[81] goes even a step further: "I cannot see the slightest reason for discrediting this account, as is usually done, because most scholars are *a priori* disinclined to believe in Indian tradition and sometimes prefer the most marvellous accounts of foreign authors to Indian lore. Almost every detail can be verified from other sources. A Śaka empire in the Indus country is... known from classical sources. Ptolemy speaks of the extension of the Śaka power to Kathiawar, and the use of the imperial title 'king of kings' among the Śakas is attested by coins. And the Purāṇas speak of the Śaka kings as the successors of the Gardabhīla dynasty."

Of course, if the three other arguments remained unchecked, the indulgent views of Rapson, Egerton and Konow would have to be set aside. But these views speak of the impression which the Jain story makes in isolation and in its own proper right, and once those arguments are out of the way what these three European scholars utter is of great importance.

The situation in regard to Hāla's *Gāthāsaptaśatī* and Guṇāḍhya's *Bṛhatkathā* undergoes also a transformation. With Chandragupta II removed to the third century B.C., we have no fear about the dating of Hāla anywhere between the first century A.D. and the commencement of the sixth century A.D. Of course now the identification with Hāla Sātavāhana is impossible because it would carry the *Saptaśatī* beyond 500 B.C., but the Vikramāditya mentioned by this book, whether the book was written immediately after 57 B.C. or over five

80. *Vikrama's Adventure*, H.O.S., Introduction, pp. lxiv, lxvi.

81. *Corpus Inscriptionum Indicarum*, Vol. II, Part I: Historical Introduction, p. xxvii.

centuries later, cannot be anyone save the Śakāri founder of that Era. Guṇāḍhya's book can now introduce both the Vikramādityas with impunity, with no exposure to the charge of interpolation by others, for both would precede its composition any time before 500 A.D. The anterior period of Chandragupta II to that of Vikramāditya of Ujjayinī would account for the sparseness in the *Bṛhatkathā* of the former's presence and the richness of the latter's: the posterior date of Vikramāditya of Ujjayinī keeps his memory more alive for Guṇāḍhya.

It seems that to defend convincingly any part of Indian tradition the necessary procedure is not to pick and choose from its pattern and chronology, but to embrace the whole of that chronology and that pattern.

We may be told: "If we put Chandragupta II Vikramāditya in the third century B.C., the legends arising in mediaeval India about a Vikramāditya of Ujjayinī who founded the Era of 57 B.C. can be traced, in its differences no less than in its resemblances, to a memory of the great Gupta. The large lapse of time would tend to haze the memory and provide a ground for the dissimilarities, a ground upon which the strong national propensity of the Mālavas and the national character of the Era concerned could act very effectively to create dissimilarities. No need will then be there to think of a historical Vikramāditya of Ujjayinī other than the great Gupta."

We should counter this statement thus: "Our point was that the proximity of the great Gupta to the time of the birth of the late Vikramāditya-tradition rendered belief in the historicity of the traditional Vikramāditya logically untenable or at least much less tenable than the belief in his derivation from Chandragupta II. If this proximity is gone, then, as you say, the long lapse of time between Chandraguta II and the mediaeval legends may, in conjunction with other factors, account for the difference no less than the resemblance; but no cogent circumstance would be left to render such a possibility the only one and, unlike the case in the previous situation, the historicity of a Vikramāditya of Ujjayinī other than the great Gupta can logically be argued – at least with equal force as his derivation wholly from Chandragupta II. Now the proximity of the great Gupta would be to the ancient date at which the mediaeval legends place their hero and not to the legends themselves about his date: the legends thereby escape the suspicions of being coloured by any proximity and being led to invent extrapolations backward to the date. Besides, the placing of the great Gupta in the third century B.C. according to the Purāṇic history, opens the way, as we have seen, to belief on our part in an early no less than a late Vikramāditya-tradition, stories in the first five centuries after Christ serving as predecessors to the mediaeval legends and linking them to the pre-Christian time about which they speak."

Apropos of Kālidāsa, the Purāṇic history brings about a tremendous simplification. Reasons have been urged to show that Kālidāsa knew about some of the glorious Guptas and that he has affinities with an age of efflorescence of Sanskrit literature such as the Gupta Age was.* Reasons have also been urged to show that he could not have existed in the period our historians allot to the Guptas. The Purāṇic history, by putting the Guptas almost three centuries before the first century B.C. in which the traditional Vikramāditya would fall, grants validity to both sides of the controversy so far as the Guptas and their conventional period are concerned.

Where other matters are concerned, the answer to all arguments for refusing to Kālidāsa the first century B.C. and for dating him more than four hundred years later is very effectively framed by Pandey. We may quote him also in the matter of the Hūṇas, which is related to the political circumstances and not the cultural ones of the Gupta Age.

There is the argument of Kālidāsa's posteriority to Aśva-

* We speak of an "efflorescence" and not a "renaissance", because the belief in an eclipse of Sanskrit literature in the pre-Guptan Age cannot be maintained (*cf.* Pandey, *op. cit.*, pp. 69-70), and is no longer regarded as technically correct (*cf. The Classical Age*, p. 271).

ghośa. "The *Buddhacharita* of Aśvaghośa bears a close resemblance to the *Raghuvaṁśa* of Kālidāsa, both the works being court-epics. On comparison it has been established that the *Buddhacharita* is inferior to the *Raghuvaṁśa* in literary merits. It is, therefore, supposed that Aśvaghośa flourished in an age when the Sanskrit Kāvya (poetic) style was still in its infancy, and Kālidāsa, coming later, imitated and improved upon his model. According to the Buddhist traditions, Aśvaghośa was a contemporary of Kanishka who is assigned either to the second half of the first century or the first half of the second century A.D. Kālidāsa who followed him in style and theme must have come later than he by at least a few centuries."[82]

Pandey replies: "The line of the contention here is entirely against the course of the development of the Buddhist literature. It is a well-known fact that the early Buddhist literature was produced in Pālī Prākṛt for the consumption of the masses. The Buddhist writers, in the course of time, realised that Sanskrit was a more refined and effective medium of expression than Prākṛt and they began to write in the Sanskrit language on the model of literary Sanskrit works. This tendency became prominent with the rise of the Mahāyāna school of Buddhism. Aśvaghosha's composing a Buddhist Kāvya in Sanskrit presupposes the existence of a Brahmanical Sanskrit Kāvya to serve him as a model. The close resemblance between the *Buddhacharita* and the *Raghuvaṁśa* indicates that the latter was used as a model for the former. If the *Buddhacharita* is inferior to the *Raghuvaṁśa*, it is the fault of an imperfect imitation. A superb poetic genius like Kālidāsa could not select the *Buddhacharita* as a model. Moreover, Kālidāsa respectfully refers to poetic geniuses who flourished before him – Bhāsa, Saumilla, etc.,[83] but he does not mention Aśvaghośa. This omission points to the non-existence of Aśvaghośa before Kālidāsa. In view of these considerations

82. E.B. Cowell, Introduction to the *Buddhacharita of Aśvaghośa*.
83. *Malavikāgnimitram*, Introduction.

Kālidāsa cannot be placed after Aśvaghośa. He must have existed some centuries earlier to set a model to be followed by later writers."

There is the argument from Kālidāsa's mention of the Hūṇas in connection with the world-conquest of Raghu. "It is said that the Hūṇas invaded India for the first time in the middle of the fifth century, when they were repelled by Skandagupta. Indians became familiar with the Hūṇas after this event. The age of Kālidāsa, therefore, must be posterior to 540 A.D."[84]

Pandey's reply is: "The mention of the Hūṇas has been misconstrued. In the description of the world-conquest of Raghu they are mentioned in the list of peoples defeated by Raghu and not as invaders or conquerors of India. They are also located outside India. It is known from Chinese history that the Hūṇas had built up a powerful empire beyond Bactria from the middle of the third century B.C. to the middle of the first century A.D.[85] The Hūṇa empire was just on the threshold of India and the Indians were familiar with the Hūṇas. To suppose that the Indians had no knowledge of peoples outside India is to do scant justice to the geographical and racial knowledge possessed by them. The Pārasīkas, the Pahlavas, the Pāradas, the Śakas, the Hūṇas, the Kambojas, the Kirātas, the Chinas – the neighbouring peoples of India were very well known to them.* Kālidāsa makes fine distinctions between the Pārasīkas, the Hūṇas and the Kambojas and gives their peculiar characteristics.[86] It is perfectly justified to conclude that Kālidāsa, while referring to the Hūṇas, was drawing upon his knowledge of the tribal disposition of central Asia in the first century B.C., and he cannot be dragged to the fifth or the sixth century A.D. simply because he makes a reference to the Hūṇas."

84. *Literary Remains of Dr. Bhau Daji*, p. 49; Pathaka, Introduction to "Megha-duta", pp. vii ff.

85. Gultzlaff, *History of China*, 1834, pp. 220-9.

* *Cf.* Reference to the various races and people in the *Mahābhārata*.

86. *Raghuvaṁśa*, IV.60-70.

There is the argument from Astronomical Data. "It is generally assumed by many Indologists that India came in close contact with the western world of Greece and Rome during the Kushāṇa period and it was during this period that she borrowed many astronomical principles from Greece and Rome. The works of Kālidāsa betray the knowledge of these principles; therefore, he belongs to the post-Kushāṇa period of Indian history, and the only suitable period for him is the Gupta period."[87]

Here is Pandey's reply: "That the Indians had no mental aversion to borrow sciences and arts from foreigners is an undoubted fact, but the time for borrowing astronomical principles has been brought down without justification. The arguers forget the fact that the Greeks and Romans themselves borrowed astronomical and astrological principles from the Chaldeans and the Babylonians in 700 B.C. The Indians had direct contact with these middle-east countries much earlier than the advent of the Greeks in India (326 B.C.), and there was nothing to prevent them from learning astronomical knowledge from them. The resemblance between Indian and Greek astronomical principles is due to their common origin.[88] The *Rāmāyaṇa*, which was composed earlier than the first century B.C., contains advanced knowledge of astronomy.[89] Kālidāsa refers to an astronomical term, 'Jamitra' which has been identified with the Greek term 'diametron'. But some scholars have also suggested that these two terms may have independent origin, 'diametron' may be a Graecised form of the Sanskrit word 'Jamitra'.[90] Kālidāsa is also not indebted to Āryabhaṭṭa (476 A.D.) for his astronomical references, because he was not dealing with scientific principles, but pointing to current notions of astronomy, which were formulated later on."

87. Jacobi, *ZDMG* XXX, 303 ff.

88. *Cf.* S.V. Dikshit, *Early History of Indian Astronomy*, pp. 137-39; Max Müller, *India, What Can It Teach Us?*, p. 327.

89. Balakanda: 18.9.15; Ayodhya Kanda: 15.3.

90. S.P. Pandit, Introduction to the *Raghuvaṁśa*.

We may remark that if one puts Varāhamihira in the first century B.C., as Pandey himself does, Āryabhaṭṭa who is mentioned by Varāhamihira must precede Kālidāsa, and Kālidāsa may owe something to him. Pandey not only interprets Varāhamihira's "Śaka Era" to be one of 550 B.C. and hence his death in Śaka 509 according to Āmarāja to be in 41 B.C.; Pandey also writes: "That Varāhamihira cannot be placed in the fifth or sixth century A.D. is shown by internal evidences contained in the *Bṛhatsaṁhitā* composed by him. The territorial divisions of India with reference to Madhyadeśa are detailed in this work, which do not fit in with the territorial divisions known from the epigraphical records of the Gupta period." This means that if the Guptas are in the fifth or sixth century A.D., Varāhamihira has to go out of it. Since we do not put the Guptas there, it only means for us that Varāhamihira cannot be wherever the Guptas are. And our theory, though removing both him and them from the fifth or sixth century A.D., still divides him from the Gupta Vikramādityas and so from the synchronism against which we are warned. With Varāhamihira separated from the Guptas everywhere and brought to the first century B.C. we have a further argument for giving credence to the Indian tradition which places him and Kālidāsa and Vikramāditya together in that period. In addition, it removes one objection to considering as not quite devoid of authenticity the astronomical work *Jyotirvidābharaṇa* ascribed to Kālidāsa. For doubt[91] has been cast on its authenticity on account of its reference to Varāhamihira who is usually taken to have lived in the sixth century A.D. Or, if it is taken as Kālidāsa's, the reference to Varāhamihira is understood as proving Kālidāsa's existence in that century. When Varāhamihira is placed in the first century B.C., we may accept as genuine amidst later contributions to this treatise the original authorship of Kālidāsa and accept as true the date[92] which it gives of its composition: Kali Era 3068=24 Vikrama Saṁvat=33 A.D.

91. Dikshit *op. cit.*, p. 475 ff.
92. XXII.21.

A final argument against the traditional date of Kālidāsa is from the reference to "Diṅ-nāga." "In his *Meghadūta* Kālidāsa refers to Nichula and Diṅ-nāga. The learned commentator Mallinātha, while dwelling upon these words, suggests that Nichula was an admirer and friend of Kālidāsa and Diṅ-nāga (a Buddhist monk and writer) was a rival and detractor of the poet, at whom he wanted to hurl insults. On the basis of Dharmakirti's commentary on the *Pramaṇasamuchchaya* of Diṅ-nāga, the latter has been assigned to the fifth or the sixth century A.D. So, Kālidāsa should be placed in the same period."

What Pandey replies runs: "In the *Meghadūta* the natural meaning of the word 'Nichula' is 'a kind of tree' and that of 'Diṅ-nāga' is 'a quarter-elephant' or 'Dik-pāla'. The cloud-messenger was advised by the Yakśa to take rest under the Nichula trees, and to avoid the waving trunks of the quarter-elephants. The reference to Nichula and Diṅ-nāga as personages in a figment of the imagination of the commentator Mallinātha cannot be taken seriously, especially in view of the fact that Kālidāsa is not noted for such references. No poet or patron of the name of Nichula can be traced in the history of the Sanskrit literature and Diṅ-nāga is only very vaguely hinted in the Buddhist work as the writer Diṅ-nāgāchārya whose extinct work was commented upon by Dharmakirti, whose work is also missing. But even supposing that Diṅ-nāga was a person, it is only suggested that he flourished before Dharmakirti; no definite date can be assigned to him and Kālidāsa cannot be brought down to the Gupta period." Of course, if the Guptas are put earlier than Vikramāditya of 57 B.C., the closing phrase should omit the epithet "Gupta" and run: "the period between 320 and 569 A.D."[93]

We need not pursue the subject of the time of Kālidāsa further. There is no directly determining force in any argument for placing him in this period, even if we put the Guptas there. But the Guptas there, with Chandragupta II among

93. *The Classical Age*, p. 44.

them, would tend to pull Kālidāsa into this period because of the strong association of him with some Vikramāditya or other. The pulling may be resisted on the ground of the dissimilarities between the legendary figure of Vikramāditya and the actual Chandragupta II. But the resistance will still not be able logically to do the justice which one feels as due to the cause of the Vikramāditya-tradition. By turning to Purāṇic history we can more definitely establish a Vikramāditya in 57 B.C. and fix in his reign the time of Kālidāsa.

TO PĀṆINI'S TIME FROM PĀṆINI'S PLACE

1

Many approaches have been made to the problem of dating Pāṇini, but we are still short of a chronological consensus. It would seem that all possible directions of historical thought have already been followed – except just one. Even here the starting-point has been found, yet there has been no proper progression from it. We may try to go as far as we can and see how much certainty can be arrived at.

The path we have in mind may be considered the shortest cut. For, it begins nearest home – Pāṇini's home. Pāṇini's native-place was Śalātura, which A. Cunningham[1] has identified with Lahur, a small town four miles north-west of Ohind, in the angle of the river Kabul meeting the Indus in the province that in antiquity, including Pāṇini's time, was known as Gandhāra. Our approach to his time is with the double question: "What does he say of Gandhāra and into what age of history does his account of its political position fit?"

V.S. Agrawala, who – after asking some other questions – assigns[2] Pāṇini to *c.* 450 B.C., tells[3] us: "Pāṇini mentions both the Vedic form Gāndhāri as the name of the *janapada* and its people in *sūtra* IV.1.169, and its later form Gandhāra in the *gaṇas* to IV.2.133 and IV.3.93... Two towns of Gandhāra are mentioned, *viz.*, Takshashilā, its eastern capital, and Pushkalāvatī, the western. The latter occurs in a *gaṇa* as the name of a river on which the town stood... Pāṇini knows Gāndhāri as a kingdom (IV.1.169). It seems that soon after the death of Darius Gandhāra became independent as would appear from the manner of its mention as an independent *janapada*."

Agrawala is referring to the Achemenid emperor of Persia,

1. *Ancient Geography of India*, edited by S.N. Majumdar (Calcutta, 1924), pp. 66-7.

2. V.S. Agrawala, *India as Known to Pāṇini* (Lucknow, 1953), pp. 455-75.

3. *Ibid.*, p. 49.

Darius I, who ruled from 522 to 486 B.C. In his very first inscription, the one of Behistun (*c.* 520-518),[4] Darius mentions "ga(n)dara" as a province of his empire: his later epigraphs of Persepolis and Naksh-i-Rustam (*c.* 518-515)[5] add the province of "Hi(n)du", whatever was called Sindhu in his day. Thus Gandhāra was a *janapada* dependent on Persia from at least 520 to 515 B.C. That, along with Sindhu, it continued to be so not only up to the end of his reign but even beyond can be gathered from what we learn about his successor Xerxes (486-465 B.C.). According to Herodotus (VI.65-6), "Gandarians" as well as "Indians" fought in Xerxes's army against Greece. With his father's conquests as the background, we have no reason to suspect, as does R.C. Majumdar,[6] that these might be mercenaries rather than regular subjects. Besides, we have epigraphic evidence to go by.

S. Chattopadhyaya[7] directs us to the Persepolis Inscription of Xerxes, discovered in 1935: "in it Xerxes gives the names of the countries under his rule. The list includes... Gandhāra... and 'Hidu'." Chattopadhyaya[8] further writes: "...after giving a list of the subject countries, Xerxes states in his Persepolis inscription: 'And within these countries was (another) where formerly Daivas were worshipped. Afterwards by the will of Ahura Mazda I destroyed the place of Daiva(-worship). And I proclaimed: Daivas thou shalt not worship. Where formerly Daivas were worshipped there I worshipped Ahura Mazda and the divine fulfilments.' The references to Daivas or Devas seem to point out that the religious revolution took place in some part of the Indian districts of the Achaemenid empire."

H.C. Raychaudhuri[9] comments on the same passage:

4. R.K. Mookerji, "Foreign Invasions" in *The Age of Imperial Unity* edited by R.C. Majumdar and A.D. Pusalker (Bombay, 1953), p. 41.

5. *Ibid.*

6. "The Achaemenian Rule in India", *The Indian Historical Quarterly*, Vol. 25, p. 157.

7. "The Rule of the Achaemenids", *Ibid.*, p. 196.

8. *Ibid.*, p. 202.

9. *An Advanced History of India,* edited by R.C. Majumdar, H.C. Raychaudhuri and Kalikinkar Datta (London, 1946), p. 64.

"Xerxes refers to the suppression of religion in lands 'where, before, the Daivas were worshipped; then, by Ahuramazda's will, of such temples of the Daivas, I (the King) sapped the foundations.' The Daiva-worshipping lands may have included the Indian satrapies."

A.F. Olmstead[10] has a different vision. He notes two new peoples in the list of Xerxes. One is the tribe of "the Dahae beyond the Araxes", inhabitants of what in medieval times was called Dahistan, east of the Caspian. (History knows of them as a Scythian nation: Olmstead[11] himself so characterises them.) The other additional satrapy is "that of the men of the Mountain Land (Akaufaka), which must be located north of Kabul in modern Afghanistan", equivalent to medieval Kohistan. Olmstead[12] then takes us to what Xerxes says at the end of his list: "Xerxes goes on to tell us that 'within these lands was a place where formerly the daevas were worshipped...'." After quoting Xerxes on how the daeva-worship was suppressed, Olmstead[13] concludes: "Obviously, the land in question must be on the Iranian border, where the supremacy of Ahuramazda had not yet been acknowledged; in the daeva-worshippers we must therefore see the hitherto unconquered Dahae."

The conclusion does not inevitably follow. If Olmstead considers the Akaufaka no less than the Dahae country as an additional conquest, why restrict the daeva-worship to the latter? Further, are we to believe that in each satrapy of the empire the supremacy of Ahuramazda had to be acknowledged? It is impossible to think all the nations mentioned in Herodotus's famous Army Roster of Xerxes – the Arabians, Ethiopians, Libyans, Paphlagonians, Syrians, Phrygians, Lydians, etc. – were followers of Ahuramazda. We cannot even think of the Scythian tribes other than the Dahae as

10. *History of the Persian Empire* (Phoenix Books, Chicago, Third Impression, 1960), p. 231.

11. *Ibid.*, p. 515.

12. *Ibid.*, p. 232.

13. *Ibid.*

having been so. Ahuramazda would be asserted only against those with whose religion he might be particularly in conflict. We know that the Zoroastrian cult was to a great degree a forcible break-away from the Vedic. Although retaining the cult of fire, it stressed more than ever the Irānian reversal of the meaning of the Vedic word "deva" and, with a larger insistence, made it signify "demon" instead of "god". Conversely we see in the Vedic cult the gradual degradation of the word "asura" whose Irānian form is "ahura". Some anti-"asura" resurgence in districts between Persia and India may have fanned the flames of the anti-"deva" attitude of Zoroastrianism whose champion Xerxes was. The satrapies of "Ga(n)-dara" and "Hi(n)du" were the only ones likely to provide a field for the Achemenid emperor's religious zeal to turn fanatic.

Perhaps the men of the Mountain Land (Akaufaka) come into the picture not because they were freshly conquered but because within an already conquered region belonging to one of these satrapies they constituted a community in which his religious zeal was directly challenged. And, when we read what Olmstead says of "Gandara" under Darius, we cannot help taking "Akaufaka" to have been that part of it which was now picked out and temporarily set off on its own. "Administratively," writes Olmstead[14] of "Gandara", "it was joined to Bactria, and it was not until shortly before 508 that it was organised as an independent satrapy, not under its ancient Iranian name of Paruparaesanna but with the native form of Gandara... In the tenth year of Darius [512 B.C.] a Babylonian slave woman was called Bahtarian (Bactrian)...; four years later (508) she was more accurately known as the Gandarian..." "Gandara" thus extended right up to Bactria and in another direction towards the way to Herat, which, as Agrawala[15] informs us, were the "low peaks... which in Irānian geography were called *Uparisaena*, 'The Falcon's Perch', and by the classical writers Peropamisus, with special reference to their

14. *Ibid.*, p. 144, with fn. 37.
15. Agrawala, *op. cit.*, pp. 40-1.

low height." In its extension towards Bactria – Pāṇini's "*Bāhlīka*... in the extreme north of Afghanistan", as Agrawala[16] says – "Gandara" runs up to the dividing mountain-line[17] "in the north-east of Kabul called Hindukush"[18] – "Hindukush and its martial tribes occupying the valleys of Kohistan-Kafiristan".[19]

So Xerxes's "Akaufaka" (=Kohistan) was definitely a part of Darius's "Gandara" and no new territory. What was new was its isolation as an administrative unit. And the isolation was most probably due to the daeva-worship becoming anti-Irānian and, through religious rampage, a force of political disruption.

If we realise what land Akaufaka was immediate neighbour to, we shall be more inclined to see some upset there. Olmstead[20] quotes from the same inscription: "Says Xerxes the king: When I became king, there was within these lands which are written above one which was restless. Afterward Ahuramazda brought me help. By the favour of Ahuramazda I smote that land and put it in its place." Olmstead[21] explains: "The restless land was Bactria. At the accession of Xerxes, his brother Ariamenes had set forth from that satrapy to contest the throne..." It is very probable that Akaufaka caught from Bactria the contagion of restlessness and tried to take religio-political advantage of the Bactrian situation.

In any case, the administrative isolation of Akaufaka by Xerxes spotlights the presence of "Gandara". We may assuredly take, for several reasons, both Gandhāra and Sindhu to have remained in Achemenid hands till 465 B.C., the close of Xerxes's reign, Agrawala[22] too admits this. But then we are pretty near his date for Pāṇini. Can it be shown that "soon after" 465 B.C. – within the next 15 years or so – Gandhāra

16. *Ibid.*, p. 447.
17. *Ibid.*, p. 48.
18. *Ibid.*, p. 40.
19. *Ibid.*
20. Olmstead, *op. cit.*, p. 231.
21. *Ibid.*
22. Agrawala, *op. cit.*, pp. 467-8.

shook off the Persian yoke and Pāṇini could characterise it as an independent kingdom?

The successor of Xerxes was Artaxerxes I (465-424 B.C.). Herodotus (*c.* 484-431) was his contemporary. Here we may listen again to Chattopadhyaya. Glancing at N.C. Debevoise's *Political History of Parthia* (p. 6), he[23] writes: "It is generally believed that the tribute list, as preserved in the account of Herodotus (III. 89-95) is clearly from his own time, that of Artaxerxes I..., not, as he states, from the time of Darius." In that list also we find "Gandarians" – within the empire's seventh province.

From A.T. Olmstead we get a glimpse of some of the reasons why Herodotus is considered to be reflecting conditions under Artaxerxes I. The Behistum Inscription gives twenty-three satrapies whereas Herodotus makes Darius I administer only twenty.[24] "When compared with the six satrapal lists published by Darius, the list of Xerxes, and his army roster, the official list incorporated by Herodotus shows decided administrative changes."[25] The larger number of Darius is reduced by the union of some hitherto separate satrapies and there are some signs of territorial loss. For example, Arachosia is absent.[26] Among the instances of re-organisation are "two satrapies... united in the case of the Sattagydians, Gandarians, Dadicae, and Aparytae".[27]

With the "Gandarians" vouched for, we are already past Agrawala's date for Pāṇini: *c.* 450 B.C. So Pāṇini could not have lived between 520 and 424 B.C.

Can we even declare that "soon after" Artaxerxes I Gandhāra regained its liberty? Indeed, Olmstead,[28] with his eye on the tribute-list of Herodotus, asserts: "The Gandarians thus make their last appearance as Persian tribute-paying subjects

23. *The Indian Historical Quarterly*, Vol. 25, p. 196.
24. Olmstead, *op. cit.*, pp. 110, 291.
25. *Ibid.*, p. 291.
26. *Ibid.*, p. 292.
27. *Ibid.*
28. *Ibid.*

in the lists of Artaxerxes, though the land continued to be known under the name of Gandhara down to classic Indian times. The Indians of Hindush nevertheless remained loyal to the reign of the last Darius, who recognised their loyalty and their fighting ability by placing them next to the Thousand Immortals who guarded his person."

Olmstead's view of Gandhāra's history is very much at fault. It is even difficult to understand when we look at his location of Hi(n)du or "Hindush". At the end of the above passage he[29] writes in reference to Herodotus's knowledge of the Indians: "There is, however, no mention of the chief city of Hindush, Taxila, which was rapidly taking the place of Paucela, the former capital of Gandhara." Olmstead's Hindush is the Punjāb east of the Indus – as his first Map, "Satrapies of the Persian Empire", makes perfectly clear. It is actually what at one period in antiquity was a part of Gandhāra itself: Gandhāra lay on both sides of the Indus, with Pushkalāvatī (Olmstead's "Peucela") its principal city to the river's west and Takshaśilā ("Taxila") its main one to the river's east.[30] It is possible that in Achemenid times as certainly in some later periods[31] Gandhāra lay wholly beyond the Indus, the river forming its eastern boundary. But, if Hindush was the Punjāb, Gandhāra east of the Indus would practically be its gateway. Was it not at Ohind, four miles South-east of Pāṇini's Gandhāran native-place Śalātura, that Alexander crossed the Indus to march towards Taxila? With Gandhāra lost, how could the Achemenids after Artaxerxes I hold Hindush and command its loyalty?

Besides, Gandhāra – in Olmstead's Map – is bounded on all sides and not only on its east by the Achemenid empire. It has Thatagush (Sattagydia) to its south, Haraiva (Areia) to its west, Bakhtrish (Bactria) to its north-west and Śaka Haumavarga (Scythians) to its north and north-west. If all these satrapies, over and above Hindush, were intact, could Gan-

29. *Ibid.*
30. B.M. Barua, *Aśoka and His Inscriptions* (Calcutta, 1946), Part I, p. 93.
31. *Ibid.*

dhāra become independent or, having somehow revolted, keep its independence long?

Finally, Olmstead is not quite correct in telling us that we hear no more of Gandhāra in relation to the Achemenids. It appears once again on the South Tomb at Persepolis, "usually assigned to Artaxerxes II (404-359 B.C.) on artistic grounds", as Chattopadhyaya[32] observes. Exactly as in the Tomb Inscription of Darius I we get "Ga(n)dariya" no less than "Hi(n)duviya".[33] Majumdar[34] protests: "...though the inscription may belong to the time of Artaxerxes II..., the list of peoples is copied *verbatim* from the inscription of Darius. No sure inference can therefore be drawn from this record..." Majumdar's objection, by itself, is hardly conclusive. And, in any case, he is really concerned to doubt the inclusion of "Hi(n)duviya" in the post-Darius Persian empire: he has particularly in mind the question of "Indians" east of the Indus anywhere whatever and not only in the region of Taxila and in his opinion the "Indians" of "the last Darius" were mercenary troops: he does not expressly exercise scepticism over "Gandarians" who would be west of the Indus. But indeed no scepticism at all is warranted in any respect about either satrapy although a study of history shows, as we shall see, a state of great instability and even of disintegration in many parts of the empire during the reign of Artaxerxes II, proving a strong element of empty brag in his inscription.

It is precisely because of Olmstead's historical knowledge that he has made that sweeping assertion about the "Gandarians". He is aware of the inscription we are discussing. In three places he[35] refers to it and, in one, passes his judgment:[36] "The tombs of Xerxes, Artaxerxes I and Darius II at Naqsh-i-Rustam were without inscriptions; Artaxerxes II returned to

32. *The Indian Historical Quarterly*, Vol. 25, p. 197.

33. *Ibid.*

34. Majumdar, *op. cit.*, pp. 164-5.

35. Olmstead, *op. cit.*, p. 229, fn. 50; p. 424, with fn. 18. In fn. 50 of p. 229, there is a printing mistake: III instead of II is put after "Artaxerxes".

36. *Ibid.*, p. 424.

the practice of Darius I, but only to copy untruthfully the names and reliefs of the subject peoples who supported the throne of his more powerful predecessor." Olmstead accuses Artaxerxes II of untruthfulness because the empire under him suffered "numerous revolts"[37] and the "subject peoples" could never have been quite the same as under Darius I. But in all of Olmstead's recital of those revolts there is no mention of any hostile stir in Gandhāra. And, in his general summing-up of the period the unfavourable vicissitudes are not allowed to weigh too heavily against achievements. He[38] introduces a balancing note: "Artaxerxes was reaching the end of his long and, despite numerous revolts, moderately successful reign." There were no such conditions in 404-359 (or 358) B.C. as might lead us to suspect, even in the teeth of a complete lack of supporting facts, that Gandhāra had revolted.

Some historians, persuaded by a yet darker vision of the period, have gone yet further than Olmstead without any grounds. The *Encyclopaedia Britannica*[39] informs us of "the rebellion of certain provinces under the later Achemenids": "Under Artaxerxes I and Darius II [423-404] these insurrections were still rare. But when the revolt of the Younger Cyrus against his brother (401) had demonstrated the surprising ease and rapidity with which a courageous army could penetrate into the heart of the empire... then indeed the imperial impotence became manifest. After that the revolts of the Satraps in Asia Minor and Syria were of everyday occurrence... When in 400 Xenophon marched with the mercenaries of Cyrus from the Tigris to the Black Sea the authority of the King was non-existent north of Armenia, and the tribes of the Pontic mountains, with the Greek cities on the coast, were completely independent. In Paphlagonia the native dynasts founded a powerful though short-lived kingdom, and the chieftains of the Bithynians were absolutely their own masters. The frontier provinces of India were also lost. Egypt...

37. *Ibid.*, p. 422.
38. *Ibid.*
39. *Encyclopaedia Britannica* (1960), Vol. 17, pp. 555, 556.

finally asserted its independence in 404... Thus the reign of Artaxerxes II ended in 358 B.C. with a complete dissolution of the imperial authority in the West."

True, in the very next breath the article tells us: "His successor, Artaxerxes III Ochus, succeeded yet again in restoring the empire in its full extent... At his death in 338, immediately before the final catastrophe the empire in all appearance was more powerful and more firmly established than it had been since the days of Xerxes." Yes, the black period was only from 404 to 358 B.C. and we must infer from this article that – contrary to Olmstead's view – Gandhāra no less than Sindhu was restored to the Achemenids and remained in the empire till "the final catastrophe", the defeat of "the last Darius" by Alexander the Great. But by throwing in "the frontier provinces of India" among the losses suffered, the article prompts the idea that for some years during 404-358 B.C. Gandhāra enjoyed independence and could make room for Pāṇini's date. How wrong the idea is can easily be brought home in more than one way.

The conclusion of the tale of defections speaks of "the complete dissolution of the imperial authority in the West". Why is the East omitted? And, if it is omitted, what is the basis of the previous pronouncement on the frontier provinces of India? That they are added with sheer gratuitousness is revealed the moment we turn to the *Encyclopaedia*'s own detailed article[40] on Artaxerxes II. There we have not only a closing picture less gloomy and more in conformity with Olmstead: "When the long reign of Artaxerxes II came to its close in the autumn of 358 the authority of the empire had been restored almost everywhere." We have also an utter reticence on the frontier provinces of India: not the slightest hint is there of any loss: they are not on the scene at all. And towards the end we read: "About the history of Artaxerxes II we are comparatively well informed from Greek sources." Then the various sources are named. Evidently, none of them

40. *Ibid.*, Vol. 2, pp. 448-9.

breathes a word suggesting the defection of Gandhāra or Sindhu.

Among them the author most in a position to report such an event was Ktesias, who spent seventeen years at the Persian court and was physician to Artaxerxes II.[41] "He wrote a treatise on India, fragments of which alone have survived in the writings of later authors."[42] Ktesias's *Indica*, no doubt, is described by Rawlinson as being "full of extravagant stories of monstrous people and strange animals" and as adding "practically nothing to our knowledge of India".[43] But the significant fact is that, sitting in Persia at a time of trouble for the empire, he could collect materials for his book. A.W. William Jackson cites this as one of the proofs of a "close and continued connexion" between Persia and its Indian dominions: "Ctesias, who was resident physician at the Persian court about the beginning of the fourth century B.C. could hardly have written his *Indica* without the information he must have received regarding India from envoys sent as tribute-bearers to the Great King or from Persian officials who visited India on state business as well as from his intercourse with travellers and traders of the two countries."[44]

We may add: "The direct touch with tribute-bearing envoys, returned Persian officials and persons moving to and fro between suzerain Persia and subject Gandhāra and Sindhu need not be called in question just because it is from Ktesias's work that, in Majumdar's words,[45] 'the grotesque legends about India, which were favourite topics of many classical and medieval authors, are mostly derived.' These legends are not necessarily inventions without roots in India itself. Megasthenes whom Seleucus Nicator sent as ambassador to Sandrocottus (Chandragupta) of Palibothra (Pāṭaliputra) has

41. Olmstead, *op. cit.*, p. 380.

42. *The Classical Accounts of India*, edited by R.C. Majumdar (Calcutta, 1960), Introduction, pp. xi-xii.

43. *Ibid.*, p. xii.

44. *The Cambridge History of India* (1935), edited by E.J. Rapson, pp. 340-1.

45. *The Classical Accounts* ..., p. xii.

also been blamed for purveying fantastic tales. Yet nobody denies his actual stay in India over years, his day-to-day contact with Indians. And we may say of Ktesias what we can assert about Megasthenes. All the strange stories of Megasthenes can be traced to Indian literature. Even the 'gold-digging ants', in relation to which the most serious charge against him has been framed, are, as E.R. Bevan[46] observes, 'mentioned in the Mahābhārata'."

Nor is it true that Ktesias has communicated nothing of historical value. A statement of his on some presents received from India by his royal patron is of considerable importance – especially to our inquiry. D.H. Gordon,[47] asking how far back in time goes the presence of iron in India and remarking that archaeologically Indian iron is not very ancient, brings in a counterbalance: "it does seem likely, if certain early writers are to be believed, that iron must have been known in India prior to the earliest evidence yet found." Then Gordon[48] discusses the testimony of Herodotus and Ktesias. They are the earliest writers to make indisputable mention of iron in connection with India. "In the case of the iron-tipped arrows mentioned by Herodotus as being carried by the Indian contingent of Xerxes's army, these of course could have been produced anywhere though probably made in India; on the other hand Ktesias makes a point of stressing the excellence of the two swords of Indian steel presented to Artaxerxes Mnemon, which looks as though the reputation for good quality of steel that was to bring an important trade in iron and steel with the West to the Cheras (Seres) was already in a fair way to being established. In view of all this, unless it can be shown that the iron arrowheads of Xerxes's Indians were acquired by them in foreign parts, and that when Ktesias spoke of swords of Indian steel, he did not know what he was talking about, iron must have been in use by 450 B.C. in all the more civilized urban centres of India, in spite of the

46. *The Cambridge History of India,* I, p. 396, fn.
47. *The Prehistoric Background of Indian Culture* (Bombay, 1958), p. 155.
48. *Ibid.*

negative evidence obtained so far by excavation." Finally, Gordon[49] pronounces: "It is... not known from what part of India the Ktesias swords came, and it is possible that they came from the North."

For our purposes we may assess Gordon's information in three steps: (1) the "Presents" to Artaxerxes II of Indian manufacture have the appearance of a tribute; (2) their being "swords of Indian steel" links them up to Xerxes's Indian contingent's "iron-tipped arrows"; (3) just as those weapons came as a mark of service to Xerxes from Indian subjects, so too these weapons seem to have come from the same subjects as a tribute to Artaxerxes II.

All things considered, the Achemenid sway over "the frontier provinces of India" must be considered intact right down to 358 B.C. And, when we are told that under Artaxerxes III Ochus the empire was restored in its full extent, we may well believe that not only till the end of this king's reign in 338 B.C. but also till the end of the last Achemenid Darius III in 330 B.C. did "the frontier provinces of India" stay under Persian rule. All the more must we think so on learning from Arrian (*Anabasis*, III.8) of the troops Darius III massed against Alexander the Great. One detail we have gathered through Olmstead. Some more are there. Among these troops were "the Indian tribes on the Bactrian border", along with the Sogdians and the Bactrians, all under the command of the satrap of Bactria.[50] In addition, there were "the Indian hillmen", with the Arachosians, commanded by the satrap of Arachosia.[51] Then, again, "the Indian troops from the hither side of the Indus" were present with some fifteen elephants.[52]

It may be objected: "The name 'Gandarian' does not figure in Arrian's history. Whatever else of 'the provinces of India' may still be serving the Achemenids as subjects, Gandhāra has disappeared."

49. *Ibid.*, p. 163.

50. *Arrian's Life of Alexander the Great*, translated by Aubrey de Sélincourt (Penguin Classics, Harmondsworth, 1958), p. 98.

51. *Ibid.* 52. *Ibid.*

The point of this objection is obviously at work also in the mind of Olmstead, leading him to that remark of his: "The Gandarians... make their last appearance as Persian tribute-paying subjects of Artaxerxes [I]... The Indians of Hindush nevertheless remained loyal to the reign of the last Darius."

There are three slips in the objection. In the first place, to include the Persian subjects of "Hi(n)du" in Arrian's list and omit those of "Ga(n)dara" is to render meaningless the clear-cut phrase of Arrian: "the Indian tribes on the Bactrian border." Of Gandhāra Olmstead himself has recounted how "administratively it was joined to Bactria" before 508 B.C. and how a Babylonian slave-woman who was called Bactrian in 512 was redesignated more accurately as a Gandarian four years later when Gandara was organised as an independent satrapy. Gandhāra is proved to have touched Bactria under the Achemenids. So "the Indian tribes on the Bactrian border" must be inhabitants of Gandhāra in the extreme north-western part of that province. Perhaps there was an overflow of Gandhārans beyond the Hindukush and these constituted Arrian's first category. By no stretch of the geographical imagination can the people of "Hi(n)du" be located on the Bactrian border. In Olmstead's own vision,[53] "Hindush" lies to the east of the Indus, with Taxila its capital.

In the second place, to charge Arrian with ignoring the "Gandarians" is to miss the import of his "Indian hillmen". We can specifically identify these from two sources. One source is Achemenid epigraphy itself. We have gathered from Olmstead that the people to the north of Kabul in modern Afghānistān and in what was in medieval times Kohistān, were named by Xerxes in his Persepolis Inscription "the men of the Mountain Land (Akaufaka)" and we have shown that, if Darius's "Ga(n)dara" extended right up to Bactria, these men who can be equated with Arrian's "Indian hillmen" must belong to Gandhāra. Our second source is Pāṇini. Agrawala[54]

53. Olmstead, *op. cit.*, pp. 144, 145.
54. Agrawala, *op. cit.*, pp. 434-5.

writes: "Pāṇini refers to a number of *Saṅgha*s as *āyudhajīvin* (V.3.114-117), meaning those who lived by the profession of arms... The most advanced *āyudhajīvin Saṅgha*s belonged to the Vāhīka country (V.3.114), which comprised the region from the Indus to the Beas and Sutlej... These were the Yaudheyas, Kashudrakas, Mālavas, etc. A very important group of martial *Saṅgha*s comprised those occupying *Parvata* [(IV. 3.91)] or some mountainous region in the north-west... Evidently this Parvata region must have been outside the plains of the Vāhīka country, which brings us to the highlands of the north-west as the homeland of the *āyudhajīvin*s. The *Kāśikā* mentions the *Hṛdgolīya*s of Hṛdgola, probably Hi-lo of Yuan Chwang (modern Hiḍḍa south of Jalalabad); *Andhakavartīyāḥ* of Andhakavarta, perhaps Andhkui, a district in the north-east of Afganistan (*Imp. Gaz.*, Afghanistan, p. 80), and *Rohitāgirīya*s of Rohitāgiri, which last is important as reminiscent of Roha, old name of Afghanistan. All this portion of the country is up to the present day peopled by hardy and warlike mountaineers... Arrian mentions these mountainous Indians as fighting in the army of Darius against Alexander the Great... It was these Parvatīya Āyudhajīvins that offered stout resistance to Alexander in Bactria and Gandhāra. The approximate location of these Parvatīyas should be in the region of the Hindukush on both sides of it. Roha, of medieval geographers, Rohitāgiri of Pāṇini, the ten *maṇḍala*s of Lohita (Sabhā, 24.16) and Rohitāgirīyas of the *Kāśikā*, all together point to the mountainous regions of central and north-east Afghanistan as being the *Parvata* country, which name survives in Kohistan."

One wonders why Agrawala brings in both sides of the Hindukush instead of only one and couples Bactria with Gandhāra. Pāṇini's *Gaṇapātha* (V.3.117) gives Parśvādi as among the Āyudhajīvin Saṅghas and the *Kāśikā* mentions Bāhlīka (Balkh, Bactria) as one of the twelve peoples of Parśvādi[55] but it is not called Parvatīya. It is central and north-

55. *Ibid.*, p. 447.

east rather than north Afghānistān that constitutes the mountainous country which stoutly resisted Alexander as well as fought in the army of Darius III. But the occurence of Arrian and Gandhāra in Agrawala's treatment of mountainous Indians implies that Gandhāra was still in Persian hands when Alexander attacked the last Achemenid.

Here is a puzzling implication in view of Agrawala's assertion that "soon after the death of Darius [I] Gandhāra became independent". Here Agrawala would seem to contradict himself and unconsciously advance an argument against his own dating of Pāṇini.

Thus Arrian is proved to mean the "Gandarians" as having been the subjects of Darius III and having fought for him not just in one batch but in two.

Perhaps even the third batch – "the Indian troops from the hither side of the Indus", with some fifteen elephants – hailed from Gandhāra. There is a regular geographical succession, from the Bactrian border through central and north-east Afghānistān to the region immediately west of the Indus. This region below Kohistān is the limited Gandhāra most commonly known to history. If, as Olmstead conceives, "Hi(n)du" lay to the east of the Indus, Arrian's third batch has necessarily to be "Gandarian". Then we have to think that either "Hi(n)du" had broken away from the Achemenid empire or it received no summons from Darius III. But, if Olmstead's idea is wrong, "the Indian troops from the hither side of the Indus" could be from "Hi(n)du", a region which might be more closely linked to the river and therefore directly designable as its western "side". It would not be below Kohistān but elsewhere along the river.

To guess at its location we may advert to a phrase in the Susa Inscription of Darius I, which can make Arrian's "elephants" a geographical pointer. After saying that for the construction of his palace he got "teak" from "Ga(n)dara", Darius tells us that "ivory" came from "Hi(n)du".[56]

56. *The Indian Historical Quarterly*, Vol. 25, p. 195.

"Hi(n)du" must be a country of elephants to be specified as a supplier of "ivory". And its precise situation may be illuminated by the fact that, along with "Hi(n)du", Darius mentions "Arachosia" as sending "ivory".[57] To the east and south-east of Arachosia was the lower Indus valley which, as Majumdar[58] observes, "was specifically known as Sindhu and was mentioned as such in *Baudhāyana Dharma-Sūtra...*" This Sindhu, adjoining Arachosia, may well constitute with the latter a source of ivory for Darius. Besides, do we not have from Herodotus (IV.44)[59] as Darius's specific accomplishment in Indian territory that he had the Indus explored right down to the sea and that he "subdued the Indians" in the course of his project for "regular use of the southern ocean"?

To return once more to our proper theme: in the third place, Arrian's omission of the name "Gandarians" is nothing strange in the historians of Alexander's invasions. Cunningham[60] has emphasised: "The district of Gandhāra is not mentioned by Alexander's professed historians." But it is certain that they knew of the district: Arrian[61] himself names several times the chief Gandhāran city Pushkalāvatī as Peucelaitis near the river Cophen (ancient Kubhā, modern Kabul). A century earlier than Arrian, Pliny[62] unmistakably indicates that "Indian" implies "Gandarian". He has the phrase: "the river Cophes and Peucolaitis, a city of India."

Thus we have no grounds to speak of the defection of Gandhāra from the Achemenid empire at any time from practically the start of the reign of Darius I (522 B.C.) to the termination of that of Darius III (330 B.C.). And we should be fully justified to endorse Chattopadhyaya's explanation[63] of "one curious fact" out of which some historians have made

57. Olmstead, *op. cit.*, p. 168.
58. Majumdar, *op. cit.*, p. 157.
59. *Herodotus: The Histories*, translated by Aubrey de Sélincourt (The Penguin Classics, Harmondsworth, 1960), p. 256.
60. Cunningham, *op. cit.* p. 56.
61. *Anābasis*, IV. xxii, xxviii; *Indica*, I. IV.
62. *Natural History*, VI. 17 (21). See *The Classical Accounts...*, p. 341.
63. *The Indian Historical Quarterly*, Vol. 25, pp. 202-3.

capital. He writes: "When Alexander crossed the Hindukush, he met no Persian officials east of the mountain and this has led to the theory that the Indian provinces were finally lost to the Achaemenians in the reign of Artaxerxes II... The Persians seem to have left the native states on the Indian borderland and the Punjāb to retain their autonomy evidently on the condition of payment of tribute and the satraps represented the imperial personage on the Indian soil. So long as these Indian chiefs obeyed their suzerain, there was no necessity of Persian officials, and the offices of the satraps were worked evidently by the Indian staffs. Bühler has pointed out this state of affairs long ago, and it was to this Indo-Persian intercourse that he ascribed the birth of the new script of Kharoṣṭhī."

We may make a supporting comment: "The appointment of Indian satraps for political or administrative reasons was practised also by Alexander." Mookerji[64] writes: "He divided Greek India into six Satrapies, three on the west side of the Indus, and three on the east. The three western Satraps were Greeks, but not the eastern Satraps who were all Indians."

Now to sum up: in the period from 522 to 330 B.C. Pāṇini's independent kingdom of Gandhāra is impossible.

Can we put it later than 330 B.C.? Almost immediately after this date Alexander took over the Persian possessions. And, among the satrapies to the west of the Indus, the name "Paropamisadae" is, as Mookerji[65] tells us, "the Greek equivalent of Babylonian *Parruparaesana* = Old Persian *Gandāra* = Sanskrit *Gandhāra* with its capital at Pushkalāvatī." After Alexander's death in June 323 B.C., Paropamisadae passed into the hands of one of his generals, Seleucus Nicator. Seleucus, in *c.* 305 B.C., struck a treaty with the Indian king Sandrocottus, whom modern historians identify with Chandragupta Maurya, and transferred this satrapy, along with the others in his charge, to that emperor.[66]

64. *Chandragupta Maurya and His Times* (Madras, 1943), p. 45.
65. *Ibid.*, p. 59, fn. 1.
66. *Ibid.*, pp. 59-60.

With the Mauryas on the throne of Magadha, the chance of an independent Gandhāra in the period after *c.* 306 B.C. is nil. Aśoka whose accession is usually dated to 269 B.C., claims in his Rock Edicts V and XIII Gandhāra as a part of his dominion – and Aśoka reigned up to 233 B.C. After this point Pāṇini is unthinkable. In fact, nobody has even dreamt of placing him lower than 300 B.C. At present, according to Agrawala's own survey[67] of the opinions of scholars, "the range of Pāṇini's date is... limited to a period of three centuries between the seventh and the fourth century B.C." And Agrawala has himself taken care not to violate the lower limit. He is there at one with Raychaudhuri[68] who judges that Pāṇini must have lived after the Persian conquest of Gandhāra but before the fourth century B.C. and that all the evidence accomodates itself with a date in the fifth century. A. A. Macdonell,[69] who had once gone so far as to give Pāṇini *c.* 300 B.C., later revised his estimate to 450.

What had led Western scholars to put the grammarian so late was his use of the term *Yavanānī*, which Kātyāyana and Patañjali interpreted as *Yavanānī-lipi* or "Yavana script" and which those scholars understood as "Greek script" because "Yavana" or its Prākṛt form "Yona" has often connoted "Greek" in Indian literature and is strongly believed to mean the same in Aśoka's Edicts. But it has been realised that the Behistun Inscription of Darius I also employs the term "Yauna", from "Ionia", to denote the Achemenid emperor's Greek subjects and that, through his possession of Gandhāra, this term could have passed on to Pāṇini the Gandhāran and got Sanskritised in the *Aṣṭādhyāyī* (IV.1.49). Hence the willingness all around to go beyond Alexander's time yet stay on the hither side of Darius's inscription.

However, as we have seen, the hither side has no room for the Gandhāran grammarian. The approach to his time from

67. Agrawala, *op. cit.*, p. 456.
68. *Early History of the Vaishnava Sect*, 1936, p. 30.
69. *India's Past* (Oxford, 1927), p. 138.

his place carries us beyond Darius I. How much earlier can we go?

2

Preceding Darius we have Cambyses and then the father of Cambyses, the great Cyrus. Ktesias (Fragment 37, ed. Gilmore, 1888) writes of Cyrus the Great having fought a battle with the Indians.[70] Xenophon (*Cyropaedia,* I.I.14), a contemporary of both Ktesias and Artaxerxes III, reports that the same Cyrus "brought under his rule Bactrians and Indians".[71] He tells us also of an embassy sent to Cyrus by an Indian king with a sum of money, and puts the event prior to Cyrus's war against Croesus of Lydia.[72] The chronology here is patently at fault, for Cyrus turned eastward after and not before subduing Croesus, but there is nothing intrinsically impossible in the event itself. Now, as is the case with Arrian writing of Darius III, does Xenophon include the "Gandarians" among the "Indians"? The answer is provided when we take together some statements by Strabo and Arrian himself.

Strabo (*Geography,* XV.1.26),[73] in the first century B.C., correctly locates Gandhāra as Gandaritis lying along the river Kophes, between the Choaspes and the Indus. Arrian (*Indica,* I)[74] informs us: "The regions beyond the river Indus on the west are inhabited, up to the river Cophen, by two tribes, the Asṭakenoi [Hāstināyana or Ārshṭaka] and the Assakenoi [Āsvakāyana]... They were in old times subject to the Assyrians, then after a period of Median rule submitted to the Persians, and paid to Cyrus... the tribute from their land which Cyrus had imposed."

Arrian's "two Indian tribes" are certainly "Gandarians" and Strabo even goes on to name – "in the dominions of the Assakenoi" – "their city, Peucelaitis". So Cyrus's suzerainty

70. Mookerji, *The Age of Imperial Unity,* p. 39.
71. *Ibid.*
72. Majumdar, *op. cit.,* p. 154.
73. *The Classical Accounts...,* pp. 256-7.
74. *Ibid.,* p. 214.

over Gandhāra is affirmed. And a reference by Pliny fits in well with the tradition Arrian has handed down. Mentioning Kāpiśā under the Pāṇinian form Kāpiśī (IV.2.99), Agrawala[75] writes: "According to Pliny Kāpiśī was destroyed by the Ashaemenian emperor Cyrus (Kurush) in the sixth century B.C. It is identified with modern Begram, about 50 miles north of Kābul on the ground of a Kharoshṭhī inscription found there naming the city (Sten Konow, *Ep. Ind.*, Vol. XXII [1933], p. 11)." Majumdar[76] proffers the reservation that some identify Pliny's Kāpiśā with Kāpiśā-kani, the name of a stronghold in Arachosia mentioned in the inscriptions of Darius. But, since Kāpiśā-kani is never heard of outside Darius's inscriptions, of which no Classical writer was aware, and since Pliny uses a clear-cut form with no ambiguity arising from any variation, we may safely adhere to the majority opinion by which, as Majumdar himself says, "this is usually taken to be the well-known Kāpiśā north of Kabul." Then we are at once led to remember from Olmstead how in Darius's day Gandhāra's north-western frontier marched with Bactria's south-eastern so that Kāpiśā would fall within Gandhāra.

Agrawala too confirms Olmstead when he explains the terms "Gandhāra, Kāpiśā, Bālhīka" in dealing with Pāṇini. He[77] writes: "...Gandhāra extended from Takshaśilā, its eastern capital to the river Kunar, its western boundary, and from the river Kābul in the south to Swat in the north. Next to it was the kingdom of Kāpiśā, coinciding with modern Kafiristān and occupying the whole area between the river Kunar and the Hindukush. The latter mountain identified as Rohitāgiri separated Kāpiśā from Bālhīka. Sometimes Kāpiśā politically formed part of Gandhāra, as in the reign of Darius [I], and then the name Gandhāra was applied to both of them."

What obtained in the time of Darius was most likely to have been the general geographical disposition in the political state of affairs in the sixth century B.C., which included

75. Agrawala, *op. cit.*, p. 69.
76. *The Indian Historical Quarterly*, Vol. 25, p. 156.
77. Agrawala, *op. cit.*, p. 48.

also the time of Cyrus. Cyrus's destruction of Kāpiśā could be considered as pointing to a conquest by him of Gandhāra.

Doubtless, Pliny and Arrian are several centuries removed from the age of Cyrus. Majumdar[78] makes much of this fact and argues: "Our oldest authority, Herodotus, merely refers to Cyrus's campaign against the Bactrians and Sacae. His further statement that Cyrus conquered every nation in Upper Asia is too vague and general, and evidently does not refer to India, which he mentions later in connection with Darius. To this may be added the explicit statement of Nearchus that Cyrus planned an expedition against India through Gedrosia (Balūchistān) but lost his entire army, excepting seven men, in that region. Megasthenes also explicitly states that the Persians did not invade India but merely approached it when Cyrus was marching against the Massagetae."

As against all this evidence Majumdar sees nothing except Ktesias and Xenophon and he dismisses them with some critical observations. But it is not so easy to set them aside. First of all, are they in direct contradiction to Herodotus? True, "our oldest authority" refers only to the campaigns against the Bactrians and the Sacae. Still, there is the eye-opening passage (I.179):[79] "While Harpagus was turning upside-down the lower or western part of Asia, Cyrus was engaged with the north and east, bringing into subjection every nation without exception. Most of his minor conquests I will say nothing about, but mention only those of his campaigns which gave him the greatest trouble and are in themselves the most interesting." Surely, this is different from being just a vague and general statement, which Majumdar tries to make it out to be. It explicitly suggests very wide conquests and it clearly provides us with a reason for whatever things Herodotus is silent about. He is silent about them not because they never occurred but because he did not

78. Majumdar, *op. cit.*, p. 156.
79. *Herodotus: The Histories*, p. 85.

regard them as of an importance comparable to that of those which were arduous and whose account would make absorbing literature. What Ktesias and Xenophon have reported is perfectly possible and does not in the least run counter to Herodotus's deliverances.

When we look at the actual words of Ktesias we note still further how Herodotus quite allows our crediting the former. Majumdar[80] reports: "Ctesias states that 'Cyrus died in consequence of a wound inflicted in battle by an Indian in an engagement when the Indians were fighting on the side of the Derbikes* and supplied them with elephants'." Herodotus,[81] after describing Cyrus's death at the hands of the Massagetae, adds: "There are many accounts of Cyrus' death; I have given the one which I think most likely to be true." Thus the account – one of the "many" existing – which Ktesias accepted has a legitimate status and is not excluded by anything transmitted by Herodotus.

Once that status is granted on Herodotus's own pronouncement, Xenophon's declarations that "Cyrus brought under his rule Bactrians and Indians" and that an Indian king sent an embassy with money to him could easily reflect earlier events and make good an omission on Herodotus's part when he spoke of Cyrus's campaigns against the Bactrians and the Sacae.

Nor must we forget that "our oldest authority" does not much precede in time the two other writers. Ktesias is almost as old as he; even Xenophon was a younger contemporary. And Xenophon as well as Ktesias is an older authority than either Nearchus or Megasthenes, both of whom were contemporaries of Alexander the Great.

Moreover, Herodotus does not stop coming to our aid with the passages we have quoted. In connection with Darius I he has a sequence of events with a very significant implication. After recounting the horse-groom's trick by which

80. Majumdar, *op. cit.*, p. 155.

* The Derbikes have not yet been satisfactorily located.

81. *Herodotus, op. cit.*, p. 100.

Darius "became king of Persia", Herodotus (III.88-90)[82] writes: "Following the conquests of Cyrus and Cambyses, his dominion extended over the whole of Asia, with the exception of Arabia... Now that his power was felt in every corner of his dominions, his first act was to erect a stone monument with a carving of a man on horseback... This was in Persia; he then proceeded to set up twenty provincial governorships, called satrapies. The several governors were appointed and each nation assessed for taxes... During the reigns of Cyrus and Cambyses there was no fixed tribute at all, the revenue coming from gifts only; and because of his imposition of regular taxes, and other similar measures, the Persians have a saying that Darius was a tradesman, Cambyses a tyrant, and Cyrus a father..."

To get the implication on the whole more sharply we may substitute for Sélincourt's opening sentence the version by George Rawlinson:[83] "Thus was Darius, son of Hystaspes, appointed king; and, except for Arabians, all they of Asia were subject to him; for Cyrus, and after him Cambyses, had brought them all under."

We may put the total implication in brief: Darius possessed an extensive empire chiefly because he was subsequent to the conquerors Cyrus and Cambyses as their heir, but he also asserted his power in all the parts of this empire and he reorganised on an efficient paying basis the administration of almost the very provinces which Cyrus and Cambyses had administered differently.

We have used the qualifications "chiefly" and "almost" because the "twenty provincial governorships" include, as Herodotus's list[84] tells us, "the Indians" as the last and twentieth satrapy – the Indians who figure in another passage of Herodotus's as a people freshly subjugated. The last and

82. *Ibid.*, pp. 217, 218.

83. *Herodotus: History of the Greek and Persian Wars,* translated by George Rawlinson, edited and abridged with an introduction by W.G. Forrest (New York, 1963), p. 151.

84. *Herodotus, op. cit.*, pp. 214-15.

twentieth satrapy is the single province added by Darius. Herodotus unmistakably shows it to have been an addition: he has the story[85] of Darius sending an expedition under the Caryandian navigator Skylax to explore the river Indus down to the sea "from Caspatyrus in the district of Pactyica". This is the sole occasion on which Herodotus says: "...Darius subdued the Indians."

And we receive a confirmation of it from those of Darius's inscriptions which are later than the one of Behistun. To quote Majumdar[86] "Two inscriptions of Darius, one at Persepolis, and another near it at Naksh-i-Rustam, include both Gandhāra and Hi(n)du or Sindhu among the countries subject to the emperor. Another found at Hamadan describes his empire as extending from Sindhu to Sparda. These epigraphic references leave no doubt that some time after the issue of the Behistun inscription, which mentions Gandhāra but not Sindhu, the latter region was conquered by Darius who was already master of Gandhāra."

If we may judge from the words of Herodotus, Darius's mastery of Gandhāra may be viewed in a double light: although he inherited the province he had to make his power felt in it once more. To reconquer provinces that Cyrus or Cambyses had owned was nothing unusual. Thus we know from Herodotus[87] that Babylon whose conqueror had been Cyrus "was captured for the second time" by Darius.

Our "double light" on Gandhāra explains a subtle difference in the phraseology at Behistun from the turn of expression at other places. As Majumdar[88] points out, the Persepolis Inscription says, "By the will of Ahuramazda these are the countries that I have conquered with (the help of) this Persian army" and the Naksh-i-Rustam Inscription reads, "By the will of Ahuramazda these (are) the countries that I seized afar from Persia", while the Behistun Inscription runs, "These

85. *Ibid.*, p. 256.
86. Majumdar, *op. cit.*, p. 240.
87. *Herodotus, op. cit.*, p. 240.
88. Majumdar, *op. cit.*, p. 156.

countries that came to me; by the will of Ahuramazda, I was their king." Majumdar interprets the last-named according to the import of the other two, but with an eye upon Herodotus we may incline to agree with the passage in the *Cambridge Ancient History* (IV.183) with which Majumdar finds fault: "Among the countries enumerated on the Behistun inscription as having come to him with the crown are Gandhāra and Sattagydia, from which it may be inferred that Cyrus had already pushed the Persian conquests to the north-western frontier of India and even to the southern slopes of the Hindu Kush."

Olmstead's rendering[89] of the Behistun Inscription is a little different: "These are the lands which obeyed me..."* But his interpretation is still that Darius intends here an inheritance. Olmstead,[90] calling the inscription Darius's "autobiography", says: "In his autobiography Darius, immediately after the protocol, states that Ahuramazda handed over to him the lordship... He then lists the twenty-three satrapies. Darius would have us believe that at his accession all these countries were loyal..."

And what Olmstead goes on to observe supports our thesis that Gandhāra was a heritage from Cambyses and Cyrus but had to be somehow reclaimed. Olmstead finishes the sentence: "all these countries were loyal and later rebelled." Then we are told: "Further on in the narrative he admits that, when he had killed the Magian, Elam and Babylonia revolted; but he still insists that it was not until after the capture of Babylon that the other revolts occurred: of his own homeland Prasa, of Elam for a second time, of Media, Assyria, Egypt, Parthia, Margiana, Sattagydia, and the Śaka." Gandhāra is not mentioned among the rebellious lands recovered.

89. Olmstead, *op. cit.*, p. 110.

* Olmstead renders the Persepolis Inscription also rather differently: "By the favour of Ahuramazdah, these are the lands which I hold, together with this Persian army which fears me..." (*Ibid.*, p. 175). However, the Naksh-i-Rustam Inscription, in Olmstead's version, has the word "seized" (*Ibid.*, p. 229).

90. *Ibid.*, p. 110.

But, from Persepolis and Naksh-i-Rustam, we may gather that it too had to be brought to heel at a later date.

Our reading of Herodotus is borne out. And there is no substantial bar to attributing the possession of Gandhāra to Cyrus. As for Nearchus and Megasthenes they make no odds. Nearchus only means that Cyrus never got beyond the Indus into India proper: his attempt to do ended in a *débâcle*. The attempt itself – through Balūchistān – was pretty distant from the regions where Gandhāra lay and can have no bearing on our discussion. Megasthenes can also be accepted without any change in our view. In fact, he can be shown to give the negative side of the very picture whose positive side we gather from Arrian. To declare[91] that the Persians did not lead an army into India but only approached its borders when Cyrus marched against the Massagetae is to mean that Cyrus was close to the Indus on the western side on his way northward where the Massagetae lived. And to be thus close is to be just where Arrian locates his Astakenoi and Assakenoi who are said to have been under Cyrus and to have paid him tribute.

Nor is Megasthenes making a mistake here, as Majumdar thinks. Majumdar[92] comments, apropos of the Massagetae: "As this people occupied the country between the Oxus and the Jaxartes, obviously the writer must have meant by India not the Punjāb but Kafiristān, as the borders of the latter, and not of the former, would have been appoached by Cyrus on his way to the Massagetae." We must remember that Herodotus (I.201) affines the Massagetae to the Sacae (Śakas) and that S.N. Majumdar,[93] elucidating Ptolemy's *Geography*, has remarked, "The Massagetae were the Maśakas described in Indian Literature as the warrior tribe of the Śakas", and that the *Mahābhārata*, as Agrawala[94] informs us, speaks of the

91. Majumdar, *op. cit.*

92. *Ibid.*

93. McCrindle, *Ancient India as Described by Ptolemy*, edited by S.N. Majumdar (1927), p. 397.

94. Agrawla, *op. cit.*, p. 68.

locality Maśaka in the *Śakadvīpa* (Śaka-land) and that in the time of Alexander and Megasthenes there was the city which the Greeks (Arrian, *Anabasis*, IV.26) called Massaga and which they described as the capital of one of the very tribes – the Assakenoi – which Arrian has made tributary to Cyrus. The Massagetae, who lived between the Oxus and the Jaxartes, appear to have had an outpost, as it were, in "the regions beyond the river Indus on the west up to the river Cophen".

Their name itself seems fully echoed in the Indian appellation "Maśakāvatī", which the grammarian Patañjali (*c.* 150 B.C. by the usual chronology) mentions in his *Mahābhāshya* (II.287) and which the *Kāśikā* (IV.2.85) links on to Pāṇini along with other river-names like Pushkarāvatī. "Maśakāvatī," writes Agrawala,[95] "seems to be identical with the name of the river on which Massaga or Maśaka, capital of the warlike people known as the Āśvakāyanas, was situated. It is possible that Pushkalāvatī and Maśakāvatī were the designations of only those particular portions of the river Swat where it flowed past by these two great towns of Gandhāra in the south and north respectively." Mookerji[96] also identifies the Greeks' Massaga with the Indian Maśakāvatī. Thus the Massaga familiar to Alexander's historians and to Megasthenes gets connected in very name with the Massagetae against whom not only Megasthenes but also Herodotus sends Cyrus fighting.

A proof of the connection is in the manner in which the Assakenoi fought Alexander. According to J.H. Haskins,[97] scholars, while fully accepting the Massagetae as Scythians, distinguish them in one particular from other Śakas such as the Western tribe whom Herodotus called the Royal Scythians and reported as having proceeded westward after their defeat in Asia by the Massagetae. This particular is the position of women among them. The women of the Massagetae stood

95. *Ibid.*, p. 42.

96. *The Age of Imperial Unity*, p. 45.

97. "The Royal Scythians", *Natural History* (New York), October 1950, p. 16.

very high. Haskins[98] writes: "we are explicitly told [Herodotus, I.214] that they were led in battle by a queen." Now let us glance at the battle given by the Assakenoi army of Massaga to the Macedonians. Mookerji[99] relates: "This army was led by the late king's mother, queen Cleophis [Kṛpā?]... The example of the queen-commander leading the struggle for freedom in person brought the entire womanhood of the locality into the fighting..."

We cannot help harking back to Herodotus's Massagetae and their queen Tomyris whose son had been captured by Cyrus through a ruse: "The queen's son Spargapises, when he was sober again and able to realize his position, begged Cyrus to have his fetters removed. The request was granted, and, as soon as he had the use of his hands, he killed himself. The queen, on hearing that Cyrus had ignored her terms, engaged him in the field with all the forces she possessed."[100]

Arrian's association – through his geographical details – of Gandhāra with Cyrus is in tune, though indirectly, with both Herodotus and Megasthenes. It has a foundation going back in one way or another to pretty ancient times. It only brings into focus an old piece of information that was either negatively present or tacitly couched before him and first found a suggestive shape in general as far back as Xenophon and Ktesias.

Nor in the age after these two is Pliny alone in supporting Arrian by his light on Cyrus and Kāpiśā. A string of events in the wake of Cyrus's conquest of Gandhāra unrolls in brief in what Strabo (XV.I.6)[101] writes: "...although the Persians summoned the Hydraces [or Oxydrakai = Kshudrakas] as mercenary troops from India, the latter did not make an expedition to Persia but only came near it when Cyrus was marching against the Massagetae." The word "mercenary" forbids us from thinking Cyrus master over the Punjāb region where the

98. *Ibid.*
99. Mookerji, *op. cit.*, p. 46.
100. Sélincourt, *op. cit.*, pp. 100-1 (I.214).
101. *The Classical Accounts...*, p. 245.

Ravi joins the Chenāb, but his connection with India is strongly suggested and there is a complementary relation between the Hydraces coming near Persia and, as in Megasthenes's account, Cyrus coming near India.

Having quoted Strabo, Pliny and Arrian – all late witnesses and therefore unreliable in Majumdar's eyes – we may draw attention to one point overlooked by their critic. It is not as if they were offering evidence in opposition to Nearchus and Megasthenes whom Majumdar favours. What we learn from Nearchus is through Arrian himself and his likes: the earlier writer's report appears only in Arrian's *Anabasis* (VI.24.2-3) in Strabo's *Geography* (XV.I.5). Neither has Megasthenes's original *Indica* come down to us except in the accounts by subsequent authors – Diodorus, Strabo, Pliny, Arrian, Aelian. And, when Arrian tells us of the Aspasioi and the Assakenoi having been subject to Cyrus, he does so at the very start of that part of his own *Indica,* at the end (XVII) of which he says: "It is sufficient for me to have set forth these facts regarding the Indians, which, as the best known, both Nearchus and Megasthenes, two men of approved character, have recorded." And the facts about those two tribes occur in the company of facts about the Nysaioi and Dionysus, which we definitely know to be in Megasthenes.

Cyrus's suzerainty over Gandhāra may have been rather loose, so that after his son's somewhat disordered reign and the more or less disordered sequel of claim and counter-claim to the throne Darius I had to reassert the royal right with military force. However, for all historical purposes we may push Gandhāra's dependence on the Persians – and therefore Pāṇini's date – a fair number of years beyond Darius I. And Cyrus himself, from Arrian's account, would seem to have merely reasserted a suzerainty exercised before him by the Medes whom he supplanted in Persia and, still earlier, by the Assyrians.

Actually, there are passages in the Avesta seeming to indicate a political hold obtained by old Irān on Northern India before the Achemenids. Although corroboration or details of this connection have hitherto been lacking, some scholars have taken those passages as genuine evidence.[102] The earliest reference is the statement in the Avestan *Vendidad* that Hapta-Hindu (Sapta-Sindhu) – land of the seven-rivered Indus-system – was one of the countries Ahura Mazda created – a statement which points to the prevalence of the religion of Ahura Mazda at least in portions of the north-west along the Indus, including Gandhāra.

Contact between these portions and ancient Assyria before the Medes came into power is also suggested by certain facts. R.A. Jairazbhoy[103] writes: "The cotton tree was introduced from India into Assyria (*c.* 700 B.C.) by Sennacherib (704-681 B.C.), who is reported to have said that trees that bear fleece were sheared and shredded for garments... The earliest date [for the Indian peacock's arrival in Assyria] may be 738 B.C., when there is a possible reference to a peacock among the wonderful birds received as tribute by Tiglath Pileser III." Gandhāra may well have sent this peacock-tribute. Also, we know from Olmstead:[104] "In 737 Tiglath-pileser III... received tribute from Median chiefs as far east as Mount Bikni..."

Even if we ignore Arrian's testimony about the Medes and the Assyrians, Pāṇini can scarcely be later than the part of Cyrus's reign – *c.* 546-540 B.C.[105] – when that king may be thought to have turned his ambition to the East.

The one serious obstacle that might be built in the way of all such claim for Cyrus is, as R.C. Majumdar[106] says, "the Buddhist account of the kingdom of Gandhāra, which comprised both Peshawar valley and the Western Punjāb". Majumdar's argument[107] is: "Special importance attaches... to the information... that Pukkusati, King of Gandhāra, sent an

102. Mookerji in *The Age of Imperial Unity*, p. 39. See also Chattopadhyaya, "Foreign Notices of Achaemenid India", *The Indian Historical Quarterly*, Vol. 26, No. 1, pp. 18-19.

103. *Foreign Influence in Ancient India* (Bombay, 1963), p. 30.

104. Olmstead, *op. cit.*, p. 22.

105. *Ibid.*, pp. 47-9.

106. Majumdar, *op. cit.*, p. 153.

107. *Ibid.*

embassy and a letter to King Bimbisāra of Magadha and also defeated Pradyota, King of Avanti. As Pradyota was the contemporary of both Bimbisāra and his son Ajātaśatru he did not probably come to the throne before 540 or 530 B.C., and Pukkusati may also be regarded as ruling in Gandhāra about that time. He would thus be a contemporary of Cyrus who established his power and authority in 549 B.C. and died twenty years later in 529 B.C. On general grounds, therefore, we can hardly credit Cyrus with the conquest of the trans-Indus borderlands in the region round Peshawar, until some positive evidence is forthcoming."

Contrary to Majumdar's idea, there definitely is – as we have shown – evidence of this kind. Apart from it, too, we can neutralise if not nullify Majumdar's contention. What is the basis of Majumdar's chronology? All modern historians date Buddha's death to the 8th year of Ajātaśatru's reign, and most of them identify this year as 483 B.C. So Ajātaśatru ascended the throne in 491 B.C. and Pradyota who was the contemporary of both Ajātaśatru and his father Bimbisāra would be ruling Avanti round about this date and his reign would commence fairly earlier. Pukkusati of Gandhāra would, therefore, be able to deal with both Bimbisāra and Pradyota in the quarter century before 491 B.C. We get the epoch of Darius I, when Gandhāra was indisputably in Persian possession. Even in the quarter century after 491 B.C., leading us to the end of the reign of Artaxerxes in 465 B.C., Pukkusati could never have ruled in a Persia-free Gandhāra. We must surely discount the Buddhist story.

The alternative date of Buddha's death, still entertained by some historians, is 543 B.C. Then Ajātaśatru becomes king in 551 B.C. and Pradyota still earlier. So Pukkusati would be sovereign of Gandhāra before and after this year. As Cyrus's conquest of Gandhāra falls in the period 546-540 B.C. we can have Pukkusati sending an embassy and a letter to King Bimbisāra of Magadha and defeating Pradyota, king of Avanti, all before Cyrus's achievement.

Even if Majumdar's chronology – 540 or 530 B.C. – is

accepted, it is possible to accommodate both Pukkusati and Cyrus. Pukkusati could lose the trans-Indus borderlands in the region round Peshawar to Cyrus and yet remain a powerful king of Gandhāra by possessing the Western Punjāb. And, on Majumdar's chronology, he who is already associated with embassy-and-letter-sending eastward to Bimbisāra would be just cut out to play the role of Xenophon's Indian king who sent an embassy westward to Cyrus with a sum of money.

So, on all counts, we should be justified to push Pāṇini upwards of 546-540 B.C. Here is the irreducible lower limit we can pose by making his "Gāndhāri" and "Gandhāra" our *point de départ*.

What, then, about that famous term of Pāṇini's, which has compelled so many scholars to date him after the Behistun Inscription: "Yavanānī"? Is it possible to suppose that it might not have connoted "Greek script"?

A most serious ground for doubt of this connotation is forthcoming from Pāṇini himself. Let us listen to what Barua[108] conveys:

"The Gaṇapātha on Pāṇini's rule, II.1.72 – *Mayūravyaṁśakādi*, speaks of persons who were shaven-headed like the Kambojas and Yavanas (*Kāmboja-muṇḍaḥ, Yavana-muṇḍaḥ*). This was evidently based upon a legend like the one in the *Harivaṁśa* (XIII.763-64, 775-83) purporting to say that King Sagara who was bent upon annihilating the Śakas, Yavanas, Kambojas, Pāradas and Pahlavas relented and so he released the first after having half of their head shaved, the second and third after having the whole of their head shaved, the fourth after compelling them to keep their hair dishevelled, and the fifth after compelling them to keep their beards.* The tradition gained ground in later Indian literature that these were the distinctive habits of these five peoples."[109]

The greatest commentators, like Vāmanajayāditya of the

108. Barua, *op. cit.*, p. 99.

* The same legend is met with also in the Vāyu Purāna.

109. Max Müller, *History of Ancient Sanskrit Literature*, p. 28.

Kāśikā and Bhattojidīkshita of the *Siddhānta-kaumudi*, have accepted the *Gaṇapātha*'s phrase as authentic Pāṇinian material. But can we ever conceive complete shaven-headedness as characterising the Greeks in Pāṇini's eyes? "Yavana" must have meant to him something else than "Greek". Side by side with the *Gaṇapātha*'s phrase, the *Aṣṭādhyāyī*'s *Yavanānī* cannot signify anything Greek.

Nor is it odd that Pāṇini should yield a non-Greek view of "Yavana" (and "Yona"). The Pali *Majjhima Nikāya* (II.149), which is admittedly pre-Mauryan, presents to us Buddha telling Assalāyana of "the Yona, Kamboja and other border countries". Buddha, at the latest, is dated to 563-483 B.C. Can any historian point to an organised Greek state on the borders of India in that period? Individual Greeks might be about in the second half of it, perhaps small groups of them might also be there, scattered in various places; but a whole country, a *janapada*, of them, organised – as the *Majjhima Nikāya* goes on to say – on a twofold basis of "masters" and "servants" instead of on a system of four castes as in India, such an established, developed and regulated state is out of the question. The Pali *Chullanidessa*,[110] one of the oldest Buddhist commentaries, numbers Yona no less than Kamboja as having been a country of the Indian subcontinent shortly before Buddha's birth. So, at the latest, we are driven upwards of 563 B.C., a time when Cyrus had not even brought his Persians into their first contact with the Lydians and no Greeks could have been known in his country: the "Greek script" would be non-existent for the Persians and still more for a Gandhāran like Pāṇini.

Non-Buddhist Hindu literature – the *Manusaṁhitā* (X.43-44) and the *Mahābhārata* (XIII.33.21) – go even further in depicting the Yavanas as non-Greek. They show them as degraded Kshatriyas, an Indian tribe which – like the Kambojas and others – lost its Aryan status by not consulting Brāhmaṇas. The *Mahābhārata* (I.79.42) gives them even a specific Indian ancestry: it designates them as descendants of

110. B.C. Law in *The Age of Imperial Unity*, p. 1.

the very ancient Turvasu, the son of Yayāti Nahusha.

A mention of "Yavana" still older than Pāṇini's is in the *Gautama-Dharma-Sūtra* (IV.17), perhaps the oldest writing of the *Sūtra* type. Neither of the two authorities – G. Bühler and P.V. Kane – regards the mention as an interpolation.[111] Gautama states that the offspring of a Kshatriya father and a Śūdra mother is called Yavana. Here a social rather than a tribal significance is stressed. It is analogous to the same author's definition (I.9.17.2) of the offspring of a Brāhmaṇa father and a Śūdra mother as a Nishāda. Nobody has questioned the existence of the Nishādas as a tribe merely because a new shade of meaning is brought out by Gautama. The tribe of Nishādas have been listed as early as the later *Saṁhitā*s and *Brāhmaṇas*.[112] Evidently Gautama is supplying us with an extension of the concept of Yavana for a special purpose: it complements rather than contradicts the tribal existence of the Yavanas. But in this social no less than in the tribal context the term, just as much as "Nishāda", is far from the least Greek colour.

We know that in times succeeding those when "Yavana" or "Yona" did mean "Greek" this term had a general implication of "foreigner".[113] Similarly in times preceding them it indicated a non-Greek tribe of the Indian frontier or a mixed class in Indian society.

Pāṇini's "shaven-headed Yavanas" is in the typical Indian tradition, reflecting one aspect out of several pointing away from Greece. It is no freak to be goggled at. In the most natural fashion it supports our chronology and helps us to reduce to absurdity the common reading of "Greek" in his *Yavanānī*.

We cannot determine what script, out of the several identified ones of antiquity, Pāṇini intended: we should first need to know the upper limit of his date and the cultural

111. Ram Gopal, *India of the Kalpasūtras* (Delhi, 1959), p. 54.

112. *The Vedic Age,* edited by R.C. Majumdar and A.D. Pusalker (London, 1952), p. 261.

113. *The Age of Imperial Unity*, p. 101.

character of the Yavanas. But it is quite on the cards that he had no script in mind. We may attend to Barua's words:[114] "In Pāṇini's time Yavanānī was the only feminine form of Yavana, while Kātyāyana, Patañjali and other later grammarians found it necessary to recognise Yavanī as another form, and to restrict the use of Pāṇini's form to the writing of the Greeks." Barua is, of course, accepting the modern interpretation of "Yavana" and so he brings in the Greeks. What he means is: "the writing of the Yavanas." And the point he makes suggests that Pāṇini might not have intended "writing" at all.

Pāṇini's rule merely shows the formation of certain feminine endings. As Kane[115] observes, he mentions twelve words, to most of which the affix *ānī* is added in the sense of "wife". Agrawala[116] himself has cited several of these words. Discussing "Religion", he writes: "Of the female deities the older goddesses mentioned are Indrāṇī, Varunāṇī (IV.1.49)..." Among the post-Vedic deities, "the most important... is goddess Pārvatī four of whose names are mentioned, *viz.* (1) Bhavānī, (2) Śarvāṇī, (3) Rudrāṇī and (4) Mṛiḍānī (IV.1.49). This worship was a feature of the Sūtra period. The Vedas refer to their male counterparts such as Bhava, Śarva, Rudra and Mṛiḍa."

The female deity-names Agrawala has listed are, in that very order, the first six of Pāṇini's twelve words. The next six in their Pāṇinian sequence are: *Himānī, Arāṇyānī, Yavānī, Yavanānī, Mātulānī, Āchāryāṇī*. Leaving aside *Yavanānī* for the moment, we may quote Agrawala on the rest. "Pāṇini... refers to... glaciers as *himānī* (IV.1.49)...[117] Pāṇini shows knowledge of the mountainous regions called Himālaya, with its perpetual snow (*himānī*, IV.1.49)...[118] Pāṇini calls a large forest *araṇya* (IV.1.49) and Kātyāyana *arāṇyānī* (*Bhāshya*, II.220)...[119] Pāṇini

114. Barua, *op. cit.*, p. 97.
115. *History of the Dharmasāstra* (Poona), Vol. V, p. 516, fn. 743.
116. Agrawala, *op. cit.*, p. 357.
117. *Ibid.*, p. 204.
118. *Ibid.*, p. 39.
119. *Ibid.*, p. 210.

refers to *Yavānī* (IV.49), a kind of crude and coarse barley according to Kātyāyana...[120] *Yavānī* (a kind of inferior barley. IV.1.49)...[121] *Mātulānī* (maternal uncle's wife, IV.1.49)...[122] Women also occupied the exalted position of teachers and were called *āchāryā* (IV.1.49), a counter-example of *āchāryāṇī*)...[123] Pāṇini also speaks of *āchāryāṇī* as the wife of an *āchāryā* (IV.1.49)."[124]

Himānī, Arāṇyānī, Yavānī pertain to objects. *Yavanānī, Mātulānī, Āchāryāṇī* stem from persons; but their bearing is not on personal names as with those six female counterparts of particular gods that open the list. The last two are common and not proper nouns. The first is from a proper noun, the name of a people or a country or the general designation of an individual belonging to either, but here too no unique individual standing out from all others by a special name is concerned: the individual belongs to a class and, if we keep that in view, the word *Yavana* can be grouped with *Mātula* (maternal uncle) and *Āchāryā* (teacher). Since, like the other six words pertaining to persons, *Mātulānī* and *Āchāryāṇī* imply "wife" by the *ānī*-affix, why should not *Yavanānī* which is groupable with these two carry the same implication? Kane takes Pāṇini's *Yavanānī* to mean the wife of a Yavana, unlike Kātyāyana's term which means the Yavana alphabet, as Kane puts it. From Kane's remarks it would seem highly debatable whether in Pāṇini's time we can speak of a script of the Yavanas.

Agrawala[125] argues: "Kātyāyana's *vārttika* mentioning the *lipi* of the Yavanas (*Yavanāl-lipyām*) is only an explanation of Pāṇini's use of the term *Yavanānī*. It is unwarranted to assume that he is supplying some new information not known to Pāṇini. Such an assumption goes against the very style of

120. *Ibid.*, p. 206.
121. *Ibid.*, p. 104.
122. *Ibid.*, p. 95.
123. *Ibid.*, p. 89.
124. *Ibid.*, p. 86.
125. *Ibid.*, p. 312.

Kātyāyana's other *vārttikas* on this *sūtra*, designed to explain and not supplement the words of Pāṇini's rule, as *himānī, araṇyānī, yavānī*."

But has not Agrawala himself written: "Pāṇini calls a large forest *araṇya*... and Kātyāyana *araṇyānī*"? And does not Agrawala say of Pāṇini's *yavānī*: "a kind of crude and coarse barley according to Kātyāyana"? What certitude do we have that Kātyāyana is not giving the meaning which a word has come to possess in his day? Further, there are a number of new words and forms offered by him. He mentions *Āchāryā* as an alternative to *Āchāryāṇī*. He adds the examples: *Upādhyānī, Upādhyāyī – Aryāṇī, Aryā – Kshatriyānī, Kshatriyā Mudgalānī*. Apropos of Pāṇini's rule, Kātyāyana brings sufficient infusion of his own for us to suspend judgment in the case of *Yavanānī*. In general, too, he is known to be no simple follower or expositor. Agrawala[126] has himself summed up: "He subjected Pāṇini's work to a searching examination, modifying and supplementing the *sūtras* where there was need for it in the process of time, initiating discussions on contentious grammatical theories, at times developed in as many as fifty-nine *vārttikas* (cf. *sūtra* I.2.64), and in other cases justifying and defending Pāṇini against his critics." On the whole, Kātyāyana cannot be regarded as prohibiting Kane's position.

Perhaps we shall be told: "*Yavanānī* has been proved to have done duty in literature for a script. Agrawala[127] points out its occurrence under the form *Javaṇāṇiyā* in the list of scripts in the *Samavāyāṅga sūtra* (*Samavāya* XVIII) as well as in the *Paṇṇavaṇā sūtra*. B.G. Puri[128] cites the *Lalitavistāra* (p. 125) for a reference to it as one of the 64 scripts in which the Śakyan prince Gautama was proficient. How can we doubt the script-sense in the *Aṣṭādhyāyī*?"

The answer is: "Puri[129] also says: 'The *Mahāvastu* [Vol. I, p. 135] has... mentioned *Yāvani* besides other scripts...' If the

126. *Ibid.*, pp. 4-5.
127. *Ibid.*, p. 312.
128. *India in the Time of Patañjali* (Bombay, 1957), p. 162.
129. *Ibid.*

form *Yavanī* could lead to a term meaning a script, so might *Yavanānī* without ceasing to have meant the wife of a Yavana in the first place. Kātyāyana's usage – and, after him, Patañjali's – cannot definitively determine Pāṇini's sense."

All in all, the problem of finding an identifiable alternative to "Greek" is not obsessive; if necessary, it can be ignored.

In any case, Pāṇini's term can in no manner restrain us from fixing for him the lower time-limit: 546-540 B.C.

3

Within our universe of discourse, is there a way to the upper limit?

We have noted that the Achemenid Gandhāra covered Kohistān-Kafiristān. Hecataeus of Miletus, whose life (549-486 B.C.) spanned the reigns of Cyrus, Cambyses and Darius I, is said to refer to Kaspapyrus (Kasyapapura, *i.e.*, Kāśmīra) as "a Gandaric city".[130] Gandhāra thus may be thought to include the capital of Kāśmīra. This political situation is reflected in some of the Buddhist *Jātaka*s recounting past history. In *Jātaka* No. 406, as Raychaudhuri[131] observes, Kāśmīra is included in the kingdom of Gandhāra. A few other *Jātaka*s represent the two countries as being ruled by one king.[132] As the *Jātaka*s talk of "kingdom" and "king", they have pro-Cyrus independent Gandhāra in mind, which yet, like the Achemenid satrapy, was inclusive of Kāśmīra or composite with it in that earlier age. Where it differs is in the prominence the *Jātaka*s give to the city of Takshaśilā (Taxila) on the eastern side of the Indus.[133] Taxila was the captial of the territory which went into Gandhāra on that side in certain historical epochs. The trans-Indus territory seems to have been of secondary importance, for it plays little part in the *Jātaka* stories. The Achemenid Gandhāra, as far we know, was confined to this territory, though some indirect Persian influence has been observed in the old

130. Barua, *op. cit.*, p. 93.
131. Raychaudhury, *op. cit.*, p. 124.
132. Barua, *op. cit.*, p. 93. Reference: *Jātaka* III, pp. 346, 378.
133. Rhys Davids, *Buddhist India* (Calcutta, 1950), p. 133.

Taxila dug up by the archaeologist's spade.[134] Now, does Pāṇini's Gandhāra agree with the pre-Cyrus Gandhāra of the *Jātakas*?

Pāṇini does mention Takshaśilā (IV.3.93) and his manner of reference implies a past history of it; for, as Agrawala[135] says, "Pāṇini applies the term *Tākshaśilā* to those whose ancestors lived at Takshaśilā." But Pāṇini has also the trans-Indus capital Pushkalāvatī in his vision: it "occurs in a *gaṇa* as the name of a river, on which the town stood."[136] His vision is thus somewhat different from that of the *Jātakas*. The difference is not very significant: it is natural for a trans-Indus man like him. What is of central moment is the relation we might deduce from him between Gandhāra and Kāśmīra.

Pāṇini's *Gaṇapātha* (IV.2.133; IV.3.93) knows of Kāśmīra, but we do not gather that it was a kingdom on its own. Agrawala[137] informs us: "As monarchical states, Pāṇini mentions the following: Sālveya, Gāndhāri, Magadha, Kaliṅga, Sūramasa, Kosala, Ajāda, Kuru, Sālva, Pratyagratha, Kālakūṭa, Aśmaka, Kamboja, Avanti and Kunti. Besides these names included in the *sūtras*, there might be others which were implied in Pāṇini's rules, of which Patañjali mentions Videha, Pañchāla, Aṅga, Dārva, Nīpa, Sauvīra and Ambashṭhe, the latter two being mentioned in the *Aṣṭādhyāyī* in a different context." Kāśmīra is, to all appearance, not a kingdom for Pāṇini. But, as a *janapada*, it might well be a republic. Does Pāṇini name it among his *Saṅghas*, the republican *janapadas*?

No.[138] Shall we then take it as a *janapada* dependent on some other and falling under its administration? Yes. But we have no hint even that it depended on Gandhāra. Would we be justified to accept as implicit in Pāṇini what is explicit in the *Jātakas*?

134. Olmstead, *op. cit.*, p. 381.
135. Agrawala, *op. cit.*, p. 70.
136. *Ibid.*, p. 49.
137. *Ibid.*, p. 425.
138. *Ibid.*, pp. 434-54.

We must consider the relation between the two. Agrawala[139] says: "In many respects Pāṇini's language is earlier than that of the *Jātaka*s, but in some cases the coincidence between the two is striking and helpful for chronology. Attention may be drawn here especially to the material for mounting chariots, *viz, dvaipa, vaiyāghra* and *pāṇḍukambalā*, which is mentioned in Pāṇini and the *Jātaka*s. The expressions cited above represent older conditions, and as a matter of fact these words occur in the *Gāthā* portions of the *Jātaka*s which are admittedly earlier than the prose portions." Here the upholstery-mounting with the special woollen stuff known as *pāṇḍu-kambalā* after which the chariots in Pāṇini are called *pāṇḍu-kambali* (IV.2.11) is very apposite. For, Agrawala[140] tells us: "According to the *Vessantara Jātaka, pāṇḍukambalā* was a kind of red-coloured blanket imported from Gandhāra (*Vessantara Jātaka*, VI.500, *Indagopaka-vaṇṇābhā Gandhārā pāṇḍukambalā*), which, as the commentary adds, were of red colour and used for the army (*Jat. Commentary*, Vol. VI. p. 501, *Gandhāraṭṭhe uppannā satasahassagghanikā senāya pārutā ratta-kambalā*)."

Inference from the *Jātaka*s to Pāṇini about Kāśmīra's dependence on Gandhāra would be legitimate. And then we should have the grammarian belonging to the period pictured by the *Jātaka*s. Within the current framework of chronology this period can fairly be dated. Rhys Davids[141] sums up the researches of Lüders, Pick and Bühler: "As regards the allusions to political and social conditions, they refer, for the most part, to the state of things that existed in North India in and before the Buddha's time." In connection with King Pukkusati who is said in Buddhist books to have been the King of Gandhāra in the time of King Bimbisāra of Magadha who was Buddha's contemporary, we saw that to place him in the last two decades of the fifth century B.C. on the assumption that Buddha died in 483 B.C. would make nonsense of

139. *Ibid.*, p. 473.
140. *Ibid.*, p. 150.
141. Rhys Davids, *op.cit.*, p. 130.

the inscriptions of Darius I. Majumdar too carries him towards the middle or the third quarter of the sixth century B.C. (*c.* 540 or 530 B.C.). Obviously Majumdar is going by the alternative Nirvāṇa-date for Buddha: 543 B.C. We have argued that if, as commonly held, Buddha died in the eighth year of the reign of Bimbisāra's son Ajātaśatru, Pukkusati can be placed so as not to clash with Cyrus's annexation of Gandhāra. He could quite safely be set reigning before 550 B.C. And, with Buddha's death fixed to 543 B.C., Buddha's birth would be eighty years earlier in 623 B.C. Then the political and social conditions to which the *Jātaka*s allude would obtain from *c.* 700 to *c.* 543 B.C. These 157 years would be roughly the upper limit of Pāṇini's time. As 543 is very close to the mean year we have chosen for his lower limit we may broadly accommodate his whole life within those 157 years.

This is so far as Gandhāra strictly is concerned. But, if we allow ourselves to take into account the other monarchical states Pāṇini mentions along with Gandhāra, we should focus our attention on an acute observation of Agrawala's. Listing the *janapada*s he[142] says about Pāṇini's reference to Kāśi (IV.2.116): "Pāṇini does not mention Kāśi as an independent monarchy like Kosala, and Magadha." Now, in the time pictured by the *Jātaka*s, Kāśi plays a prominent role. Apropos of its inclusion in their list, Rhys Davids[143] remarks: "In the time of the Buddha this famous old kingdom... had fallen to so low a political level that the revenues of the township had become a bone of contention between Kosala and Magadha, and the kingdom itself was incorporated into Kosala. Its inclusion in this list is historically important, as we must conclude that the memory of it as an independent state was still fresh in men's minds. This is confirmed by the very frequent mention of it as such in the Jātakas." The condition of affairs presented in the *Jātaka*s must, therefore, be prior to

142. Agrawala, *op. cit.*, p. 60.
143. Rhys Davids, *op. cit.*, pp. 17-18.

the circumstances in which Pāṇini found himself. If we can go back to *c.* 700 B.C. for the former we must stop earlier for the latter.

Before seeking to decide where we should stop, we may put out of the way a suggestion of Agrawala's about the omission of Kāśi from Pāṇini's "monarchies". "The omission," he[144] says, "may be accidental, or due to political reasons reflecting the condition when Kāśi lost its separate identity and was under the control of Magadha." Magadha twice took Kāśi over. The Purāṇas report Mahāpadma Nanda, founder of the dynasty immediately previous to the Mauryas, as conquering Kāśi as well as a host of other Kshatriya states.[145] Agrawala,[146] considering the age of Magadhan imperialism initiated by Mahāpadma Nanda, finds Pāṇini's enumeration of a large number of independent kingdoms inconsistent with placing him after this *ekrāṭ* or emperor. Before Mahāpadma it was Ajātaśatru who had started annexing neighbour-countries to Magadha. Agrawala calls it "only a passing phase". But a passing phase would be enough to cause a reference in Pāṇini. So we must ask if its character answered to the political data of the *Aṣṭādhyāyī* and the *Gaṇapātha*. Agrawala[147] informs us: "Ajātaśatru as a Magadhan king had annexed... the kingdoms of Kāśi and Kosala." Pāṇini, however, according to Agrawala himself, mentions Kosala no less than Magadha as an independent monarchy. Therefore we have to fly past Ajātaśatru's annexation and, doing so, rule out Magadha and, ruling it out, conclude that on political data Pāṇini cannot be posterior to Buddha who died in Ajātaśatru's eighth regnal year. This conclusion, we may remark, agrees with our inferences from a study of Gandhāra's political status.

Kāśi's incorporation into Kosala as a reason for Pāṇini's treatment of that state must be earlier than 543 B.C. In Rhys

144. Agrawala, *op. cit.*, p. 60.
145. *Ibid.*, p. 465.
146. *Ibid.*
147. *Ibid.*

Davids we have already the hint that the incorporation was a fact of Buddha's life time. A more explicit and precise statement we find in A.D. Pusalker's narration[148] of the ups and downs of Kāśi *vis-à-vis* Kosala: "...The final stage marks the total absorption of the Kāśi kingdom under the Kosala king Mahākosala who has been mentioned as the sovereign of both Kāśi and Kosala... Mahākosala was the father and immediate predecessor of Prasenajit (in Pali Pasenadi)." Prasenajit was a contemporary of Buddha and died a few years before him.[149] As Buddha lived for 80 years we may think of Mahākosala as having been on the throne before Prasenajit during Buddha's own life. So the incorporation to which Rhys Davids refers does not seem to go beyond Buddha's birth. Hence Pāṇini's time, coinciding with it, should have that birth as its definite upper limit. In other words it is the same period as Buddha's: 623-543 B.C.

However, this very period is divisible into two parts – the first 35 years before the Enlightenment and the last 45 of mission and ministry. To which part does the *Aṣṭādhyāyī* belong? The answer depends on the signs we can read in it of knowledge of Buddhism. Agrawala,[150] putting him in *c.* 450 B.C. – that is, after Buddha's death – has tried to show that the grammarian was aware of the new doctrine. Ram Gopal[151] has opposed Agrawala's case. As what Agrawala says can be argued just as well to make Pāṇini a contemporary of Buddha during the years when the latter had succeeded in making his mark, Ram Gopal must be given a hearing in order that we may decide whether Pāṇini's book is nearer (623-35=) 588 B.C. or 543 B.C.

Ram Gopal comments:

"Dr. Agrawala's strongest argument consists in that in one sūtra (IV.4.60) Pāṇini betrays his acquaintance with the chief doctrine of the Ājīvikas and that in another sūtra (VI.1.154)

148. In *The Vedic Age* (London, 1952), p. 323.
149. Davids, *op. cit.*, pp. 2-3.
150. Agrawala, *op. cit.*, pp. 458-9.
151. *India of the Vedic Kalpasūtras* (Delhi, 1959), pp. 86-7.

the grammarian refers to the name of Maṅkhali Gosāla, the founder of the Ājīvika sect, who was a contemporary of the Buddha;[152] and the other important argument advanced by Dr. Agrawala is that Pāṇini's 'reference to such specifically Buddhist terms as Maskarin, Kumārī Śramaṇā (maiden nun), Nikāya and Nirvāṇa suggest that Pāṇini came after the Buddha'.[153] It is rather difficult to find corroboration for the above arguments of Dr. Agrawala. There is no cogent proof to substantiate the assumption that the word *Maskarin* in Pāṇini's grammar stands for Makkhali Gosāla who was a contemporary of Buddha. According to Pāṇini, the word Maskarin is synonymous with the word Parivrājaka denoting a wandering mendicant, and Patañjali restricts the sense of the word Maskarin to a particular type of mendicants who denounce action. No authority on Pāṇinian grammar interprets Maskarin as a proper noun. Moreover, the Buddhist and Jaina traditions are not unanimous in regard to the name Makkhali Gosāla; some Buddhist texts have the forms Gosālikāputra and Gosāliputra, while the Jain scriptures refer to the Ājīvika teacher as Gosāla Maṅkhaliputta.[154] In this connection Dr. Basham observes that Makkhali or Maskarin, a fairly common appellation of a staff-bearing ascetic, was rather a title than a proper noun.[155] There is no basis for Dr. Agrawala's assumption that the term *Dishṭa* in Pāṇini's grammar (IV.4.60) refers to the doctrine propounded by Makkhali Gosāla; for it has been shown by Dr. Basham that Makkhali Gosāla had many predecessors and was not the first teacher to propound the doctrine of determinism.[156]

"Dr. Agrawala's other argument that Pāṇini refers to such specifically Buddhist terms as Maskarin, Kumārī Śramaṇā, Nikāya and Nirvāṇa is far from convincing; for it is not yet

152. Agrawala, *op. cit.*, pp. 458, 462, 381-383; *cf.* Jayaswal, *Hindu Polity*, p. 30, fn. 1.
153. *Ibid.*, pp. 475, 459.
154. Basham, *History and Doctrine of the Ājīvikas*, pp. 34, 78.
155. *Ibid.*, p. 78.
156. *Ibid.*, pp. 27 ff.

certain that the above terms were first coined by the Buddhists and that Pāṇini uses them in the Buddhist sense. There is, on the contrary, ample evidence to show that some of the above terms are definitely pre-Buddhistic..."

We may add a note from E.J. Rapson[157] on the definitely pre-Buddhistic *Śatapatha Brāhmaṇa*: "Many of the terms which subsequently became characteristic of Buddhism, such as *arhat* 'saint' and *śramaṇa* 'ascetic', first occur in the Śatapatha..."

The upshot of Ram Gopal's censures seems to be not that Agrawala has been disproved but that his case remains unproven and the onus of proof lies on him. We need not hesitate to put Pāṇini's book round about 588 B.C.

It was in the opening quarter of the sixth century B.C. that, in Gandhāra on the other side of the Indus ruled over by a king who controlled also Kāśmīra and whose fellow-king of Kosala controlled also Kāśi, Pāṇini lived to compose the most astonishing ancient work on Grammar.

We have gone by the accepted system of chronology, within its terms we may opine that if *Yavanānī* denoted a script or alphabet the most probable candidate for this "writing" is Aramaic, which was fast spreading from Syria. Pāṇini is shown by Agrawala to have used some Semitic words but not a single word from Greek. We may cite Agrawala[158] on the former:

"*Jābāla* denoted a goatherd, and *mahājābāla* (VI.2.38) one who was the owner of a big sheep-run. *Jābāla* does not seem to be a word of Sanskrit origin. It may be traced to a Hebrew word *yobel* or *jobil*, signifying ram's horn, whence 'jubilee' ...*Hailihila* and *mahā-hailihila* are words of unknown meaning and origin, mentioned by Pāṇini as special names of some article (VI.3.38). The word is not explained in any Sanskrit dictionary, nor is there any instance of its being used in literature. It appears that *hailihila* was a Semitic word appea-

157. *Ancient India* (Cambridge, 1916), p. 57.
158. Agrawala, *op. cit.*, pp. 220-1, 124, 146.

ring in a sanskritised form, as the name of a poison which was imported from the West. In Arabic *halāhila* means deadly poison (cf. Hebrew *halūl,* deadly poison). Steingass derives without reason the Arabic word from Skt. *halāhala* (F. Steingass, *Persian-English Dictionary,* p. 1506). The Skt. word itself is exotic as shown by its variant spelling, e.g., *hālāhala, halāhala, hālahala, hālahāla, hāhala, hāhāla* (Monier-Williams, *A Sanskrit-English Dictionary,* 1899, revised edition, p. 1293). Pāṇini's *hailihila* seems to come nearest to the original Semitic form of the word, which may have been Aramaic...

"*Goṇī* is mentioned as a container or sack *(āvapana)* made from *goṇa* (IV.1.42), obviously a cloth. It is unknown in the Vedic literature, but occurs in the *Brahmajāla Sutta* XV as *goṇaka,* explained as a woollen cloth made from the hair of long-haired goats. It was probably the same as *kaunakes,* a one-piece loin-cloth worn by the early Sumerians and the Accadians, and made of suspended loops of wool hanging from a woollen skirt (Marshall, *Indus Valley Civ.,* I.33, 342; pl. 95, fig. 10). The word seems to have travelled to India through commerce in pre-Pāṇinian times."

To supplement Agrawala's information we may turn to Olmstead. In an imaginative reconstruction of the entombment of Cyrus, he lists the garments that must have gone with the king to his final rest. Among them he[159] mentions "Babylonian tapestries and *kaunakes* clothing". Again, during the reign of Darius II, an Athenian embassy went in *c.* 423 B.C. to Persia: "Aristophanes thereby learned of the very expensive *kaunakes* garment woven at Ecbatana."[160] Evidently, *kaunakes* was in use all over the Middle East from pretty early times. If it can be spoken of in relation to Cyrus, there is no reason why it cannot be connected with Pāṇini some time earlier. We have already seen that Assyria was in direct touch with India certainly in *c.* 700 B.C., under Sennacherib and very probably even in 738 B.C. during the reign of Tiglath Pileser III.

159. Olmstead, *op. cit.,* p. 66.
160. *Ibid.,* p. 357.

Contrary to Agrawala's idea,[161] Achemenid Persia is not in the least necessary as a go-between.

But then the natural question would arise: Why should the Yavanas have the Aramaic script as theirs? We may provide the answer with the help of several considerations. First, there is the Aramaic version of the bilingual inscription recently discovered at Kandahār – a version well sprinkled with words of specifically Avestan (Zoroastrian Mazdean) nature. Here is the Aramaic script of a community following the Avestan religion. Such a community is known to be the Kambojas. The Buddhist *Jātaka* (VI.208.27-30) tells us that many Kambojans kill insects, moths, snakes and worms as a religious practice. This practice, as E. Benveniste[162] points out, may be recognised as Avestan or Mazdean from passages in Avestan books like the *Videvdāt* (XIV.5-6) as well as from the remarks of Herodotus (I.140) about the Persian religion. Now, we may remember the pre-Mauryan *Majjhima Nikāya* (II.149) making Buddha tell Assalāyana of the frontier countries *yonakambojeṣu* – Yavana-Kamboja – and their common customs. The two peoples – the Yavanas and the Kambojas – are frequently joined together in Indian literature, Pāṇini himself in his *Gaṇapātha* links them. And it is extremely probable that they had religious practices also in common. A religion strongly coloured by the Avestan could easily have been followed by the Yavanas and expressed in Aramaic script like the one at Kandahār and with a similar infusion of Irānian words of an Avestan character. All the more is that script likely when we realise from Dupont-Sommer[163] how archaic are some of the turns of the Aramaic words themselves at Kandahār, as if the language used had come from a fair antiquity and were in accord in that respect with the obvious antiquity of its Irānian-Avestan component which, as Benveniste[164] remarks,

161. Agrawala, *op. cit.*, p. 124.

162. *Journal Asiatique* CCXLVI, 1958, I, p. 48: "Une bilingue gréco-araméenne d'Aśoka."

163. *Ibid.*, pp. 25, 27, 30.

164. *Ibid.*, pp. 44-5, 36-7.

seems older than the Irānian of the Achemenids. A script like the Kandahār epigraph's could most reasonably be assigned both to the Kambojas and to the people intimately associated with them, the Yavanas. This proposition drives home to us on our harking back to the list of 64 scripts which the Buddha who spoke of *yonakambojeṣu* is reported to have learnt; the *Lalitavistāra* includes *Yavanānī* among them. The *Yavanānī* of Pāṇini, who speaks of *Kāmboja-muṇḍaḥ Yavana-muṇḍaḥ*, appears also as cogently to be that script.

The possibility that the Yavanas and Kambojas of Pāṇini's day were under Irānian-Avestan influence can be entertained on the strength of Pāṇini's own allusion to Parśu (V.3.117). Agrawala[165] comments: "The whole tribe was called *Parśavaḥ*, and a single member *Parśava*. The Parśus may be identified with the Persians. The Parśus are also known in Vedic literature (*Ṛgveda*, VIII.6.46) where Ludwig and Weber identify them with the Persians. Keith discussing Pāṇini's reference to the Parśus proposes the same identification (*Vedic Index*, I.505)."

Finally, we may emphasise that the Aramaic script, with Avestan linguistic infusion, which we are attributing to the Yavanas no less than to the Kambojas, was found in the very precincts (Kandahār) of Pāṇini's native *janapada*, Gandhāra. And Gandhāra was closely set with the provinces of those two peoples – so placed and related as to be directly aware of their life-details, including whatever script they might have. Does not the *Mahābhārata* (XII.207) give us the combination: *Yauna-Kāmboja-Gāndhārāḥ*?

This combination is most likely to have applied to Pāṇini's own day just as much as to other periods. Agrawala[166] writes: "Pāṇini knows of a *Bhārata* and a *Mahābhārata* (VI.2.38), and refers to its three principal characters, Vāsudeva, Arjuna (IV.3.98) and Yudhishṭhira (VIII.3.95). This admittedly old reference to the Epic throws light on its evolution..." Thus the Epic's *Yauna-Kāmboja-Gāndhārāḥ* could be pre-Pāṇinian, un-

165. Agrawala, *op. cit.*, p. 445.
166. *Ibid.*, p. 340.

like the post-Pāṇinian *Yona-Kamboja-Gandharānāṁ* of Aśoka's Rock Edict V (Girnār). And, stretching down to Aśoka's time, it could be apt also to the intermediate age that was Pāṇini's. Then it might constitute, by its Kamboja-link between Yavana and Gandhāra, a key to the right procedure in the interpretation of the Gandhāran grammarian's *Yavanānī*. In him, well might we trace to the Yavanas a script which is surely relevant to the Kambojas.

4

Two or three times we have spoken of the present framework of chronology. What we meant is the time-scheme which puts Aśoka's accession in 269 B.C. and his grandfather Chandragupta Maurya's not long after Alexander's invasion of India. The starting-point is the identification of Chandragupta Maurya with the Sandrocottus whom the historians of Alexander mention as the latter's contemporary who founded a new dynasty at Palibothra (Pāṭaliputra). The coronation of Sandrocottus would most probably be in some year between 325 and 315 B.C. But there is a school of historical thinking, basing itself on clues in the Indian Purāṇas and equating Sandrocottus with Chandragupta I, founder of the Imperial Guptas who are at present counted from 320 A.D. If, by any chance, this school should be correct, Aśoka would go farther back in the past by several centuries. Between his 269 B.C. and the Gupta Era of 320 A.D. we have 589 years. So in the Purāṇa-based scheme he would come in the period between (325+589=) 914 and (315+589=) 904 B.C. Then, naturally, the *Aṣṭādhyāyī* would have to be dated without bringing Persian and Greek sources into the picture. We should have to go without their bearing on the political condition of Gandhāra, and determine Buddha's date first and then go by the *Jātakas* as we have done.

In dating Pāṇini within the terms of the current scheme we have considered 543 B.C. as a suitable year for Buddha's death. But once the Persian and Greek sources are set aside we need not put (543-269=) 274 years between this event and

Aśoka. Most historians today accept 218 years. But it is the considered opinion of E.J. Thomas,[167] agreeing with the two scholars, Rhys Davids and G. Bühler who have devoted most study to the subject, that the 218 years cannot command implicit credence. Thomas's own view, based on the best testimony available in Indian Buddhism, testimony which finds support even in Ceylonese Buddhism according to him, is that only 100 years elapsed from Buddha's Nirvāṇa to Aśoka's accession. Takakusu informs us that in the Chinese Tripitaka there are four dates for Aśoka: 116, 118, 130 and 218 years after the Nirvāṇa.[168] "The last date, however, is found apparently only in the Chinese Sudarśana-vibhāsā Vinaya, which is a translation of Buddhaghosa's Samanta- pāsādikā."[169] Thus Chinese as well as Indian no less than a school of Ceylonese Buddhism situates Buddha's death between 130 and 100 years before Aśoka. With the latter in 914-904 B.C. the former would be between 1144 and 1004 B.C. Then, corresponding to our *c.* 588 B.C. (45 years before Buddha's death) for the *Aṣṭādhyāyī*, we should have some year between (45+1144=) 1189 and (45+1004=) 1049 B.C.

In the light of such a chronology Aśoka's *yonakambojeṣu* would not differ in its racial implication from the *Majjhima Nikāya*'s. And his *yonakambojagaṁ dharānāṁ* could carry on the significance we might read in the *Mahābhārata*'s compound on the same three tribes.

Much would be of a piece, but new problems would face us in dealing, principally, with Aśoka's own Yona rājā Aṁtiyoka, the four rājās beyond him with their almost equally Greek-sounding names, and the Greek version accompanying the Aramaic in the Kandahār inscription of Aśoka.

As for *Yavanānī*, it might still be the Aramaic script. For,

167. "Theravādīn and Sarvāstivādīn Dates of the Nirvāṇa", *B.C. Law Volume*, Part II (Poona, 1946), pp. 18-22.

168. W. Geiger, *Mahāvaṁśa* (Colombo, 1950), Introduction, p. lxi.

169. *Ibid.*

the Arameans poured from South Arabia into the Fertile Crescent in *c.* 1400 B.C. and by the period 1189-1149 B.C. their language might have penetrated into the province of the Mazdean Yonas on India's borders. But, of course, we cannot be so sure as when the *Aṣṭādhyāyī* is dated to *c.* 588 B.C. It would be quite on the cards that Pāṇini's *Yavanānī*, unlike the use of the term in later writing, meant no script at all and bore the sense which Kane sees in it.

WHAT IS THE HISTORICAL VALUE OF THE CEYLONESE CHRONOLOGY?

1

A critical consideration of the Ceylonese chronology has to face three questions:

(1) What is its date for Buddha's death?
(2) Is its date for this event correct?
(3) Whether correct or no, does it make the right starting-point for the events of Ceylonese history?

According to the Ceylonese Chronicles, 543 or else 544 B.C. marks, as Rhoads Murphy[1] says, "the landing of Vijay, an Aryan-speaking prince and his seven hundred followers somewhere on the north-west coast..." We are also told by the Chronicles that, in Max Müller's phrase,[2] "there was a prophecy of Buddha that Vijaya should land in Ceylon on the same day on which Buddha entered the Nirvāṇa".

But apropos of this double tradition we may attend to the words of Rhys Davids.[3] The earlier Buddhist books contain a good amount of geographical information relating to the times immediately before, right through and soon after Buddha's life. For the period not only prior to Buddha's life but also during it we find "the whole of South India and Ceylon ignored". The same blank exists for the next stage when the geographical knowledge has advanced: "there is still no reference whatever either to South India or to Ceylon..." All this evidence throws light on "the date of the colonisation of Ceylon". The colonisation "cannot have taken place in any considerable degree before the period in which the Nikayas were composed... The Ceylon chronicles, therefore, in dating the first colony in the very year of the Buddha's

1. *The Journal of Asian Studies*, Vol. XVI, No. 2, Feb. 1957, p. 183.
2. *A History of Sanskrit Literature* (Edition 1917), p. 137.
3. *Buddhist India* (Calcutta, 1950), pp. 21, 23, 24.

death... must be in error". We have evidently "a wrong synchronism", an arbitrary and artificial construct.

Can we urge that 543 B.C. is mistaken in regard to the first Aryan colonisation of Ceylon but correct for Buddha's death? Whether some group of colonisers from Upper India arrived in Ceylon or no in 543 we have to look – in the matter of Buddha's death – at two reports by B.M. Barua:[4] (1) "...the Pali Chronicles definitely state that Aśoka's consecration took place 218 years after the demise of the Buddha"; (2) "According to the Dīpavaṁśa tradition, when prince Priyadarśana, son of king Bindusāra, was consecrated for the first time in 219 B.E. (Dīpava., VI.1) just four years after his accession to power (ibid., VI.21), he was consecrated under the name or title of Aśoka (Aśokam abhisiñchayuṃ, ibid., VI.22)." The 218th elapsed year or the 219th current from the stipulated Buddha Era (B.E.) of 543 B.C. leads us, in the Ceylonese chronology, to the consecration of Aśoka who is known to that chronology as Priyadarśana (Piyadassi, to give the exact Pali form). But then we reach (543-218=) 325 B.C. In the eyes of modern historians this is an impossible date. They place Aśoka more than half a century later. Even by itself 325 B.C. is out of the the question; for, up to September of that year Alexander the Great was still in India and his prefects ruled in the Punjāb and Sind for some years afterwards. The India of Aśoka's day had no independent Greek rulers. 543 B.C. for Buddha's death must be an error.

The situation is hardly saved by saying, as some scholars do: "Is not Aśoka's grandfather, Chandragupta Maurya, once named Priyadarśi in Act VI of the late Indian drama *Mudrārākshasa*? As Chandragupta Maurya can be identified with Sandrocottus whom the historians of India's invasion by Alexander the Great mention as the Macedonian's contemporary, 325 B.C. may be taken as the date of his consecration as king of Magadha. Then, with his own reign as well as Bindusāra's intervening between 325 B.C. and Aśoka's, Aśoka

4. *Aśoka and His Inscriptions* (Calcutta, 1946), Part I, pp. 6, 16.

will fall into just the period modern history requires. For, Chandragupta reigned for 24 years and Bindusāra for 28, according to the Pali books: we thus come down to (325-24-28=) 273 B.C. for Aśoka's accession to power and (273-4=) 269 for his consecration. There is no reason to discredit 543 B.C. as the year of Buddha's death." The fault with this argument is: the Ceylonese Chronicles do not recognise any other Priya-d na than the "son of king Bindusāra" who "was consecrated under the name or title of Aśoka". The *Mudrā-rākshasa* is irrelevant to these Chronicles' 218 years.

A possible pair of alternatives have been pointed out to substitute either 218 years or 543 B.C. E.J. Thomas[5] has observed that the Sarvāstivādīn Buddhists, as distinguished from the Theravādīn, take Aśoka to have flourished one century after Buddha's demise and that such a tradition may be traced in the Ceylonese Chronicles themselves. But 100 years render matters still worse. They put Aśoka in 443 B.C. W. Geiger,[6] following J.F. Fleet,[7] has argued that 543 B.C. is a late invention and that the only and original Buddha Era in Ceylon was 483 B.C. No doubt, 218 years from this date brings us to 265 B.C., which is regarded as quite plausible for Aśoka's consecration. But is 483 B.C. itself beyond doubt as a Ceylonese datum?

H.C. Raychaudhury[8] comments: "Geiger's date... is not explicitly recognised by tradition." S. Paranavitāna[9] rejects the theory that there was a Ceylon era reckoned from this date. S.N. Pradhan,[10] who was willing to grant such an era, was yet obliged to add: "it has not been settled whether the era had any connection with the date of the death of the

5. "Theravādīn and Sarvāstivādīn Dates of the Nirvāṇa", *B.C. Law Volume*, Part II (Poona, 1946), pp. 18-22.

6. *Mahāvaṁśa*, trans., Introduction, p. xxiif.

7. *Journal of the Royal Asiatic Society*, 1906, pp. 984 fn.

8. *An Advanced History of India*, edited by R.C. Majumdar, H.C. Raychaudhuri and K. Datta (London, 1953), p. 58.

9. *A New History of the Indian People*, edited by R.C. Majumdar and A.S. Altekar (Lahore, 1946), Vol. VI, p. 262.

10. *Chronology of Ancient India* (Calcutta, 1927), p. 248.

Buddha..." Consequently, we have either to brush away 483 B.C. as being no part of the Ceylonese records or else dissociate it from Buddha. 543 B.C. alone remains as Ceylon's testimony to Buddha's death and, if the island was colonised in that year and if Buddha died 218 years before Aśoka's consecration, this date cannot be right for Buddha.

2

A new issue can be brought up between 543 and 483 B.C.: "Leaving Buddha aside, which of the two is the starting-point which yields correct results for the events of Ceylonese history subsequent to Buddha's death?" If 483 comes out better, we shall have some cause to think that it must have been in the minds of Ceylonese annalists.

Here we must heed the warnings of Max Müller as well as Sylvain Lévi. The former[11] states: "The Ceylonese possess a trustworthy and intelligible chronology beginning with the year 161 B.C. Before that time, their chronology is traditional and full of absurdities." Lévi, as quoted by Vincent Smith,[12] remarks: "There is not, I believe, any reason to doubt the substantial accuracy of the Ceylonese dates... from... the time of Duṭṭhagāmanī, about 161 B.C., although the dates prior to his reign are not to be trusted." Of course, both Max Müller and Lévi wrote before Fleet suggested 483 B.C. But Fleet's suggestion can only help to bring down the date of Duṭṭhagāmanī to 101 B.C. for the beginning of the period in which the chronology is not "full of absurdities": it can scarcely change the fact that the chronology before him is "not to be trusted". The real test, therefore, lies in the A.D. period.

Paranavitāna,[13] who favours the tables of Wijesinha, writes in connection with the theory of Geiger and his group, which principally includes Wikramasinghe:

"The theory has landed both these scholars in consider-

11. Max Müller, *op. cit.*, p. 137.
12. *The Indian Antiquary*, 1902, p. 199.
13. Paranavitāna, *op. cit.*, pp. 262-64.

able difficulties in effecting a transition from the Buddhist era to the other. Chinese references to Ceylon during the period between the fifth and eighth centuries published by Sylvain Lévi (*Journal Asiatique*, 1900, pp. 297 ff, 401 ff) furnish us with indisputable evidence to prove that Wijesinha's dates are preferable to those of Wickramasinghe and Geiger. *Pien-e-tien*, chap. 66, records that in the fifth year of Iuen-kia (428 A.D.), the king of Ceylon, Mo-ho-nan by name, sent an embassy to the Chinese court. There is no difficulty in recognising the name Mahānāma in 'Mo-ho-nan' and there was only one king of Ceylon by this name. According to Wijesinha's tables, Mahānāma reigned from 412 to 434. The date of the Chinese embassy falls correctly within this period. Computing on the basis of a Buddhist era beginning 483 B.C. Wickramasinghe makes Mahānāma ascend the throne in 468 A.D., forty years after his envoy arrived in China.

"The *Nikāya Saṅgraha*, a work of the fourteenth century, gives 818 B.E. [Buddha Era] as the date of Mahāsena's accession. Adding up the lengths of intervening reigns as given in the *Mahāvaṁśa*, the first year of Mahānāma would fall in 953 B.E., *i.e.* 410 A.D. which enables the latter to be on the throne in 428 A.D. when his envoys were received by the Chinese emperor. On the same computation Siri-Meghavaṇṇa should have ascended the throne in 845 B.E. (302 A.D.)..."

This is practically in conformity with Wijesinha's 304 A.D. for the same king. Paranavitāna continues: "There is no valid ground to doubt the general accuracy of the chronicles for the three or four centuries preceding Mahānāma's reign. The great majority of the kings of this period are mentioned in contemporary records and when regnal years are given in these records, they do not come in conflict with the data furnished by the chronicles. Sylvain Lévi, who has tested numerous dates from the fifth to eighth centuries by means of Chinese references, concludes that 'the accuracy of the Sinhalese annals is triumphantly vindicated by this test'."

An example of the difficulties in which Geiger has been landed by his era and of the artificial manner in which he seeks to solve them concerns Mahānāma himself. Geiger[14] tells us that after Siri Meghavaṇṇa, whom he puts in 352-379 A.D., there are three kings – Jyeshthatishya II, Buddhadāsa and Upatishya I – before we come to Mahānāma, and that Meghavaṇṇa's reign and theirs cover, in the Ceylonese annals, respectively 28, 9, 29, and 42 years making altogether 108 years. According to him, these four kings must actually have ruled for only 47 years but were given 61 years more in order that the calculation might be able to reach back to 544 B.C. instead of 483 B.C. It is hard to see why, if 61 years have to be cut off, they are distributed over the reigns of the three kings after Meghavaṇṇa, leaving his own 28 years practically intact; and also why, instead of diminishing their reign-periods, that of Mahānāma is not severely curtailed. Obviously, Geiger is anxious to fit Meghavaṇṇa in with the period of Samudragupta before Chandragupta II, his son, has his accession in 376 or 380 B.C. by the commonly accepted Gupta Era of 320 A.D. fixed by Fleet. Samudragupta, the second of the Imperial Guptas, is believed to be the San-meou-to-lo-kiu-to whom the Chinese writer Wang-hiuen-t'se makes the contemporary of the Ceylonese king Chi-mi-lis-po-mo who is generally equated to Siri Meghavaṇṇa. Geiger does not wish to break the "synchronism" and at the same time he is eager that Mahānāma should not miss the embassy to China in 428 A.D. So, by hook or by crook, he gets both Siri Meghavaṇṇa and Mahānāma in the required places. Instead of acting with logical consistency and making Mahānāma ascend the throne 40 years after that embassy, he fixes him in 409-431 A.D.

A straightforward look at things is bound to support Paranavitāna's conclusion not only that the era of 483 B.C. was never in use in the early history of Ceylon but also that the dates computed in the era of 543 B.C. are correct onward from 161 B.C. as the accession-year of Duṭṭhagāmaṇī.

14. See *The Classical Age,* edited by R.C. Majumdar and A.D. Pusalker (Bombay, 1960), p. 285, fn. 1.

There is only one Chinese reference relevant to the times concerned, which cannot be brought into harmony – "a Chinese notice referring to King Kia-che Kai-lo-ha-li-ya who sent an embassy to the Chinese court in A.D. 587."[15] D.C. Sircar[16] says: "Kiache no doubt indicates the name Kāśyapa..." But in Wijesinha's chronology[17] Kassapa (=Kāśyapa) reigned in 479-497 A.D. So Kia-che does not merge in him. This, however, must not lead us to regard the other chronology as satisfying the demand of the Chinese notice. Having first fixed Mahānāma where convenient, the manipulators of that chronology have to date Kāśyapa to almost the same period as does Wijesinha – 478-496 A.D.[18] – since no purpose is served by making him earlier and no excuse is available to push him forward to 527 A.D. Thus Kia-che still goes a-begging.

Sircar[19] mentions how the problem is sought to be solved: "...it has been suggested that the King of Ceylon here referred to is the same as a later ruler Śilākāla." The new chronology puts Śilākāla in 524-537 A.D.[20] But, even if for some reason this king may serve, what ground is there to date him thus to match the Chinese information? Sircar[21] himself admits that his accession to the throne according to a tradition in the Ceylonese *Rājaratnākarya* took place 1088 years after Buddha's death. Traditionally, says Sircar, the event should be in the 108th year. Then we shall have (1089-543=) 546 A.D. by the old chronology and (1089-483=) 606 by the new, neither date allowing the reign to include 527 A.D. Sircar adds about the *Rājaratnākarya*'s indication: "According to some writers the date refers to the introduction of the Vetulla canon (actually a Vetulla work entitled *Dhammadhātu*), which tradition assigns to the king's 12th regnal year. But even this emendation does

15. *Ibid.*, p. 286.
16. *Ibid.*
17. Paranavitāna, *op. cit.*, p. 261.
18. *The Classical Age*, p. 285.
19. *Ibid.*, p. 286.
20. *Ibid.*
21. *Ibid.*

not suit the chronology of Geiger who, therefore, assumes an error in the tradition." Geiger's arbitrariness is obvious: he does what he wants with Śilākāla.

Except for Kia-che who eludes both the chronologies, Wijesinha is amply vindicated and Paranavitāna's championship of him is historically justified. The Ceylonese annalists could have counted only from 543 B.C.

3

If 483 B.C. is disqualified even by history the next step to be taken is one which Paranavitāna himself fights shy of. He[22] says in relation to Siri Meghavaṇṇa's reign-period, which is 302-330 A.D. according to the *Nikāya Saṇgraha* or 304-332 according to Wijesinha: "This is not in conflict with the fact that he was a contemporary of Samudragupta..." Now, could Samudragupta – dated by Fleet's Gupta Era of 320 A.D. – have been on the throne within this period?

Yes, if he and not his father Chandragupta I founded the Era or else if Chandragupta I founded the Era but married before doing it, so that Samudragupta might be old enough to ascend the throne by 332 A.D.

There are a couple of dated copper-plate inscriptions in Samudragupta's name from Nālandā and Gayā respectively in addition to the couple of undated ones, the epigraphs of the Allāhābād Pillar and Eran. They give the fifth and the ninth years. If they are genuine and are taken to refer to the Gupta Era, either Samudragupta must have himself founded it or his father, after founding it, must have reigned for barely five years. The first alternative seems most unlikely: while Chandragupta's ancestors are known only as Mahārājas, he is the first of the family to be entitled Mahārājādhirāja ("Supreme King of Great Kings") and stands marking the commencement of a new chapter in its history. The second alternative would demand that Chandragupta married many

22. Paranavitāna, *op. cit.*, p. 264.

years earlier than the Era, for Samudragupta would have to reach at the time of his own accession an age compatible with the remarkable ability and prowess for which, as the Allāhābād Pillar *praśasti* recounts,[23] he was chosen out of a number of princes by Chandragupta and crowned king. Against this alternative, as also to a considerable extent against the first, it may be urged that since Kumāragupta I, the grandson of Samudragupta, was on the throne in the year 136 of the Gupta Era we would get for three generations a duration far above the average. Hence the odds are pretty heavy against the two copper-plates. And we are not surprised when we find Sircar[24] declaring – quite apart from the points we have made – that they are spurious.

R.C. Majumdar[25] is in some doubt whether we can assert positively that the first of these is forged. And Sircar also grants at least the possibility that both may be forged copies of lost genuine inscriptions. But there is nothing obliging us to take the possibility seriously. And in any case, since the two other much more important epigraphs of Samudragupta use no dates, it is as likely that the hypothetical genuine inscriptions are using Samudragupta's regnal years as that they are using the Gupta Era. No real argument can be built upon them.

And, once they are held as either spurious or invalid, it becomes all the more unthinkable that anybody except Chandragupta I founded the Era. We are equally forced either to agree with Raychaudhuri,[26] as most scholars do, that Chandragupta married Kumāradevī of the Lichchhavi family soon after his own accession which this Era marked – or to believe that the marriage with her coincided with this Era. But then for Samudragupta to be king by 332 A.D. in time for contemporaneity with Siri Meghavaṇṇa's reign he would have to be less than 12 years old and therefore quite unfit to

23. Sircar, *op. cit.*, pp. 262, 264.
24. *Ibid.*
25. *A New History of the Indian People*, p. 132.
26. *The Political History of Ancient India* (5th Ed.), p. 530.

be the remarkable hero the *praśasti* proves him at his accession. He must be substantially more than a stripling of 12 when he wore the crown. In other words, he became king fairly later than 332 A.D. And in that case he could not be the San-meou-to-lo-kiu-to of Wang-hiuen-t'se, and the synchronism which Lévi was the first to urge falls out of accord with Fleet's epoch of the Imperial Guptas.

4

With the failure of the alleged Siri Meghavaṇṇa-Samudragupta synchronism we are emboldened to see in a new light the alleged synchronism between the Ceylonese king Devānaṁpiyatissa and Aśoka. Counting from 543 B.C., we get for Devānaṁpiyatissa "the period 308-7 B.C. to 268-7 B.C."[27] The tail-end of his reign just reaches into the period our historians assign to Aśoka. But Aśoka's contact with Ceylon could not have occurred before the war with Kalinga which, by his own evidence in Rock Edict XIII, formed a turning-point in his life and led him to become a Buddhist and a promulgator of Dhamma. This war was waged in the eighth year of his consecration. In the Rupnath Edict Aśoka says that for two and a half years he had been a lay disciple but had not developed much zeal at first. In Rock Edict VIII he records his pilgrimage to Sambodhi, the sacred spot of Buddha's Bo-tree, in the tenth year of his consecration. So we may take the zeal to have developed at least a year after the Kalinga war. His Dutas or emissaries could not have gone out to foreign countries before his ninth year. Thus, even dating him as early as (24+28=) 52 years after 325 B.C. which is the earliest possible accession-year for his grandfather Chandragupta Maurya – that is, even dating Aśoka's accession to 273 B.C. – we go quite past 268-7 B.C. which terminates Devānaṁpiyatissa's reign, in order to reach first the consecration of Aśoka and then the time appropriate to his missionary activities, the

27. *The Age of Imperial Unity*, p. 236.

period after (273-4-9=) 260 B.C. By the only valid Ceylonese Era we cannot bring Aśoka into touch with Devānaṁpiyatissa.

We may also observe that Aśoka has no reference to the name of this king, with whom he is supposed to have been in the most friendly relationship and who is even reported to have asked for a reconsecration of himself by the Indian king.[28] Aśoka gives five king-names in R.E. XIII but Devānaṁpiyatissa is not among them. Nor is there in any place a reference to his son (or brother) Mahendra whom the Chronicles call a monk and declare to have been sent to convert Devānaṁpiyatissa to Buddhism. And we may add that the very words "Taṃbapaṃṇi" and "Taṃbapaṃṇiya" figuring in Aśoka's Edicts need not have a bearing on Ceylon which was once known as the island of Tāmraparṇī: they could well be for the region and the people about the river Tāmraparṇī in South India. The Tāmraparṇī-region in the present Tinnevelly District is the original and primary Taṃbapaṃṇi: after it a part of Ceylon opposite it came to be known by its name. Unless a specific indication is given in the Edicts that Ceylon is meant we have no right to go beyond South India. The specific indication could be by the use of the term *dvīpa* (*dīpa* in Prākṛt), "island" – a term which in all Indian writings accompanies "Tāmraparṇī" whenever and wherever Ceylon is meant. Aśoka does not use this indication. Again, we have Davids's information[29] about the early Buddhist books: "The books never mention any person, or any place, in Ceylon; or even in South India." Aśoka's mission to the South-Indian Tāmraparṇī is just conceivable while that to Ceylon is highly improbable.

Might we not then think that Devānaṁpiyatissa really flourished in the period the Chronicles allot him and that not Aśoka but some other Indian king who had connection with Ceylon was his contemporary and therefore even that Aśoka

28. *Ibid.*
29. Rhys Davids, *op. cit.*, p. 118.

may not have lived in the epoch modern historians consider to be his?

5

The last point would occur all the more when we put the query: "If the Ceylonese 543 B.C. cannot be the date of Buddha's death, can any other year in its neighbourhood serve? Will 483 B.C. or else the so-called Cantonese date 486 B.C. make a plausible year?"

Barua,[30] dealing with the same subject as Davids and basing himself on B.C. Law's *India as described in the Early Texts of Buddhism and Jainism*, tells us: "The geographical references... in the pre-Aśokan Pali Canonical texts... hardly take us further south than the river Godavarī." If this period is to run from 486 or 483 B.C. to Aśoka's reign as currently dated – that is, to 273 B.C. or thereabouts – how shall we account for the mention by Onesicritus and Megasthenes of the island of "Taprobane"? And, when Pliny quotes them, we note not only their dealing with some details but also the West's awareness of the place, however vaguely, before their time in India – 326-300 B.C. Pliny[31] writes: "Taprobane, under the name of the 'Land of the Antichthones', was long regarded as another world. The age and achievements of Alexander the Great made it clear that it is an island. Onesicritus, the commander of his fleet, had stated that its elephants are larger and more bellicose than those of India, and from Megasthenes we learn that it is divided by a river, and that its inhabitants are called Palaeogoni, and that it is more productive of gold and pearls of great size than India itself." We have the strange situation that the West knew of Ceylon earlier than India did.

The situation would lose all its strangeness if the interval between Buddha's death and Aśoka's reign lay in some other epoch than we think today and if Alexander's contemporary Sandrocottus were some other Chandragupta than the

30. Barua, *op. cit.*, p. 289.

31. *The Classical Accounts of India*, edited by R.C. Majumdar (Calcutta, 1960), pp. 345-6.

Mauryan. Buddha's death then would recede into greater antiquity and the ignorance of Ceylon in the pre-Aśokan Pali Canonical texts would be perfectly explicable.

Neither 486 nor 483 B.C., any more than 543 B.C., has plausibility as the year of Buddha's death. And, if for Chandragupta Maurya we substitute Chandragupta I, founder of the Imperial Guptas, we get in the period of Devānaṁpiyatissa (308-7 – 268-7 B.C.) the right kind of king. Megasthenes came to the court of Sandrocottus in *c.* 302 B.C. and stayed on for some years. The successor of Sandrocottus would fall into the period concerned. The successor of Chandragupta I was Samudragupta who, in the Allāhābād Pillar Inscription, is specifically connected with Ceylon.[32] His chronological position would be confirmed also by the Gupta records. His son Chandragupta II came to the throne in the 56th year after Chandragupta I. Sandrocottus must have ascended the throne somewhere between 325 and 315 B.C. Then Chandragupta II would start reigning between (325-56=) 269 and (315-58=) 259 B.C. His father Samudragupta thus would have the period roughly from 300 to 269-259 B.C. to reign somewhere in and be the contemporary of Devānaṁpiyatissa.

Ceylon's relationship with him is itself of the very character that Devānaṁpiyatissa has with the Indian king who was his contemporary and whom the Chronicles identify with Aśoka. We may recollect that Devānaṁpiyatissa sought to be re-consecrated at the hands of the Indian king. Now, Ceylon figures on the Allāhābād Pillar in the midst of foreign powers which sought to win Samudragupta's favour by – among other things – "soliciting imperial characters confirming them in the enjoyment of their territories."[33]

Not Siri Meghavaṇṇa but Devānaṁpiyatissa seems to synchronise most appositely with the great Samudragupta. Some smaller scion of the line, with the same name, must

32. Majumdar in *The Classical Age*, pp. 10-11.
33. *Ibid.*

have synchronised with Siri Meghavaṇṇa. This is a hypothesis which appears to be called for by even the fact that the current chronology and history of the Guptas render it impossible for the son of Chandragupta I to be on the throne when Siri Meghavaṇṇa was reigning (302-330 or 304-332 A.D.).

6

Unquestionably, the substitutions we have suggested raise a lot of problems demanding satisfactory answers. We cannot undertake to consider them here. We have brought forward ideas that naturally arise when a proper assessment is made of the historical value of the Ceylonese chronology.

If we wish to avoid too much heterodoxy we may content ourselves with summing up the results of our research thus:

(1) 543 B.C. and not 483 is the correct starting-point for calculating the events of Ceylonese history.
(2) It may or may not mark a colonisation of Ceylon by an Aryan-speaking group headed by a Prince Vijaya.
(3) What it certainly does not mark is the death of Buddha.
(4) On the basis of it, it is difficult to put King Devānaṁpiyatissa of Ceylon in the same period as Aśoka.
(5) Similarly we can hardly make Siri Meghavaṇṇa of Ceylon a contemporary of Samudragupta, son of Chandragupta I.
(6) Neither 483 nor 436 B.C. – the alleged alternatives to 543 – for Buddha's death nor, for that matter, any other date thereabouts can be right for this event.

MIHIRAKULA AND YAŚODHARMAN IN THE LIGHT OF THE CHINESE CHRONOLOGY OF THE GUPTAS

We have established, by making Hiuen Tsang's testimony our starting-point, that the formidable ruler called Mihirakula was defeated by Narsiṁhagupta Bālāditya, a member of the Imperial Gupta line, in the period 115-105 B.C. Other Chinese sources also favour such a dating for this event rather than the modern *c.* 530 A.D.

However, the field of inquiry gets widened and a new problem arises as soon as we realise that Mihirakula is mentioned not only by Hiuen Tsang but also by the king named Yaśodharman in his own inscription of Mandasor dated the year 589 of the Mālava Era. For, the Mālava Era is considered by our historians as being the same as the Vikrama Era of 57 B.C. no less than as being identical with the Era named Kṛta. Counted from 57 B.C., the year 589 brings us to 532 A.D. for Yaśodharman. And, as Yaśodharman says that he was victorious over Mihirakula, how can Mihirakula have suffered defeat so far back as 115-105 B.C. at the hands of Bālāditya? The Gupta king must have fought him in *c.* 530 A. D.

Besides, we may be asked: "Was not Mihirakula a Hūṇa, a chief of the White Huns, known also as the Ephthalite Huns or the Ye-thas, who first attacked India in the middle of the fifth century A.D. and continued their depredations off and on until the time assigned to Yaśodharman? How then can he be switched off to the end of the second century B.C.? And, if he cannot, must not the Imperial Guptas return to their usual epoch beginning 320 A.D. and the Chinese chronology of them be utterly fantastic?"

Let us begin our answer with a fundamental counter-question. It is true that Yaśodharman mentions Mihirakula, but on what grounds can we say that the Mālava Era of his inscription is the same as the Vikrama? What certain inscriptions establish is just the identity of the Mālava with the Kṛta

Era: the Mandasor inscription of Naravarman[1] dated year 461 and the Negari inscription of some Vaishyas[2] dated 481 speak of both these eras as if they were one. But no epigraphic proof is there for identifying either the Mālava or the Kṛta with the Vikrama Era. The Mālavas are an old people. Their republic is cited in the history of Alexander's invasion of India: they were then at the confluence of the Rāvi and the Chenāb. They were in the same or another region of the Punjāb as far back as the age of Pāṇini who names them (IV.2.45) among the "warrior communities" of "the land of rivers" (V.3.114). The very word *gaṇa* which occurs several times in the inscriptions of the Mālava Era – *Mālavanām gaṇasthityā, Mālava-gaṇa sthiti vasāt, Mālava-gaṇānnāte* – serves for Pāṇini to classify them (III.3.86) as republics (*saṇghas*). Even according to the modern dating of Pāṇini, the Mālava Era could very well be as old as any date upwards of the middle of the fifth century B.C. which is the lowest limit accepted for him in that time-scheme by most scholars.[3] It can certainly antedate by a good number of centuries the Vikrama Era of 57 B.C. and may be taken to mark some important event connected with the great love of liberty and independence which the Mālavas are reported by Alexander's historians[4] to have expressed to the Macedonians. If the word "Kṛta" represents a personal name, as it certainly may,[5] the Era was established by some illustrious Mālava leader who fought to preserve the cherished freedom of his tribe.

To approach its date we should take into account another Mandasor inscription – Bandhuvarman's – of the year 493 of the Mālava Era, where there is a reference to Kumāragupta. Gupta history knows of three kings with this name. So we may adjust the era to any one of them in the B.C. period

1. D.C. Sircar, *Select Inscriptions* (1942), p. 377.
2. D.R. Bhandarkar, *List of Inscriptions of Northern India*, No. 5.
3. V.S. Agrawala, *India As Known to Pāṇini* (Lucknow, 1953), pp. 455-6, 474.
4. J. McCrindle, *The Invasion of India by Alexander the Great* (Westminster), p. 154.
5. See *Mahābhārata*, XVIII.91; *Harivaṁśa*, 1.20.42; *Bhāgavata Purāṇa*, IX.24.46; *Vāyu Purāṇa*, 96.139.

where we have commenced the Gupta line on Chinese authority. Here we have to see that Yaśodharman's victory over Mihirakula does not fall too far in time from Bālāditya's of the period 115-105 B.C. Kumāragupta II, whose date[6] is the year 154 from the beginning of the dynasty in any year between 325 and 315 B.C. in which the accession of Alexander's contemporary Sandrocottus (Chandragupta I to us) must be dated – Kumāragupta II is the most appropriate. For, he takes us to the time from (325-154=) 171 to (315-164=) 161 B.C. and then by Bandhuvarman's inscription the Mālava Era will fall within the period from (171+493=) 664 to (161+493=) 654 B.C. With this date to go by, Yaśodharman of the Mālava year 589 will be somewhere in 75-65 B.C., and his defeat of Mihirakula will be some time before the right year covered by this time-span. It will thus be posterior by some decades to Bālāditya's, which is as it should be since in Hiuen Tsang's story of the latter event,[7] although no second defeat by somebody else is mentioned, we read that Bālāditya's was not the end of that formidable enemy: "Bālāditya resolved to kill Mihirakula, but released him on the intercession of his mother."

The placing of Yaśodharman in 75-65 B.C. is of peculiar interest because we are in the time of the reputed founder of the Vikrama Era – the traditional Vikramāditya of Ujjayinī in Mālava, a mighty conqueror by all legends. Curiously enough, Vikramāditya's empire, as described in the *Bṛhatkathāmañjarī* and the *Kathāsaritasāgara,* is paralleled almost uniquely, as R.B Pandey[8] notes, by the description of Yaśodharman's kingdom in his Mandasor inscription. Yaśodharman declares that he became the sovereign of an empire from the Himālayas to the Western Ocean, from the river Brahmaputra to the Mahendra mountain and including "those coun-

6. *The Classical Age,* edited by R.C. Majumdar and A.D. Pusalker (Bombay, 1960), p. 29.

7. *A New History of the Indian People,* edited by R.C. Majumdar and A.S. Altekar (Lahore, 1946), p. 200.

8. *Vikramāditya of Ujjayinī* (Benaras, 1951), p. 127.

tries which were not enjoyed (even) by the Gupta lords and which the command of the chiefs of the Hūṇas failed to penetrate".[9] It seems extremely probable that Yaśodharman of Mālava was the original of the historically elusive Vikramāditya. So far no recognised Mālava king with any greatness to his credit bearing any correspondence to the fabled prowess of that hero has been found for the first century B.C. Our chronology provides us eminently with one in the most natural way.

Of course, it will at once be objected: "Yaśodharman is the conqueror of the Hūṇa Mihirakula and his hordes. Vikramāditya is associated only with the Śakas whose destroyer he has been called: '*Śakāri*.'"

This objection brings us to a capital instance of insecure hypothesis mixed up with indisputable history. Although Yaśodharman may have come into conflict with the Hūṇas, his inscription[10] mentions no conquest over them and gives prominence to his victory over Mihirakula who nowhere in it is called a Hūṇa and whose defeat is mentioned quite separately from the reference to the Hūṇas. Majumdar,[11] in spite of working with the usual unification of Mihirakula, has honestly remarked: "In the Mandasor inscription of Yaśodharman reference is made both to Mihirakula and to the Hūṇas, but in a manner which, far from connecting the two, might even suggest a definite distinction between them." Yaśodharman has not at all declared Mihirakula to be a Hūṇa. He leaves us free to consider Mihirakula a Śaka king. As for Vikramāditya, it is wrong to assert that he is associated only with the Śakas. The *Bṛhatkathāmañjarī*,[12] in recounting his conquests, includes the defeat, at his hands, of "the mean Hūṇas with barbarous hordes". What is true is not the non-association with the Hūṇas but their minor role as compared to that of the Śakas in his life. And this is precisely the truth

9. *A New History...*, p. 203.
10. *Corpus Inscriptionum Indicarum*, Vol. III, pp. 147-8.
11. *A New History...*, p. 197.
12. *Bṛhatkathāmañjarī*, X.i, 285-6, quoted by Pandey, *op. cit.*, p. 114.

we are prompted to feel in regard to Yaśodharman by the attitude of his inscription which suggests the non-Hūṇa character of Mihirakula.

Nor is there any fact outside the inscription to favour the general belief that Mihirakula was a Hūṇa. Our historians hold him to be the son of a chief from North India who goes by the name of Toramāṇa and who too is commonly regarded as a Hūṇa. But, while regarding him as such, Majumdar[13] still tells us: "There is no conclusive evidence to this effect... We possess little definite information about him." We have as little ground to take Toramāṇa for a Hun as to take Mihirakula for one. None of the inscriptions of either of them, says Majumdar,[14] "calls these kings Huns or contains any reference to that people." Majumdar[15] further records that there is a question whether Toramāṇa and Mihirakula were Hūṇa or Kushāṇa: Sir Aurel Stein, Jayaswal and Fleet saw a Kushāṇa in Toramāṇa. Nothing prevents us from looking on them as neither Hūṇa nor Kushāṇa but Śaka. On the contrary, if we put Mihirakula's defeat by Yaśodharman before some year within 75-65 B.C. and accept the view of all historians[16] that Mihirakula was in possession of Kāshmir, he fits precisely into the picture which the Sinologist P.C. Bagchi[17] has drawn of the Śaka influx into Kāshmir by the Bolor route a little earlier as reported by Chinese historians. There is nothing incongruous in considering this king of Kāshmir a Śaka successor to the Śakas who conquered Kāshmir before 128 B.C. Besides, just as the Śakas in the Vikramāditya-legend are said to have invaded Malwa, Toramāṇa is known to have "carried his victorious arms as far as Malwa"[18] and Mihirakula's "suzerainty was acknowledged in Gwalior in the 15th year of his reign".[19]

13. *The Classical Age*, p. 35.
14. *A New History...*, p. 196.
15. *Ibid.*, p. 198.
16. *The Classical Age*, p. 35.
17. *The Indian History Congress*, 1943. Presidential Address, pp. 33-5.
18. *A New History...*, p. 199.
19. *Ibid.*

Even the name "Mihirakula" has nothing exclusively Hūṇa about it. It only means: "Of the family of the Mihiras." "Mihira" is the same as "Mer" or "Meher" and signifies "Sun". The Hūṇas were indeed sun-worshippers, but the Śakas too were most certainly such, as we know from the Purāṇas[20] where *Śaka-dvīpa* is the land of the *Maga-dvijas* who worship the sun-god. The cult of Shiva which Mihirakula seems to have practised, if we may judge from the Bull and the legend "*Jayatu Vṛṣa*" on the reverse of his copper coins,[21] has no connection with the Hūṇas but is known to be one of the characteristics of the Śakas as well as the Kushāṇas in India. The Śaka ruler Moga or Maues has coins with the figure of Shiva on them.[22] And the *Mahābhārata*[23] regards *Śaka-dvīpa* as a centre of Shaivism.

As to any title which may serve to distinguish the Hūṇa or Śaka or any other nationality of Mihirakula, we have an inscription found at Kura (Salt Range, the Punjāb) referring to Toramāṇa-Shāhi-Jau(bla).[24] There are also some coins which have the words *Shāhi Javula* and which are usually attributed to Toramāṇa. The title *Shāhi,* like *Shāhānushāhi,* is a well known one borne by the Kushāṇas. But it is also an Indian designation for a Śaka king. As Majumdar[25] informs us, the Jain *Kālakāchārya-kathā,* which tells the story of the foreign conquest of Malwa in the first century B.C. just before Vikramāditya expelled the invaders, calls the invading chief from beyond the Sindhu (Indus) a Shāhi and this chief and his 95 colleagues are said to belong to "Sagakula" and their overlord is called Shāhānushāhi.

What makes it still more probable that Mihirakula, son of Toramāṇa, was of the "Sagakula" that came to India and ruled over Kāshmir a little prior to the time of Vikramāditya

20. Agni, 119, 21; Brahmāṇḍa, II.71; Kūrma, I.48.36-7.

21. *A New History...,* p. 306.

22. *The Age of Imperial Unity,* edited by R.C. Majumdar and A.D. Pusalker (Bombay, 1955), p. 461.

23. *Mahābhārata,* VIII.II.8-38.

24. *A New History...,* pp. 198, 306.

25. *The Age of Imperial Unity,* p. 155.

and also that Yaśodharman who defeated him was this very Vikramāditya is that Toramāṇa, Mihirakula's father, is put by Kalhaṇa's history of Kāshmir, the *Rājataraṅgiṇī*, just one generation before Vikramāditya. Kalhaṇa separates Mihirakula from Toramāṇa by a good number of generations and hence far beyond any such date as either our historians or we ourselves give to Yaśodharman. But if Toramāṇa is Mihirakula's father, the Śaka-destroyer and Era-founder Vikramāditya of the *Rājataraṅgiṇī* (III) must belong to the same time as Yaśodharman. In another way too Kalhaṇa leads to the conclusion that the time of Yaśodharman was the same as Vikramāditya's. For, just as Hiuen Tsang makes the Gupta king Bālāditya a contemporary of Mihirakula, Kalhaṇa (III) suggests the contemporaneity of Bālāditya and Toramāṇa. He states that Toramāṇa forbade the currency of the coins with the name "Bala" within his territory and largely circulated the dināra coined by himself. D.N. Mookerjee[26] remarks: "It is evident therefore that Toramāṇa ruled for a few years contemporaneously with Bālāditya." And, since Toramāṇa preceded Vikramāditya by a generation, Bālāditya can be considered a contemporary of Vikramāditya also; but, since Bālāditya and Yaśodharman, both conquerors of Mihirakula, were contemporaries, the time of Vikramāditya must be the same as Yaśodharman's.

From all viewpoints, Mihirakula emerges as the Śaka king whom Vikramāditya is said to have vanquished in the first century B.C. The sole possible plea against this emergence is on the basis of the account left by Cosmas, surnamed Indicapleustes (Indian navigator), a Greek of Alexandria, in his *Christian Topography*, a book probably began in 535 A.D. but not put in its final form till 547 A.D. Cosmas in one place speaks of a White Hun King named Gollas as the lord of India and an oppressor of the people. Majumdar[27] comments: "It is generally believed that king Gollas in the above account refers to Mihirakula whose name is also written as Mihira-

26. *Bhāratīya Vidyā*, Vol. V (Miscellany), p. 113.
27. *The Classical Age*, p. 36.

gul." Here a certain semi-echo in the name may be granted; yet the identification hardly forces itself. As Majumdar[28] himself says, "the identification... chiefly rests on the assumption that Mihirakula was a Hūṇa chief." When this assumption is itself questioned the similarity of "Gollas", which is a full name, with the mere name-ending "gul" is not convincing in the least. And there is a significant fact which works against the conjectured identification. "It must be noted," observes Majumdar,[29] "that whereas the chief seat of Hūṇa power, according to both Sung-Yun[30] and Cosmas, was to the west of the Indus, Mihirakula's capital, according to Hiuen Tsang, was at Sākala (Sialkot) and that of Toramāṇa, according to the Jain book *(Kuvalayamālā)*, on the river Chenab."

Yes, there is nothing Hūṇa about Mihirakula. But an important issue arises because Yaśodharman's inscription refers to "the chiefs of the Hūṇas" and to their failure to "penetrate" the countries over which he himself is sovereign. This implies inroads by the Hūṇas into India before Yaśodharman's time and, if he is taken to the first century B.C., we have to ask: "Can we believe that there were Hūṇa inroads centuries previous to the sixth century A.D. in which Sung-Yun and Cosmas speak of Huns attacking India and in which, according to the Aphsad inscription, the Maukharis defeated them? History is not aware of any movement of the Huns into India except that of the White Huns mentioned by Cosmas, who are also named Ephthalites or, as Sung-Yun says it, Ye-thas. Sung-Yun's is the earlier notice: he reached Gandhāra in 520 A.D. and spoke of the Ye-thas having destroyed this country and set up a cruel king two generations before Sung-Yun's visit."[31]

Well, if Sung-Yun and Cosmas spoke of the Ephthalite or White Huns in India's north-west in the fifth and sixth centuries A.D., we need not conclude that in more ancient times other branches of the Hun race could not have entered

28. *A New History...*, p. 198.
29. *Ibid.*
30. *Ibid.*, pp. 194-5. 31. *Ibid.*

India. Surely Sung-Yun and Cosmas are not our sole sources and authorities for Hūṇa history. And even they do not tell us of their Huns penetrating deep into India. The latter[32] locates them only in the Indus-region, the former[33] mentions nothing more than the destruction of Gandhāra and a war with Ki-pin (Kāshmir). Chavannes[34] writes that according to Chinese history the only Indian countries under the White Huns were Gandhāra and Chitral. Our historians draw upon Indian sources when they talk of the Maukharis of the United Provinces inflicting a defeat on the Huns or when they talk of the Huns penetrating so far inland as to evoke comparisons with Gupta overlordship in the mind of Yaśodharman. It is again on Indian authority that they relate of the victory achieved by the Gupta emperor Skandagupta, son of Kumāragupta I, over the Huns: they build their account on the Bhitari Pillar inscription. Now the question is whether Indian sources and authorities dictate the dating of Hūṇa inroads exclusively to the fifth and sixth centuries A.D. The answer depends on how we frame the chronology of Yaśodharman and Skandagupta. We may leave the Maukharis where they are and let them triumph over the Ephthalites, but there is no bar to our putting Skandagupta and Yaśodharman before Christ. And with them, by historical necessity, the Hūṇas must go to the B.C. period.

Even by the current chronology which starts the Guptas in 320 A.D. we have reasons for postulating Hūṇa contact with India before the fifth century. F.E. Pargiter[35] points out that, according to the Purāṇas, when the Āndhras (Sātavāhanas) came to an end, 11 Hūṇas had lasted for 103 years. He[36] notes: "The Āndhra kingdom fell about 236 A.D. and it may be said that the Matsya account brings the historical narrative down

32. *Ibid.*

33. *Ibid.*, p. 195.

34. *Ibid.*, p. 188, fn. 2. See Chavannes, *Documents sur les Toukiues Occidentaux*, pp. 224-5.

35. *The Purāṇa Texts of the Dynasties of the Kali Age* (London, 1913), pp. 44-5.

36. *Ibid.*, Introduction, pp. xii, §19; xxv-xxvi, §45.

to about the middle of the third century A.D. and no further...Huṇas*...may have formed some small kingdom for 103 years on the frontiers of India in A.D. 260." The Buddhist *Lalitavistāra* which at present some scholars[37] assign to the 1st century B.C. and others[38] to the 1st or the 2nd century A.D. at the latest, mentions[39] *Hūṇa-lipi,* the script or writing of the Hūṇas. Then there is the *Mahābhārata*'s references. "Scholars," opines M.A. Mahendale,[40] "hold widely divergent views..., but we may accept for all practical purposes the one expressed by Dr. Winternitz in the following words: 'The *Mahābhārata* cannot have reached its present form earlier than the 4th century B.C. and later than the 4th century A.D.'" "The *Mahābhārata,*" says Bagchi,[41] "knows the Hūṇas and generally associates them with the Parasīkas." C.V. Vaidya[42] states: "Prof. Pathak thinks that the Hūṇas could not have been on the north bank of the Indus before the fifth century A.D., but the Hūṇas were there from ancient times. Even the *Mahābhārata* mentions the people to the north of India as Hūṇas and Chīnas. We must remember the fact that there were numerous tribes of the Hūṇas. The Hūṇas in fact represent the Mongolian tribes to the North of India generally including the Tibetans. The realms to the north of India are always known to India as *Chīna-huṇanisevitān.*"

Vaidya's mention of Pathak is in connection with Kālidāsa who is said by both Vaidya and Pathak to locate the Hūṇas on the north bank of the Indus while narrating the "world-conquest" of the ancient hero Raghu, the ancestor of the avatar Rāma. Some scholars read *wankshu* instead of *Sindhu*

* The reading in some copies is "Maunas", obviously a corrupt form. We may attend to what D.C. Sircar writes in a letter (17.9.1957): "The Maunas are not known from any inscription and I do not think that they have been satisfactorily identified."

37. *An Advanced History of India,* edited by R.C. Majumdar, H.C. Raychaudhuri, and K. Datta (London, 1946), p. 142.
38. *A New History...,* p. 401, fn. 1.
39. In Lefmann's edition of *Lalitavistāra,* p. 126.
40. *The Age of Imperial Unity,* p. 251.
41. *The Indian History Congress,* 1943. Presidential Address, p. 24.
42. *Annals of the Bhandarkar Institute,* 1920-1921, p. 67.

and, dating Kālidāsa to the end of the fourth century A.D. where they put the third of the Imperial Guptas, declare like Sircar:[43] "Kālidāsa, a contemporary of Chandragupta II Vikramāditya, refers for the first time to the Hūṇas in relation to Indian politics; but he places the Hun-land on the Oxus." Whatever may be meant by "Indian politics", this declaration is a mistake in chronology, as may be seen from all that we have said in the preceding paragraph. Even if we need Altekar's warning[44] "that we have so far no decisive, direct and definite evidence to place Kālidāsa in the Gupta age" – even if we opt for the traditional date of the poet, the first century B.C. with the traditional Vikramāditya, Kālidāsa's allusion to the Hūṇas will not be "for the first time" in Indian literature. Nor, we may add, will his location of their land on the Oxus in relation to the ancient Raghu imply that they were not in India before the first century B.C. And it is difficult to say how much earlier the Hūṇas were known to India. Counteracting the opinion that they came to be known only in the fifth century A.D. to which Skandagupta is commonly allotted, A.B. Keith[45] avers: "as the name (Hun) had penetrated to the western world by the second century A.D., if not earlier, there is no conceivable reason for assuming that it could not have reached India long before the fifth century A.D."

Nothing save prejudice joins the Hūṇas with India as late as the Ephthalite intrusion. Just because they came soon after the time indicated by Sung-Yun and Cosmas, why should we believe they did not come once or even twice before? There is the same prejudice operating here as for the Śakas. And it should be certain that the *Lalitavistāra*'s Hūṇas with their *lipi*, their script or writing, were quite different from the Ephthalites. For, Sung-Yun[46] clearly says of his Ye-thas: "They have no written character." All available Indian evidence permits,

43. *Select Inscriptions*, p. 315, note 1.
44. *A New History...*, p. 405.
45. *Sanskrit Drama*, p. 145.
46. Beal, p. xci.

even compels, the idea of a Hūṇa intrusion into India, however short-lived, in the B.C. period we assign, on our chronology, to Skandagupta and Yaśodharman.

Even evidence from outside India creates the likelihood of such an intrusion. We know that the Huns were active on the borders of China for over three hundred years before Christ. We may cast a glance at their activities.[47] In 318 B.C. they were troubling the Chinese empire. In 215 they were again engaged in war and suffered a defeat. Round about 212 the Emperor Shi Huang-ti was completing the Great Wall to keep them out. Foiled by the Great Wall they might easily have sought other fields of adventure to the south-east. And indeed it was while the Great Wall was being completed that they formed for the first time a nation united and strong, capable of just such an excursion. On our computation Skandagupta's reign in the years 135-147 from the accession of Chandragupta I at some point in 325-315 B.C. has its 12 years somewhere in the period from 190 to 168 B.C., exactly the time when the Huns, on a south-eastern warpath, could have struck at India in the way we might imagine from the Bhitari Pillar inscription. No *a priori* ground exists against a Hūṇa invasion in the second century B.C. Whether it actually occurred or not can be judged only according as we date Skandagupta and Yaśodharman.

The road is clear of all obstacles to our accepting from Chinese sources a light which reveals Mihirakula as a Śaka chief and his conqueror Yaśodharman as the Vikramāditya of Ujjayinī whom legend makes the hero of a victorious war with the Śakas in the first century B.C. and the founder of the Vikrama Era of 57 B.C., an Era which we find to be not at all the same as the Mālava (or Kṛta) Era used by Yaśodharman in his Mandasor inscription a decade or so before the foundation of the other.

47. M. Grenet, *La Civilisation Chinoise*, pp. 51, 112, 118, 132, 145, 156.

HIUEN TSANG ON THE TIME OF THE IMPERIAL GUPTAS

Historians today start the Imperial Guptas in 320 A.D. and terminate them in *c.* 570 A.D. Hiuen Tsang travelled in India during 630-643 A.D. He thus came practically on the heels of the last Guptas. And yet his sense of their time poses us a problem. The principal place where the problem emerges is in his account of "Bālāditya-rājā, king of Magadha".[1]

Bālāditya, to quote R.C. Majumdar[2] "is mentioned... as a great patron of Buddhism and the builder of a great *saṅghārāma* at Nālandā". He is also described[3] as having fought with and defeated the terrible Mihirakula who is usually taken for a Hūṇa chief. Majumdar[4] continues: "An inscription found at Nālandā, and belonging to about the middle of the eighth century A.D., also refers to 'Bālāditya, the great king of irresistible valour' who, 'after having vanquished all the foes and enjoyed the entire earth, erected a great and extraordinary temple at Nālandā'. We need hardly doubt his identification with Bālāditya mentioned by Hiuen Tsang." But there is another question connected with Bālāditya. Majumdar[5] speaks of a member of the Imperial Gupta line named Narsiṁhagupta who is currently dated to have reigned from about 500 A.D. and whose gold coins show that he assumed the title Bālāditya. Majumdar[6] thinks it very plausible that Narsiṁhagupta is the hero of Hiuen Tsang as well as of the Nālandā inscription. What makes it certain that he was this hero is the lineage Hiuen Tsang traces of his Bālāditya.

In his account[7] Bālāditya was the great grandson of

1. *A New History of the Indian People* (Lahore, 1946), Vol. VI, edited by R.C. Majumdar and A.S. Altekar, p. 200.
2. *Ibid.*, pp. 192-3.
3. *Ibid.*
4. *Ibid.*
5. *Ibid.*
6. *Ibid.*
7. Sen, *India through Chinese Eyes* (1957), pp. 135-39, 162.

Sakrāditya who is credited by the Chinese pilgrim with the building of the earlier monastery of Nālandā. In between Sakrāditya and Bālāditya we get from Hiuen Tsang Sakrāditya's son Buddhagupta and Buddhagupta's son Tathāgatagupta. Now, Buddhagupta, son of Sakrāditya, must be identified with the historical Buddhagupta, grandson of Kumāragupta I, especially as Kumāragupta's title Mahendrāditya includes like Sakrāditya a name of Indra.[8] So, even though historically one of the steps Hiuen Tsang puts between Sakrāditya and Buddhagupta seems missing and even though the real Narsiṁhagupta seems a brother of Buddhagupta[9] and not his grandson through some equivalent of Hiuen Tsang's Tathāgatagupta, we may be sure that the Chinese pilgrim had the Imperial Guptas in mind in connection with his Bālāditya.

However, he makes two startling statements. Majumdar,[10] touching again on the defeat of Mihirakula by Bālāditya, writes: "...the most important point to be noted is that Hiuen Tsang places this defeat 'some centuries ago', *i.e.* several hundred years before *c.* 633 A.D., when he visited Sākala. This is hardly compatible with the view that the incident referred to took place about 530 A.D."

Yes, it is hardly compatible with the current chronology, but it would be quite right if we subscribed to the theory, derivable from the traditional Indian chronology, that the Sandrocottus of the Greek historians of Alexander's Indian campaign was not Chandragupta Maurya, as our historians hold, but Chandragupta I, founder of the Imperial Guptas. For, then the Guptas would commence in the last quarter of the fourth century B.C. and Narsiṁhagupta Bālāditya's defeat of Mihirakula which is now placed about 210 years after 320 A.D. would come the identical number of years after the accession of Sandrocottus at Palibothra (Pāṭaliputra) in some year between 325 and 315 B.C.: that is, the defeat would be in

8. H.C. Raychaudhuri, *The Political History of Ancient India* (1932), p. 325.
9. *A New History...*, p. 185.
10. *Ibid.*, pp. 196-97.

the period from (325-210=) 115 to (315-210=) 105 B.C. The incident would certainly be "some centuries ago" in relation to Hiuen Tsang's visit to Mihirakula's capital Sākala in *c.* 633 A.D. And what is especially interesting and significant here is Majumdar's admission,[11] *vis-à-vis* the view that Mihirakula was defeated about 530 A.D.: "As Watters has pointed out, other Chinese authorities also seem to place Mihirakula long before that date."

How persistent is Hiuen Tsang's idea of a B.C. date for the Imperial Guptas can be seen from his next "bombshell" – about Bālāditya's great grandfather Sakrāditya whom we have equated with Kumāragupta I, the great grandson of Chandragupta I. Hiuen Tsang says that Sakrāditya built the earlier Nālandā monastery "soon after" (in Watters's translation[12]) or "not long after" (in Beal's[13]) the Nirvāṇa of Buddha. So we may conclude that Hiuen Tsang believed Buddha's death to have shortly preceded the rise of the Imperial Guptas. And, as none of the four dates he reports as prevalent in his time about the number of years elapsed since the Nirvāṇa — (1) 1,500 years, (2) 1,300, (3) 1,200, (4) 900[14] – puts the event after Christ, he must have dated the Guptas fairly earlier than the period starting from 320 A.D.

Of course, the belief that the Imperial Guptas succeeded shortly the death of Buddha may strike us as a gross mistake, but, even so, it should drive home to us with some finality Hiuen Tsang's sense of their antiquity.

And it is not possible to discredit his sense simply by arguing that, just as he was wrong to place Buddha's death shortly before Kumāragupta I, he must be wrong to place the defeat of Mihirakula by Kumāragupta's grandson some centuries earlier than *c.* 633 A.D. The first dating is confined to Hiuen Tsang, whereas the second is the consensus of Chinese authorities.

11. *Ibid.*, p. 197.
12. Watters, II, p. 164.
13. Beal, II, p. 168.
14. Watters, II, p. 28.

And even the first is not as egregious as it seems. In fact, Hiuen Tsang's words, understood in all their special association, need be no mistake at all. To begin with: he estimated, in conformity with the Nepalese tradition of the *Divyāvadāna*, the interval between Buddha's death and Aśoka's accession to be 100 years.[15] And surely, for Hiuen Tsang, Sakrāditya did not precede Aśoka. Hence "soon after" or "not long after" must mean an interval of at least 100 years plus the length of Aśoka's reign. Then there is the question of Aśoka's successors. The earlier Chinese traveller Fa-hien (*c.* 400-411 A.D.) distinctly mentions a son of Aśoka as the Viceroy of Gandhāra.[16] Thus for the Chinese the dynasty of Aśoka did not end with him. And, as the *Divyāvadāna*[17] speaks of his grandson Sampadi succeeding him and having as lineal successors Bṛhaspati, Vṛshasena, Pushyadharma and Pushyamitra, we may assume that Hiuen Tsang considered the whole Maurya dynasty of several members, if not any other dynasty, to have preceded the Guptas. This would mean altogether more than a couple of centuries as the real substance of his "soon after" or "not long after".

But how could he put such substance into words normally meaning much less? He could do so if the intention of his words was comparative and not absolute. A still greater span of time could also be covered by that intention. And it would be quite rational to take as terms of comparison the time from Buddha's death to Sakrāditya's reign and the time from Buddha's death to the duration of Hiuen Tsang's stay in India. "Soon after" or "not long after" should mean anything appreciably less than the number of years from Buddha's death to Hiuen Tsang's Indian sojourn of *c.* 630-643 A.D.

If, out of the four numbers, we select 1,500 years, we reach for Buddha's death a date during *c.* 870-857 B.C. Then, will not even six or seven centuries from it be a short time compared to the time between it and Hiuen Tsang's sojourn?

15. Beal, II, p. 85.
16. *Aśoka and His Inscriptions* (Calcutta, 1946), I, p. 36.
17. *Ibid.*, p. 55.

Actually, Kumāragupta I (Sakrāditya) became king between the 92nd and the 96th year[18] – say, the 94th – after the accession of Chandragupta I.

Thus, from all points of view, Hiuen Tsang points towards the identification of Sandrocottus with Chandragupta I. But an objection may be raised apropos of a so-called synchronism first suggested by Sylvain Lévi. The Chinese writer Wang-hiuen-t'se[19] who was in India in 647-648 A.D., speaks of the Ceylonese king Chi-mi-kia-po-mo as a contemporary of the Indian monarch San-meou-to-lo-kiu-to. The former is identified with Siri Meghavaṇṇa, more properly to be called Kittisiri Meghavaṇṇa. According to the traditional Ceylonese chronology which starts from 543 B.C., Kittisiri Meghavaṇṇa reigned from 304-332 A.D. According to the modified starting-point proposed by Fleet and Geiger – 483 B.C. – his reign-period is 352-379 A.D. San-meou-to-lo-kiu-to is equated to Samudragupta, son of Chandragupta I. As Chandragupta II, Samudragupta's son, came to the throne in the 56th or 60th year of the Gupta Era, Samudragupta would reign in the current chronology up to (320+56=) 376 or (320+60=) 380 A.D. So Kittisiri Meghavaṇṇa can be his contemporary – if we may overlook certain difficulties.

The difficulty in the way of 304-332 A.D. for him is that Samudragupta's accession within 12 years of his father's in 320 A.D. which is also very likely to be the date of the father's marriage to the Lichchhavi princess Kumāradevi, is rather improbable. The difficulty for 352-379 A.D. is: Fleet and Geiger's 483 B.C. has no traditional basis in Ceylon and scholars like Wijesinha and Paranavitāna reject altogether the notion that it was ever used by Ceylonese chronologists. Modern historians are generally prepared to overlook the difficulty in either case. With the latter situated by us somewhere in 325-315 B.C., Kumāragupta comes in *c.* 231-222 B.C. This date would be about 640 years after a Nirvāṇa dated between 870 and 857 B.C. About 640 years can with reason be

18. Majumdar, *op cit.*, p. 172.
19. Vincent Smith, *The Indian Antiquary*, 1902, p. 195.

considered "soon after" or "not long after" in comparison to Hiuen Tsang's own time which would be 1,500 years later and consequently "not soon after" or "long after".

In passing, we may note that Beal holds Hiuen Tsang himself to have actually put the Nirvāṇa 1,500 years before his own time. The Chinaman[20] says of "Manorhita, a master of Śāstras": "This learned doctor flourished in the midst of the thousand years after the *Nirvāṇa* of Buddha." And Beal[21] gives the footnote: "This expression, 'in the midst of, or during, the thousand years' had a particular reference to the period of 1000 years which succeeded the period of 500 years after Buddha's death. The 500 years is called the period of the 'true law', the 1000 years 'the period of image', *i.e.*, image-worship; after that came the period of 'no law'. The phrase 'during the 1000 years', therefore, in these records, means that the person referred to lived during the middle portion of the second period, that is, about a thousand years after Buddha. There is a useful note in Wong Pūh's life of Buddha (§204, *J.R.A.S.*, vol. xx. p. 215) relating to this point, from which it appears that the accepted date of the *Nirvāṇa* in China at this time was 850 B.C. The period of 1000 years, therefore, would extend from 350 B.C. to 650 A.D. Wong Pūh uses the expression *ke-shi* 'the latter age', for 'the thousand years'."

Face to face, however, with Hiuen Tsang we come to see the situation rather differently and to give weight to the difficulties. For, Hiuen Tsang[22] himself has essentially the same story into which Wang-hiuen-t'se, who was his contemporary, introduces his Chi-mi-kia-po-mo and San-meou-to-lo-kiu-to. In view of this fact we may ignore one or two minor dissimilarities of detail and Hiuen Tsang's bringing in no names but mentioning "a pious king" of Ceylon and the Indian monarch as "Mahā Śrī Rāja". There can be no doubt that Hiuen Tsang is referring to the very rulers that figure in Wang-hiuen-t'se. But then the whole aspect of the case

20. Beal, II, pp. 105-06.
21. *Ibid.*, p. 106, fn. 80.
22. *Ibid.*

changes. By Hiuen Tsang's chronology of Bālāditya, "Mahā Srī Rāja", *alias* "San-meou-to-lo-kiu-to", cannot belong to the 4th century A.D. And then, since Chandragupta I in this chronology is a man of the B.C. period, Hiuen Tsang's Gupta contemporary of Chi-mi-kia-po-mo must be no son of the founder of the Imperial Guptas but some minor namesake of the great Samudragupta – a namesake coming at the tail-end of the dynasty in the 4th century A.D. instead of at almost its commencement in the 4th-3rd centuries B.C. Lévi's synchronism, therefore, gets directly rebutted by reference to Hiuen Tsang who has, we may repeat, the support of all Chinese testimony about Mihirakula's epoch.

Nor is it surprising that Hiuen Tsang should be in general harmony with the Chinese sources which Lévi himself as well as Watters has noticed. For, the condition in which he found Pāṭaliputra, the capital of the Imperial Guptas no less than of the Mauryas in whom he was interested, was not at all such as to suggest the end of the Gupta line where modern historians place it: *c.* 570 A.D. Even Indologists who subscribe to the usual chronology have marked Hiuen Tsang's report. J. Charpentier[23] writes: "Prof. Konow points out that at the time when Yuan-tsang visited India... the magnificent capital of the Mauryas was already reduced to a heap of ruins." F.J. Monahan[24] draws our attention to Hiuen Tsang's mention of Pāṭaliputra as having been not only in ruins but also "long deserted". Can we conceive that in 630-643 A.D., about 180 years after its full glory at the commonly calculated end of Skandagupta's reign in 467 A.D. and less than 70 years after the last known Gupta, the capital of a mighty empire would be a wilderness of broken stones? The phrase "long deserted" goes ringing back through several centuries of ruined condition and would be valid if it could stop not later than 320 A.D. when some minor Samudragupta synchronised with Kittisiri Meghavaṇṇa.

And here it is most apt for us to turn to the earlier pilgrim

23. *J.A.R.S.*, 1923, p. 587.
24. *The Early History of Bengal* (Calcutta, 1928), p. 8.

Fa-hien. Even in his day – more than two centuries prior to Hiuen Tsang's – Pāṭaliputra did not present a really glorious sight. He[25] wrote: "This is the town in which King Aśoka reigned. In the city is the royal palace, the different parts of which he commissioned the genii (demons) to construct by piling up the stones. The walls, doorways, and the sculptured designs are no human work. The ruins still exist." R.K. Mookerji[26] quotes a somewhat different translation where the word "ruins" is omitted; but still he is forced to comment:[27] "These remarks rather suggest that Pāṭaliputra did not occupy the same position of importance in the Gupta empire as it had in the Maurya empire." The comment is at odds with Mookerji's own statement[28] on the Gupta empire: "The capital of the empire was Pāṭaliputra called Pushpa in the Allāhābād Pillar Inscription..." Pāṭaliputra could not be the Gupta capital if it was as Fa-hien pictures it in 400-411 A.D.

But then how are we to get round the assertion, in all our popular history-books, that Fa-hien visited India when the Imperial Guptas were at the height of their power, with Chandragupta II on the throne? Well, there is not a shred of proof for this assertion. Majumdar,[29] who first says that this pilgrim travelled through Chandragupta's wide dominions for more than six years, goes on to admit: "Unfortunately Fa-hien does not give any account of the political condition of India – he does not even mention the name of the great Gupta emperor." Rawlinson,[30] Mookerji,[31], Basham[32] and Sen[33] confess the same glaring omission.

Perhaps we shall be told: "There is another side to Fa-hien's picture of Pāṭaliputra. Read what he[34] says: 'By the side

25. Beal, I, chap. XXVII, p. iv.
26. *The Gupta Empire* (Bombay, 1947), p. 62.
27. *Ibid.* 28. *Ibid.*, p. 53.
29. *A New History...*, p. 172.
30. *Indian Historical Studies*, p. 64.
31. *The Gupta Empire*, p. 56.
32. *The Wonder that was India* (New York, 1956), p. 65.
33. *India Through Chinese Eyes.*
34. Beal, I, chap. XXVII, p. lvi.

of the tower of King Aśoka is built a *Saṅghārāma* belonging to the Great Vehicle, very imposing and elegant. There is also a temple belonging to the Little Vehicle. Together they contain 600 or 700 priests; their behaviour is decorous and orderly. Here one may see eminent priests from every quarter of the world; Śramaṇas and scholars who seek for instruction all flock to this temple.'" Fa-hien[35] also says "that here he spent three years studying Sanskrit, and was made happy by obtaining certain works on monastic discipline as taught by various schools, for which he had sought elsewhere in vain."

Undoubtedly Fa-hien is describing a flourishing religious centre, with Buddhism very much in the front. But if he is communicating to us an aspect of Pāṭaliputra in about 400-411 A.D., how is it that those particular Guptas, who were the principal patrons of Buddhism and who are all said to come after his time and before Hiuen Tsang's, could not keep the city in full flood of religious activity but on the contrary left it in such a state that Hiuen Tsang, less than seventy years after the last Gupta emperor, could note hundreds of monasteries, Brāhmaṇical temples and Buddhist stupas all in ruins?

There is something wrong somewhere. And Dhirendranath Mookerjee[36] puts his finger on the spot when he says of Fa-hien's account of the great *Saṅghārāma*: "The description... reminds us of the similar description of the Nālandā *Saṅghārāma* by Hiuen Tsang." The difficulty, however, is that Fa-hien talks of the *Saṅghārāma* immediately after speaking of the Maurya palace. D. Mookerjee,[37] quoting from Giles,[38] informs us: "There were originally two *Narratives of Fahsien*, the first of which in two parts has been lost, and the second, in one volume, is the work we have... A Buddhist priest of the Liang dynasty (A.D. 502-517) named Hui-Chaiao, states that there was another and more extensive Narrative of the travels of

35. *Ibid.*, chap. XXXVI, pp. lxx-lxxi.
36. *Proceedings of the Indian History Congress* (Calcutta, 1939), p. 431.
37. *Ibid.*, p. 427.
38. *Travels of Fahsien* (1923), pp. 86 ff.

Fahsien, in the various countries..." Mookerjee contends that in the abridged narrative which is in our hands certain confusions have taken place. And he drives home his contention by an example.

He says:[39] "From the discussion by General Cunningham (*A.S.I.R.*, Vol. XI, pp. 186-191) we know that in Fa-hien's travels while describing the Indra-śilā-guha (near Giryek) two different places have been jumbled up." What we can identify – from the description as well as the directions and distances given – as Hiuen Tsang's Indra-śilā-guha is called by Fa-hien "a small solitary stone hill" (Beal's translation), "a small rocky hill standing by itself" (Remuset's), "the little hill of the isolated rock" (Laidley's), "a small orphan rock hill" (Giles). Mookerjee, referring to Cunningham's Map of Gayā and Bihar in his *Ancient Geography of India*, facing page 452, says that the Indra-śilā-guha is not "solitary", "isolated", "standing by itself", "orphan" but forms part of one of the two ranges of hills stretching from Gayā. What can be so designated and is indeed designated by Hiuen Tsang as an "isolated hill" is the Bihar Hill (Dand Bihar).

Judging from this confusion of Indra-śilā-guha with the Bihar Hill, Mookerjee submits that Pāṭaliputra is confused with Nālandā, which is the next important step, by Fa-hien's abridger who had not seen these localities personally. The confusion, we may add, naturally persists when Fa-hien is spoken of as returning to Pāṭaliputra and staying at the *Saṅghārāma* for two years to collect the precepts of the Vinaya.

A most significant point[40] to be marked here is that the jumbling up of the Indra-śilā-guha and the Bihar Hill occurs in a continuation of the context in which Pāṭaliputra is first mentioned and that it occurs between the mention of two places named Ni-li and Na-lo. "Nalo" sounds much like "Nālandā" and Giles has actually translated it as "Nālandā".

39. *Proceedings of the Indian History Congress*, p. 429.
40. Beal, I, pp. lv-lviii.

But Fa-hien[41] characterises it as the village where Sāriputra was born and where he came back to enter Nirvāṇa. Now, Hiuen Tsang[42] also refers to the place "where Sāriputra, the venerable one, was born... and obtained Nirvāṇa", and the geographical setting is exactly the same as of Fa-hien's Na-lo. But Hiuen Tsang calls the place Kālapināka. Beal,[43] in a footnote, draws our attention to this fact. So Fa-hien's Na-lo cannot be Nālandā, and indeed Nālandā is not at all associated with Sāriputra's birth and death. The name "Na-lo" seems somehow to have got affixed to the wrong locality. Its resemblance to "Nālandā" leads us to think that in the four pages, describing Pāṭaliputra and confusing the Indra-śilā-guha with the Bihar Hill and labelling as Na-lo what Hiuen Tsang calls Kālapināka, we have in disguise a reference to Nālandā. The great *Saṅghārāma* which the account joins up with Pāṭaliputra is precisely the thing we should expect if Nālandā were referred to. And it is precisely the thing which, as we have already shown, we should never expect at Pāṭaliputra in Fa-hien's time if we are to credit Hiuen Tsang's report of dilapidated monasteries and desolate temples and broken-down stupas at Pāṭaliputra in his age. Nālandā and nothing except Nālandā could be suggested by Fa-hien's *Saṅghārāma* – and, in view of Hiuen Tsang's report, no capital of Gupta patrons of Buddhism could be accepted in the centuries between the earlier Chinese pilgrim and the later.

Even if a flourishing Nālandā in contrast to a declining Pāṭaliputra be not deducible from Fa-hien's book, there is no justification to take Sāriputra's place of birth and death for Nālandā in Fa-hien's period. It is incomprehensible how A.S. Altekar,[44] to prove that the Gupta patrons of Buddhism who built Nālandā lived after and not before this period, could write to Mookerjee: "...we find that when Fahsien visited Nālandā in *c.* 410 A.D. it was only an unimportant village,

41. *Ibid.*, p. lviii.
42. *Ibid.*, II, p. 177.
43. *Ibid.*, I, p. lviii, fn. 65.
44. *Proceedings of the Indian History Congress*, p. 428.

possessing only one *Stūpa* to commemorate the memory of Sāriputra. Fahsien did not see any imposing buildings there. How would you explain this?" More or less the same attitude Altekar has expressed in the chapter "Education, Literature and Sciences" he has contributed to *A New History of the Indian People*:[45] "When Fa-hien visited Nālandā in *c.* 410 A.D. there was no educational activity at the place; but by the end of the 5th century this Buddhist monastery became a famous University, thanks to the generosity of a number of Hindu emperors of the Gupta dynasty." Evidently our historians have forgotten all about Hiuen Tsang's Kālapināka, swallowed Giles's arbitrary identification of Sāriputra's village with Nālandā and overlooked the fact that Sāriputra and Nālandā have nothing to do with each other.

Fa-hien thus lends no support to the modern chronology and stands by Hiuen Tsang, rendering it as good as certain that on Chinese authority the Imperial Guptas belonged to an epoch earlier than his and had already come to an end by the time of his Indian tour.

"As good as certain" we have said. For, the final certainty on the basis of Chinese sources must wait for an answer to one more objection. I-tsing[46] who was in India towards the close of the 7th century A.D., refers to a king named Chi-li-ki-to (Śrīgupta) who flourished 500 years prior to his day. An attempt is made by some historians to identify I-tsing's Śrīgupta with Chandragupta I's grandfather whose name is Gupta. If this attempt is well founded, Chandragupta I cannot belong to the B.C. period.

However, I-tsing's chronology hardly clinches the modern dating of the founder of the Imperial Guptas. When Chandragupta's accession is put in 320 A.D., then by the normal computation of a generation as 25 to 33 years his grandfather's time will be round about (320-60=) 260 A.D. But I-tsing wants us to go back by 500 years from the closing

45. *A New History...*, p. 398.
46. Sen, *India through Chinese Eyes*, p. 162.

quarter of the 7th century A.D. This means round about 175 A.D. – a time too early for the king proposed. We should have to allot nearly a century and a half to the reigns of the two ancestors of Chandragupta I.

D.C. Sircar puts up another argument too. He[47] remarks about Chandragupta's grandfather: "The name of this prince is Gupta and not Śrī Gupta. It is therefore unreasonable to identify him with Śrīgupta mentioned by I-tsing as having lived about 175 A.D." Sircar's argument is not in itself convincing; for the Gupta kings do carry in their inscriptions an honorific "Śrī" which connotes "Illustrious". Thus Samudragupta is called "the son of the son's son of the Mahārājā, Śrī Gupta; the son's son of the Mahārājā Śrī Ghaṭṭotkacha; the son of the Mahārājādhirāja, Śrī Chandragupta..."[48] But, if we look at the argument in the context of two seals[49] that have been found, it acquires some point. One seal has the legend *Gutasya* (in mixed Sanskrit and Prākṛt) and the other the Sanskrit legend *Śrīguptasya*. There seem to be two different names here, the former with a dropped honorific and the latter with the word "Śrī" as integral part of the name. But, of course, one cannot be quite sure. And the main criticism remains the chronological, which leaves I-tsing's Śrīgupta unexplained on our placing the founder of the Imperial Guptas in 320 A.D.

This monarch, however, stands very naturally where he does if we start the dynasty somewhere in 325-315 B.C. and make him one of the members of its tail-end, a predecessor of Wang-hiuen-t'se's San-meou-to-lo-kiu-to by about 125 years.

All Chinese sources thus back up Hiuen Tsang's chronology and provide hurdles in the way of the modern dating of the Imperial Guptas.

47. *Select Inscriptions*, p. 492, giving the note to line 9 of p. 256.
48. *A New History...*, pp. 127-28.
49. *Ibid.*, p. 131.

THE GRECO-ARAMAIC INSCRIPTION OF KANDAHĀR

SOME SECOND THOUGHTS ON ITS INTERPRETATION

PART I

1

The Inscription and Its Message

A rock-inscription in two languages – Greek and Aramaic – was discovered in April 1958 at Shar-i-Kuna near Kandahār in Southern Afghānistān. It was copied, translated and commented on both by Italian and by French scholars.[1] Translation from the Greek was easy; the Aramaic presented some difficulties. But the result was hailed as one of the most illuminating in relation to the Mauryan emperor Aśoka who is generally taken to have reigned in *c.* 269-232 B.C.

In an article in the *Epigraphia Indica*[2] J. Filliozat made a more or less literal English translation of the French versions. After a clear analysis of the chronological information contained in all the Aśokan edicts, D.C. Sircar[3] assigned the bilingual inscription to the thirteenth or fourteenth year of Aśoka: that is, 256 or 255 B.C.

Basing ourselves on Filliozat's translation as well as on Sircar's more idiomatic rendering, we may read the message of the Greek and the Aramaic as follows:

GREEK

Ten years having passed (since his coronation) King Piodasses has shown piety to mankind.

1. *Serie Orientale Roma,* XXI, 1958, 8, pp. 1-35: "Un editte bilingue greco-aramaico di Asoka. La prima inscrizione greca scoperta in Afghanistan."

Journal Asiatique CCXLVI, 1958, I, pp. 1-48: "Une bilingue gréco-araméenne d'Aśoka."

2. Vol. XXXIV, Part I, pp. 1 ff.
3. *Indo-Asian Culture,* April 1960, pp. 357-68.

And, since then, he has rendered mankind more pious, and all are prospering on the whole earth.

And the King abstains from animals, and other people and all the King's hunters and fishermen have given up hunting.

And those who did not control themselves have stopped being uncontrolled, as far as they can.

And (they have become) obedient to father and mother and to the elders, contrary to what happened before.

And henceforth, by so acting, they will live in a better and more profitable way altogether.

ARAMAIC

Ten years having passed (?) it so happened (?) that our lord Priyadraśi the King became the institutor of Truth.

Since then, evil has diminished for all men, and he has caused all misfortunes (?) to disappear, and (there are) peace (and) joy on the earth.

And moreover (there is) this in regard to food: for our lord the King a few (animals only) are killed; having seen this, all men have given up (killing animals): even (?) those who catch fish, these men are subject to prohibition.

Similarly, those who were without restraint have stopped being without restraint.

And obedience to one's mother and father and to elders (reigns) in conformity with the obligations which fate imposes on each (person).

And there is no Judgment for all the pious men.

This (practice) has been profitable to all men and shall be still profitable.

2

For Whom was the Inscription Intended?

The most thorough study of the inscription appeared in the *Journal Asiatique*, the work of D. Schlumberger, L. Robert,

A. Dupont-Sommer and E. Benveniste. The first three confined themselves very efficiently to more or less the specialist's field; but the last-named not only covered this field but also went beyond it to make a brilliant excursion into general history.

The issue he raised may be summed up in his own words*: "There are two peoples to be identified, whom Aśoka addressed in two distinct languages. Who were these peoples?"[4] More specifically the issue is: "For which two peoples among those listed by Aśoka as his subjects were the Greek and Aramaic texts intended?"

This issue is of wide importance because the text in Greek brings up the problem: "The Prākṛt term 'Yona', occurring in Aśoka's own inscriptions as well as in several ancient Indian books, and its Sanskrit equivalent 'Yavana', which also occurs frequently in the literature of ancient India, have been equated by most historians to the Old Persian 'Yauna' for 'Ionian', the broad label which the nations of the Near East are known to have applied in their own tongue to the Greeks. Are the historians right in their equation? Were the early Greeks in India called 'Yoga' and 'Yavanan'?"

Benveniste introduces, among other matters, the very problem of the Yonas and argues out three propositions after reflecting on the Aśokan compound *Yonakambojeṣu* in Rock Edict XIII, which seems to take the Yonas and the Kambojas together as one whole.

The three propositions may be briefly stated thus:

1. The Yonas (Yavanas) within Aśoka's empire were the Greeks settled in the country of the Kambojas, with whom they – though culturally different – formed a single population.
2. The Kambojas were the Irānian autochthons, following the Mazdean religion, of the country around present-day Kandahār.

* The translation from the French is mine.

4. *Journal Asiatique*, p. 45.

3. The Greek text was intended for the Yonas and the Aramaic for the Kambojas.

Benveniste's arguments[5] for the propositions may be summarized: "The Greeks were called Yonas. Irānianized foreigners are also said to have been called by the same name; but the contention of Tarn and Bloch that Aśoka's Yonas might be such foreigners is disproved by the Greek part of the bilingual inscription. For whom was this text in good Greek of the third century B.C. intended except for the Yonas, the people whose very name suggests a Greek origin? The Aramaic part is full of Irānian words of an Avestan kind. Aramaic interspersed with Irānian words was in use in the Persian Empire of the Achemenids. The Kambojas, who are closely allied to the Yonas in Indian tradition, were known in that tradition as a foreign people, with peculiar customs, who raised a celebrated breed of horses, spoke – as the *Nirukta* (II, 2.8) tells us – a language with Irānian words in it (*e.g., Śavati*, 'to go') and had, according to a Buddhist *Jātaka* (VI.206, 27-30), a certain religious practice – the killing of insects, moths, snakes and worms – which we may recognize as Mazdean from passages in Mazdean books like the *Videvdāt* (XIV. 5-6) as well as from the remark of Herodotus (I. 140) about the Persian religion. Hence, for whom except for the Kambojas could the Aramaic version with its Avestan words be meant? And the inscription as a whole situates their country and shows it to be the site of a Greek settlement."

Filliozat, in his article in the *Epigraphia Indica*, has offered two additional points which may be pressed in favour of Benveniste's thesis about the Yonas. He observes in general that the bilingual inscription is chiefly close to Aśoka's R.E.s I and IV. Like the former, it speaks of the king's abstention from killing animals, followed by cessation of killing by others; but it associates this with some matters of conduct and, like R.E. IV, announces a new and prosperous era by the establishment of a new behaviour which consists in cessation

5. *Ibid.*, pp. 47-48.

of slaughter of creatures and in obedience to father, mother and elders. The sole difference between the two announcements is that R.E. IV mentions good conduct towards Brāhmaṇas and Śramaṇas, while the bilingual inscription omits reference to them. As Brāhmaṇas and Śramaṇas are prominent again and again in Aśokan texts and would be most expected – nay, inevitable – in prescriptions as here of meritorious behaviour, their omission is too glaring to be accidental. Filliozat informs us that they are omitted because, as Aśoka himself declares in R.E. XIII, they did not inhabit the Greek countries and because the present inscription was basically engraved for the sake of the Yonas – *i.e.* the Greeks – dependent on him within his empire as distinguished from the Greek kings outside it. From Filliozat one may draw the suggestion that the omission of Brāhmaṇas and Śramaṇas proves the equivalence of "Yona" to "Greek".*

He also suggests that the region in which the inscription has been found is that of the ancient site of Alexandria of Arachosia where, according to Strabo (XV.2, 9), Alexander had established Greek colonies and which was transferred by Seleucus Nicator to the Indian king named Sandrocottus by the Greeks.

As Benveniste must grant that the omission of Brāhmaṇas and Śramaṇas cannot be ignored and as thus he is sure to accept both of Filliozat's points, we propose to deal with his views in conjunction with them.

* *Cf.* D.R. Bhandarkar, *Aśoka* (Calcutta, 1932), p. 30: "In Rock Edict XIII, Aśoka tells us that there is no country in his empire except that of the Yavanas, where are not found the two congregations, – the Brāhmaṇas and the Śramaṇas. This means that the Yavana province was the only country where the Indo-Aryan civilisation had not spread. How can that be possible in a neighbouring district of India except on the supposition that it was colonised by the Yavanas and had therefore the Hellenic civilisation only prevalent there?" The view here expressed is almost universally shared by the historians of Aśoka.

3

The Yonas, the Kambojas and the Aramaic Text

We may begin with the expression spotlighted by Benveniste: *Yonakambojeṣu*. The two peoples involved are not always put into a compound like this by Indian literature: *e.g.*, the *Manusaṁhitā* (X.44) has *kāmbojā yavanā*. Nor has the compound anything special in the context of the Aśokan edicts to indicate that the Yonas and the Kambojas constituted a single population in the same province. The Aśokan edicts have many such compounds putting together quite different entities. Nobody has said that the Gandhāras were a single population with the Yonas and the Kambojas, and yet we have in R.E. V (Girnār) the compound *yonakambojagaṁdharānāṁ*. In the same edict the Mānsehrā version reads *rathikapitinikana* while the Shāhbāzgaṛhī reads *rathikanaṁ pitikanaṁ*, clearly implying that the two peoples combined in the Mānsehrā version are really distinct. In R.E. XIII (Girnār) we find *andhrapāriṁdeṣu*: should we say that the Andhras and the Pāriṁdas had no separate provinces but were inhabitants of the self-same province? In R.E. V (Mānsehrā) we have the word *bramanibhyeṣu* where, according to R.K. Mookerji,[6] two entirely different and contrasting categories – Brāhmaṇas and householders – are combined. The Brāhmaṇas and Śramaṇas too, for all their common religious purpose, are not a single body and their distinctness is preserved in the passage in R.E. XIII to which Filliozat has referred: *bamhane ch [ā] samane* (Kālsī); but in R.E. IV to which also he alludes we get the combination *bramhaṇasamanānam* (Girnār). The combination in the edicts serve various ends, of which perhaps the convenience of the moment is the most telling. None favours the interpretation Benveniste puts on *yonakambojeṣu*. Rather everything makes that word signify that the country of the Yona was merely contiguous to that of the Kambojas in Aśoka's empire.

6. *Aśoka* (Delhi, 1955), p. 140, fn. 1.

In addition, what proves the two countries to be distinct in it is a basic cultural feature which Aśoka ascribes exclusively to his Yonas. As Filliozat reminds us, Aśoka has said in R.E. XIII: "And there is no country except that of the Yonas where there are not these two orders, namely, the Brāhmaṇa and Śramaṇa ascetics..."* Whether "Yona" connote "Greek" or no, Aśoka's reference – as Filliozat realizes – is specifically to his own empire, to which alone the mention of Brāhmaṇas and Śramaṇas would be relevant. Now, if in that empire the Yonas, as Benveniste says, were settled in the province of the Kambojas and constituted a single population with them, why does Aśoka not assert that the Brāhmaṇas and Śramaṇas were absent in the country of the Kambojas no less than in that of the Yonas? Particularly if the Kambojas were Mazdean Irānians, what applies to the Yonas in this respect could apply also to them. Aśoka's deliberate and conspicuous singling out of the Yona's country marks it off from that of the Kambojas just as much as from those of other peoples.

Further, if the country round Kandahār was fundamentally Kambojan and later settled in by the Yonas and if the Aramaic part of the inscription was intended for the Kambojas, this part should mention the Brāhmaṇas and Śramaṇas. About this part Dupont-Sommer says: "The Aramaic recension, a little longer, is manifestly closer to the Indian text..."[7] It is more detailed and conforms more to the Aśokan edicts found in India itself. An instance of the detailed character, out of the several noted by Dupont-Sommer, is that, while the Greek version states in general the king's abstention from slaughter of animals, the Aramaic specifies the killing of only "a few" animals for the king's sake and is thereby almost exactly in accord with the datum of R.E. I that only three animals instead of many were killed daily for the king's curries at the time of the inscription.[8] The Aramaic version is

* Bhandarkar, *op. cit.*, p. 330 – except that I have substituted "Yona" for "Yavana" in accordance with the original Prākṛt.

7. *Journal Asiatique*, p. 34.

8. *Ibid.*, p. 26.

not at all a translation or adaptation from the Greek. It derives directly and intimately from the original Indian model and was not constrained by the contents of the Greek to omit Brāhmaṇas and Śramaṇas. Nor could any model destined for the Kambojas have omitted them. Therefore, its omission of them, in spite of the resemblance of the *Dhamma*-injunction in it to the one in R.E. IV and in spite of the presence of the Brāhmaṇas and Śramaṇas among the Kambojas in Aśoka's day, shows that it was not intended for the Kambojas' country.

The sole contrary possibility is: "The Yonas, having settled in Arachosia, expelled all the Brāhmaṇas and Śramaṇas who happened to be there. As a result, the indigenous population, among whom the Yonas had settled, came to be without those two religious congregations and the Aramaic version no less than the Greek omits them. Thus, although a people other than the Yonas lived in the latter's province in Aśoka's empire, this province would yet be without Brāhmaṇas and Śramaṇas. It may have been carved out of the original Kamboja country: that country may have had sufficient territory left to make a separate contiguous province where Brāhmaṇas and Śramaṇas still ministered, but in the portion taken over by the Yonas the resident Kambojas would be without them. Such a situation, while accepting distinct provinces for the Yonas and the Kambojas, would yet allow Benveniste's identification of the people addressed in the Aramaic version as Mazdean Kambojas and permit his exclusive equation of the Greeks to the Yonas."

Unfortunately for such a theory, the completely Mazdean character of the Aramaic version shows that there could have been no interference, by the Greeks or any other people, in the religious life of the indigenous population. The Brāhmaṇas and Śramaṇas, if they were originally there despite the population having been Mazdean, could not have suffered expulsion at any hands.

Least of all could they have suffered it at the hands of the Greeks. The Greeks are known to have been extremely tolerant of alien creeds and cults. We know from Alexander's historians[9] how keenly interested he and his men were in the Indian ascetics – the "gymnosophists", as they called them – and how Alexander wanted one of them even to accompany him back to Greece. Megasthenes has written of the Brāhmaṇas and Śramaṇas at some length, mentioning them by their very names: his terms are "Brachmanes" and "Sarmanes".[10] Even outside India, the Greeks of the post-Alexandrine epoch were interested in things Indian: Athenaeus tells us that in the processions of Ptolemy II Philadelphus, who is currently regarded as a contemporary of Aśoka's, there were to be seen Indian women, Indian hunting dogs, Indian cows and also Indian spices on camels.[11] We have it on the authority of Epiphanius that the Head of Philadelphus's Library at Alexandria was anxious to translate the books of the Hindus.[12] To some extent the Greek interest came of a proclivity to look for Hellenism at work in various garbs among other nations. The Greeks tended to see their own creeds and customs everywhere: witness their stories about the worship of Dionysus and Heracles in India. But they also had a genuine spirit of inquiry and sympathetic understanding. Their colonists in Arachosia were not at all likely to expel any Brāhmaṇas and Śramaṇas. Rather, they were likely to welcome them. And, if the Greeks of Arachosia formed part of Aśoka's empire, the Brāhmaṇas and Śramaṇas were sure to be found amongst them, free to pursue their vocations, even succeeding in Indianizing some of the foreigners.

Of course, these facts would not entitle us to say that in an inscription for the Greeks, who had a non-Indian civilization, Aśoka would go out of his way to mention Brāhmaṇas and Śramaṇas. But they do entitle us to say that the omission of

9. *E.g.*, Arrian, *The Anabasis of Alexander*, VII.ii.3-9, and Strabo, *Geography*, XV.i.68.

10. J. McCrindle, *Ancient India as described by Megasthenes and Arrian* (Calcutta, 1926), pp. 96-97.

11. *The Age of Imperial Unity*, edited by R.C. Majumdar and A.D. Pusalker (Bombay, 1953), p. 616.

12. Bhandarkar, *op. cit.*, p. 163.

these religious orders in the Aramaic text would never be due to the Greeks of the province: it would be due to the Yona character of the very people addressed in that text.

Our facts entitle us also to say that the Greeks, by their temperament and tendency, hardly qualify as the one people within Aśoka's empire, namely, the Yonas, of whom he could aver that no Brāhmaṇas and Śramaṇas lived in their country.

We may be told: "Aśoka's characterization of his Yonas has nothing to do with temperament and tendency. He has only the set-up of the collective life in view. This set-up has no room for Brāhmaṇas and Śramaṇas: that is all. And did not the Greeks have precisely such a set-up?"

Even if Aśoka's view is caught correctly here, the interpretation is rather queer in the mouths of those who, deeming the Kambojas to be Irānian and Mazdean in the set-up of their collective life and therefore without any room for Brāhmaṇas and Śramaṇas, point out still that under Aśoka none except the Yonas were without these religious orders. A self-contradiction is indulged in. If the Kambojas, for all the Irānian nationality and Mazdean religion attributed to them, could be thought of as having Brāhmaṇas and Śramaṇas among them, the set-up of the collective life should not be responsible for their absence in the Yona province.

But can we even admit, independently of the question of the Kambojas' nationality and religion, that Aśoka had nothing save this set-up in view? His actual words run in full: "And there is no country except that of the Yonas where there are not these orders, namely, the Brāhmaṇa and Śramaṇa ascetics; and there is no place in any (such) country where men have no faith in one sect or another."[13] Obviously the operative word is "faith". The Yonas have no faith in the Brāhmaṇa and Śramaṇa ascetics such as the rest of the empire has in one or another sect of them: hence the absence of these ascetics in the Yona territory. Aśoka has in view a psychological condition more than the set-up of the collective life.

13. *Ibid.*, p. 330.

To draw together the various strands of our criticism:

1. The Kambojas were in another province than that of the Yonas.
2. The Aramaic text was not addressed to the Kambojas.
3. It was addressed only to a people who did not have the services of the Brāhmaṇas and Śramaṇas in their midst: the Yonas.
4. The Greeks, having a many-sided receptive mind, could not be the Yonas of Aśoka's empire.

These conclusions, in conflict with Benveniste's, as well as with Filliozat's and those of modern Aśokan scholars in general, carry us into deep waters. How deep the waters can be we may try to gauge by some further considerations.

4

The Kambojas as Non-Irānians, Non-Mazdeans

To establish *in toto* our unconventional fourfold thesis we must take two important steps.

First, we must neutralize Benveniste's contention that Indian tradition shows the Kambojas to have been foreigners of Irānian nationality and to have followed what he termed Mazdeism, the religion of the Irānians.

Benveniste[14] is correct in telling us that the Kambojan verb *śavati* ("to go") which Yāska in his *Nirukta* (II.2.8) has transmitted to us, is Irānian usage; but must we dub the Kambojas Irānian because of it? No doubt, Grierson,[15] who originally discussed the clue from Yāska, concluded that the Kambojas could not have been Indo-Aryan, but did he mean that they were Irānian altogether with no touch of Indo-Aryanism? What he deduced from Yāska's context and other data was that the Kambojas must have used either Sanskrit with an infusion of Irānian words to which they gave Indian inflexions or else a language partly Indo-Aryan and partly Irānian.

14. *Journal Asiatique*, pp. 46-47.
15. *The Journal of the Royal Asiatic Society*, 1911, pp. 801-02.

Surely, Grierson is pretty far from Benveniste's generalization. His Kambojas would hardly qualify as the people for whom Aśoka got the Aramaic version engraved.

And we should remember V.S. Agrawala's remark:[16] "The *Nirukta*... is a commentary on a traditional list of Vedic words known as the *Nighaṇṭu*." The *Nighaṇṭu* (II.14) lists *śavati* among the verbs meaning "to go". So the implication of Yāska's statement is that *śavati* in the sense "to go" is an ancient Vedic verb once in general Indian use but later restricted to the Kambojas who, unlike other sections of the Indian people, had somehow preserved it. Whether originally Irānian or no, this verb cannot make the Kambojas Irānian any more than it can make Irānian the Vedic literature of which the *Nighaṇṭu* took stock. And it was not at all for Yāska a pointer to any non-Indianness.

How little he considered the Kambojas non-Indian is further evinced by his etymology (doubtless "folk-etymology") of their name – "Kambhoja" to him – in the same context as his comment on *śavati*. He writes: "*Kambhojāḥ kambalabhojāḥ kamanīyabhojāh vā. Kambalah kamanīya bhavati*" – "The Kambojas are fond (bhojāh) of blankets (kambala) or they are fond of pleasant (kamanīya) things. The blanket is a pleasant (*kamanīya*) thing." Yāska takes "Kambhoja" to be composed of *bhoja* preceded by an abbreviation, *kam*, of *kambala* which is at the same time *kamanīya*. This etymology, drawing confirmation from the fact that the Kamboja country was noted for many of the best kinds of blankets,[17] and basing itself entirely on Indian words, could never have been pertinent to a people thought to be Irānian.

As for raising a celebrated breed of horses, for which too the Kambojas were noted, it was not a profession special to the Irānians. In fact, the Irānians as such do not figure at all when Mookerji,[18] writing on the recruitment of horses for the Indian cavalry, observes: "The horses... had to be recruited

16. *The Cultural Heritage of India* (Calcutta, 1958), Vol. I, p. 294.
17. B.M. Barua, *Aśoka and His Inscriptions* (Calcutta, 1946), Part I, p. 99.
18. *Chandragupta Maurya and His Times* (Madras, 1943), p. 280.

from various places which are thus named by Kauṭilya (II.30): Kamboja (Afghānistān, the Kaofu of Hiuen Tsang), Sindhu (Sind), Āratta (Punjāb), Vanāya (Arabia), Balhīka (Balkh), Sauvīra (Sind or Indus delta), Papeya, and Taitala (unknown). 'Western horses' in general are highly prized in the *Mahābhārata*, but those of Sindhu and Kamboja are most mentioned (*Mbh.* III.71.12). Equally famous were the steeds from Balhi (*Mbh.* I. 221; v. 88. 6, etc)."

In regard to the origin of the Kambojas, Indian tradition is unequivocally against the foreignness Benveniste reads in it for them. A.D. Pusalker[19] writes: "The earliest mention of Kāmboja occurs in the *Vaṁśa Brāhmaṇa* of the Samaveda where a teacher Kāmboja Aupamanyava is referred to. The sage Upamanyu mentioned in the Ṛgveda (I.102.9) is in all probability the father of the Kāmboja teacher. From the fact that Kāmboja Aupamanyava is stated to be a pupil of Madragāra, Zimmer infers that the Kāmbojas and Madras were close neighbours in north-western India. The speech of the Kāmbojas is referred to by Yāska as differing from that of other Aryans and Grierson sees in this reference the Irānian affinities of the Kāmbojas, but the fact that Kāmboja teachers were reputed for their Vedic learning shows them to have been Vedic Aryans, so that Kāmboja was an Aryan settlement. Later on Kāmbojas settled in the north-west of the Indus and were the Kambujiya of the Old Persian inscriptions."

The last point is doubtful, since Benveniste[20] categorically tells us in all honesty that although he sees the Kambojas as Irānians the Persians do not know of the name Kamboja at all and he rejects the *rapprochement* proposed by J. Charpentier between the Kambojas and the name of the Persian king Cambyses, Old Persian *Kambujiya*. But all the rest of Pusalker's information is incontrovertible. And what Benveniste categorically tells us may be additional evidence against the Kambojas being not Indian but Irānian.

19. *In The Vedic Age*, edited by R.C. Majumdar and A.D. Pusalker (London, 1952), pp. 259-60.

20. *Journal Asiatique*, p. 48.

Then there is the *Manusaṁhitā* (X.43-44) grouping the Kambojas with some other tribes as degraded Kshatriyas, tribes who lost Vedic rites and customs and thereby became Dasyus. It clearly states that they lost their Kshatriya status by not consulting Brāhmaṇas. The *Mahābhārata* (XIII.33.21) calls them an Indian people that became *Vriśala*s (degraded castes) from seeing no Brāhmaṇas, and in an earlier section it gives the perfectly Indian name of two of their kings Chandravarman and Sudakshina.[21] The Purāṇas too relate how in remote antiquity King Sagara fought them as well as other tribes and degraded all of them from their original Kshatriyahood and penalized them in various ways.[22] Their giving up of Vedic rites and customs is put in the time of Sagara.

Indian tradition makes the Kambojas "foreign" by their own choice or else by compulsion from India: it does not give them a foreign origin, it does not anywhere take them to be Irānian. The utmost this tradition allows us to say is that they were Indians who, by their long stay in the north-west without Vedic ministrations, became partially Irānianized.

It is their partial Irānianization that accounts for the practice which Benveniste cites from a Buddhist *Jātaka*. This practice is indeed ancient Mazdean, though on the superficial side of the religion, a curious penance the *Videvdāt* imposed for the crime of slaughtering what it called a "water-dog". But the *Bhūridatta Jātaka* does not say that *all* Kambojas went in for it: the words are *kambojatakānam...bahunnam*, "many Kambojas". B.C. Law[23] is quite precise here: "In the *Bhūridatta Jātaka* we find that many Kambojas who were not Ariyas falsely held that people were purified by killing insects, snakes, frogs, etc." And even the *Jātaka*s do not make out the Kambojas to be Irānian in origin. To quote Law[24] again : "In the *Jātaka*s we read that Kambojas were a North-Western tribe who were

21. H.C. Raychaudhuri, *The Political History of Ancient India* (Calcutta, 1932), p. 106.

22. B.C. Law, *Tribes in Ancient India* (Poona 1043), p. 7.

23. *Ibid.*, p. 7. *Cf. Jātaka* (Fausböll), VI, pp. 208, 210.

24. *Ibid. Cf. Jātaka* (Fausböll), VI, p. 208.

supposed to have lost their original Aryan customs and to have become barbarous."

Even the "barbarous" condition, including the partial Irānianization of a good number of them with that Mazdean practice, cannot really be applied to the Kambojas in Aśoka's time. For Aśoka, by making a unique exception of the Yonas, implies that the Brāhmaṇas and Śramaṇas lived in the Kamboja country. And we need not be surprised. Indian tradition itself suggests the possibility of a reversal to Indianness. In the midst of the degradation of the tribes a shadow of Brāhmaṇical institutions was yet allowed to fall upon them. A long passage in the *Mahābhārata* recounts what the degraded Kshatriyas were required to do by way of religious observance and social duty.[25] Whatever the state of affairs before Aśoka's time, we have in the constant presence of the Brāhmaṇas and Śramaṇas everywhere in his empire except in the Yona country the active play of the Indo-Aryan civilization among his Kamboja subjects. So Benveniste's characterization of them as Irānian on the strength of a queer practice (and that too not universal) is counterbalanced.

There is nothing in Indian tradition to set up the Kambojas as candidates for the entirely Mazdean Aramaic version – and least of all when we bring it into relationship with Aśoka's R.E. XIII.

If we should like to know what kind of inscription would, in comparison to ours, go rightly with the Kambojas of Aśoka, we have only to look at a slab broken off from a rock, which was picked up a few years later in the bazaar of Kandahār where curios and antiques from near and far have often been brought for sale. Called for convenience's sake Kandahār II, this fragment, like Kandahār I, is in Aramaic containing Irānian words but it also incorporates Indian Prākṛt ones in the manner of the two Aśokan fragments in Aramaic found a long time back at Taxila and Pūl-i-Dārunteh respectively. The Prākṛt component shows that the message could not have

25. *Muir's Sanskrit Texts*, 2nd Edition, Vol. I, p. 484.

been for people completely Irānianized. A semi-Irānianized group must have been addressed. And what is most significant is that the Pillar Edict VIII openly advises, like that section, reverence for Brāhmaṇas and Śramaṇas. In its 6th line it has the compound *babhanasamanesu*.[26] Evidently, here are not moral precepts for Yonas. With equal certainty they are meant for those subjects of Aśoka who are neither thoroughly in line with the Indians nor thoroughly Irānianized and Mazdeanized: in short, the Yonas' neighbours, the Kambojas.

When Kandahār I and II are juxtaposed, the case against Benveniste's choice of the Kambojas for the former's Aramaic version seems clinched.

5

The Aramaic Text's Mazdeism and the Yonas

Our second step to ensure total support to our fourfold thesis lies in aligning the mind of the Aśokan Yonas to the Mazdeism Benveniste rightly reads in the Aramaic text.

Unlike the tolerant, inquiring and syncretic attitude of the religious Greeks as demonstrated by the historians of Alexander's invasion as well as by Megasthenes who stayed in India from *c.* 302 B.C. for several years, the attitude of the ancient Mazdean religionists towards Indian practices could easily turn unsympathetic. The Mazdean religion was to a great extent a forcible break-away from the Vedic. Although retaining the cult of fire, it stressed more than ever the Irānian reversal of the meaning of the word "deva" and, with a larger insistence, made it signify "demon" instead of "god". We may attend to the remarks of H.C. Raychaudhuri[27] on one of the Achemenid emperors, Xerxes (485-465 B.C.): "Xerxes refers to the suppression of rebellion in lands 'where, before, the Daivas were worshipped; then, by Ahuramazda's will, of such temples of the Daivas, I (the King) sapped the foundations.'

26. *Journal Asiatique* (Paris, 1966), facing p. 462.

27. *An Advanced History of India*, edited by R.C. Majumdar, H.C. Raychaudhuri and Kalikinkar Datta (London, 1946), p. 64.

The Daiva-worshipping lands may have included the Indian satrapies." Values that the Brāhmaṇas and Śramaṇas stood for might be opposed by the more orthodox among the ancient Mazdeans. What Aśoka says about his Yona subjects in R.E. XIII in connection with the Brāhmaṇas and Śramaṇas would apply eminently to such Mazdeans and, with Benveniste's brief for the Kambojas disqualified, prove the Yonas to be the Mazdeans for whom Aśoka got the Aramaic text inscribed.

Thus the Aśokan Yonas give the lie to the common assumption which equates them to the Greeks. But is there anything unnatural about this consequence? We have noted how the *Manusaṁhitā* and the *Mahābhārata*, in dealing with the loss of Kshatriyahood by the Kambojas and other Indian tribes, refer to the absence of the Brāhmaṇas among these peoples and in their countries. One of these other Indian tribes mentioned are the Yonas. Have we not here a correspondence to Aśoka's own statement on the Yonas and their country? His statement is thus in keeping with a common Indian tradition and need hold no clue to his Yonas having been non-Indian. An entirely false issue is raised when it is said that the absence of the Brāhmaṇas and Śramaṇas among his Yonas indicates Greek colonists whose civilization is different from the Indo-Aryan.

The sole problem Aśoka's statement poses for us is: "Why does he specially pick out the Yonas as living without Brāhmaṇas and Śramaṇas when ancient Indian books have combined several peoples with them in this matter?" The answer is already contained in what we have said about the possibility those books have held forth of these peoples changing their deviated religious course and about the Kambojas, all of whom were not Mazdeanized, having obviously done so, as we infer from Aśoka that unlike the Yonas they allowed the Brāhmaṇas and Śramaṇas to visit them. The Yonas must have made too radical a deviation from the Vedic religion – a deviation which, by excluding in the area between India and Persia these two religious orders, could have been only towards Mazdeism such as held by the people for whom the Aramaic version was intended.

On top of Aśoka's statement about his Yonas in agreement with old Indian books we have the fact that in those books there are several impressive signs of their Yonas having really been indigenous and non-Greek. An impartial study of the old Indian literature leads one to echo E.A. Schwanbeck[28] who marks that Yavanas were known in India much before any appreciable body of the Greeks could have arrived and concludes that those ancient Yavanas could not be the Greeks. Is there any reason to contradict Schwanbeck?

At the very start we must get rid of the notion, once popular, of a Greek colony on India's frontiers before the time of Alexander – the people mentioned by his own historians as the Nysaioi. No doubt, Alexander's soldiers played with the idea that the Nysaioi were a colony left behind by Dionysus when he returned home from the wanderings which, according to a story by Euripides in his *Bacchae,* had taken him all over the East. However, we may heed what Strabo (XV.7) has to say on the "conquests" attributed to both Dionysus and Heracles:[29] "As for the stories of Heracles and Dionysus Magasthenes with a few others considers them trustworthy; but most other writers, among whom is Eratosthenes, consider them untrustworthy and mythical, like the stories current among the Greeks." So we see that the mass of Greek minds themselves dismissed the claim of the Nysaioi's Hellenic ancestry. And there was even a counter-legend: Diodorus Siculus[30] reports that more than one Dionysus existed and that the most ancient of them was not a Greek but an Indian and moved from India to every part of the world. Moreover, the Dionysus who was supposed to have come to India and founded the Nysaioi colony on his way back was put by Pliny, Solinus and Arrian[31] more than 6,000 years before Alexander:

28. *Megasthenes's Indica,* p. 18.
29. McCrindle, *op. cit.,* p. 110.
30. *Ibid.,* pp. 34-35, fn.
31. *Ibid.,* pp. 116, 208.

six millennia in the borderland between India and Persia would be enough to make any foreign people as good as indigenous. Hence the story of the Dionysian Greek colony is self-contradictory.

It was a product of sheer wishful thinking on the basis of Greek-seeming echoes in the names involved. First, the town-name 'Nysa' reminded the Macedonian soldiery of the mythical place, Mount Nysa, where Dionysus had been nursed by a nymph when he was born, but about it M. de St.-Martin[32] rightly observed long ago: "This place ought to be of Median or Persian foundation, since the nomenclature is Iranian, the name of Nysa or Nisaya which figures in the cosmogonic geography of the *Zendavesta* being one which is far-spread in the countries of ancient Iran." Then the name of the neighbouring mountain "Meru" resembled "Meros", the Greek for "thigh", and at once got linked with the myth of Dionysus's springing from the thigh of Zeus. Further encouragement was given by the presence of the vine in that mountain-region, a plant sacred to the Wine-god that Dionysus was, but, as Strabo[33] notes, the vine was abundant throughout a great part of Armenia, Mesopotamia, Media, Persia, and Karmania and therefore nothing special here.

A typical trait of the Greek psychology lay behind all the play of fancy around the Nysaioi as around the well-known Dionysus-worship read in the cult of Shiva and Heracles-worship seen in the cult of Kṛṣṇa-Balarāma. "The Greeks," remarks E.R. Bevan,[34] "always experienced a keen joy of recognition when they could connect things with the figures of their own legends..." How eager the Greeks were on any pretext to read Hellenic things in foreign countries we can see from the manner in which they declared the tribe "Oxydrakai" to be the Nysaioi's kin and, like them, the offspring and worshippers of Dionysus.[35] The reasons offered were: "the

32. *Ibid.*, p. 183, fn.
33. *Ibid.*, p. 97.
34. *The Cambridge History of India* (1923), Vol. I, p. 353.
35. McCrindle, *op. cit.*, p. 111.

vine grew in their country, and their processions were conducted with great pomp, and their kings on going forth to war and on other occasions marched in Bacchic fashion..." Strangely enough, the statement ends with the words: "which is also a custom among other Indians." The absurdity of the claim emerges as soon as we realize that scholarship has universally recognized the "Oxydrakai" to be the Indian Kshudrakas.

Besides, if in any appreciable mass the Greeks, locally named "Yona", had been anywhere on the scene of Alexander's invasion, the local appellation by the resonance with the Greek "Iáones" would have instantly caught the Macedonian ear. On assuming their presence we have every right to expect in the records of the invasion something like "Iaonoi" and a good deal of enthusiastic assertion that the Iaonoi were settlers from distant Ionia. What happened about the Nysaioi should have been repeated on a grander scale and with greater justification. But we draw a blank on this matter from the records.

We may safely affirm that prior to Alexander there was no Greek colony in India's north-west, which old Indian literature could label as "Yona", and that what this literature does is on its own a pointer away from it. Let us give a glance at a few striking deliverances.

The Buddhist canonical work *Majjhima Nikāya* is referred to in the *Chullavagga* which does not mention the Third Buddhist Council held in Aśoka's reign, and which is therefore pre-Aśokan. The *Majjhima Nikāya*, on this showing, is pre-Mauryan.[36] It makes Buddha tell Assalayana (II.149): "*Suttante: Yonakambojeṣu aññesu cha pachchantimesu janapadesu...?*" Mookerji[37] translates: "Have you not heard this: that in the Yona, Kamboja and other border countries....?" The Yonas thus are already a state on India's borders fairly before Alexander's invasion. (In passing, mark the very term Aśoka

36. Pusalker in *The Age of Imperial Unity*, p. 408.
37. *Aśoka*, p. 161, fn. 8.

uses in his R.E. XIII and Benveniste picks out and misconstrues in his gloss on the Kandahār inscription: *Yonakambojeṣu.*) The *Chullaniddesa,* which is included in the Buddhist canon and is hence one of the earliest commentaries,[38] numbers Yona no less than Kamboja as having been a country of the Indian subcontinent before Buddha's birth.[39] Can we think of an organized Greek colony on a provincial scale in north-west India as early as such a period?

There is also the testimony of the grammarian Pāṇini. His mention of *yavanānī* (V.1.49) – equated to *yavanānī lipi,* meaning "Yavana script" – is regarded by most scholars as the very first pertinent use of the term "Yavana" in Sanskrit literature. Commonly, Pāṇini's expression is understood as "Greek writing". But everything hangs on the date we assign to him. According to V.S. Agrawala,[40] "the range of Pāṇini's date is in the opinion of scholars limited to a period of three centuries between the seventh and the fourth century B.C." As Pāṇini was a native of Śalātura, a town in Gandhāra, and as the Behistun inscription (*c.* 520-518) of the third Achemenid emperor Darius I lists both Gandhāra and Yauna as provinces of his empire, the term "Yauna" (="Ionia" or "an Ionian") broadly connoting "Greece" or "a Greek" is very likely to have reached the grammarian if he can be put subsequent to the time of the Behistun inscription. Agrawala,[41] at the end of a detailed discussion, places him around 450 B.C., thereby allowing the correspondence of his Sanskrit "Yavana" to the Persian "Yauna" through the possible intermediary Prākṛt "Yona".

Ram Gopal,[42] however, has raised a strong dissenting voice. He has countered every one of Agrawala's arguments – the chief of which are drawn from Indian religious history – and succeeded at least in neutralizing them and proving them

38. Pusalker in *The Age of Imperial Unity,* p. 408.
39. B.C. Law in *Ibid.,* p. 1.
40. *India as Known to Pāṇini* (Lucknow, 1953), p. 456.
41. *Ibid.,* pp. 456-75.
42. *India of Vedic Kalpasūtras* (Delhi, 1959), pp. 86-88.

indecisive. On the positive side he has attempted to estimate properly the interval between the grammarians Patañjali and Kātyāyana and that between Kātyāyana and Pāṇini. On several well-pleaded grounds he is inclined to fix Pāṇini to about 600-550 B.C.

But actually Agrawala himself puts before us a fact which sets Pāṇini clear of all Persian influence. It is about the very *janapada* (province) of the grammarian. Agrawala[43] writes: "Pāṇini mentions both the Vedic form Gāndhāri as the name of the *janapada* and its people in *sūtra* IV.1.169, and its later form Gandhāra in the *gaṇa*s to IV.1.133 and IV.3.93... Pāṇini knows Gāndharī as a kingdom (IV.1.169). It seems that soon after the death of Darius [I] Gandhāra became independent, as would apppear from the manner of its mention as an independent *janapada*."

Here is a piquant paradoxical situation. Gandhāra has to be under Darius I before Pāṇini in order that Pāṇini's "Yavanānī" should signify "Greek writing". Gandhāra has to be free soon after him in order that it should be the province Pāṇini knew. But everything cannot be so conveniently arranged. And we can demonstrate the inconvenience from Agrawala's own book.

Darius died in 486 B.C. What do we find soon after him in the reign of his successor Xerxes (486-465 B.C.)? We hear from Agrawala[44] that Gandhāra as a part of the Persian empire "continued under the reign of Xerxes, who recruited to his army a contingent of Indians from Gandhāra about the year 479 B.C." Again, after distinguishing Pāṇini's *Āyudhajīvi Saṅgha*s (warrior clans or groups) of "Parvata" from similar *Saṅgha*s of "Vāhīka" as those belonging to "the highlands of north-west", "outside the plains of the Vāhīka country", "which comprised the regions from the Indus to the Beas and the Sutlej", Agrawala[45] remarks that the geographical clues we possess from various writers "all together point to the

43. Agrawala, *op. cit.*, pp. 49, 446.
44. *Ibid.*, p. 466.
45. *Ibid.*, pp. 434, 435.

mountainous regions of central and north-east Afghanistan as being the Parvata country". And he[46] notes: "Arrian mentions these mountainous Indians as fighting in the army of Darius [III] against Alexander at Arbela (*Anabasis*, III.8.3-6). It was these Parvatīya Āyudhajīvins that offered stout resistance to Alexander in Bactria and Gandhāra." This implies that the fighters for Darius III from central and north-east Afghānistān included Gandhārians. So Gandhāra comes into the picture right at the close of the Achemenids (330 B.C.) just as it does during the time of Darius I. From Agrawala's own pronouncements there seems to be no evidence at all that Gandhāra was independent at any period of the Achemenid empire. Correctly does Mookerji[47] aver: "The Persian hold on India continued up to 330 B.C." From *c.* 520 B.C. of the Behistun inscription in the reign of Darius I to the last days of Darius III Gandhāra was in Persian hands.

In the interests of greater precision let us inquire about the state of affairs in the reign of the Achemenid Artaxerxes I (465-424 B.C.), which succeeded the reign of Xerxes and which would coincide with Agrawala's epoch for Pāṇini. Scholarship has disengaged an important fact in relation to the narrative by Herodotus who was in Persia during the reign of Artaxerxes I. Herodotus supplies us with a list of the tributes paid by the various provinces of the Achemenid empire. "It is generally believed," writes S. Chattopadhyaya,[48] "that the tribute list, as preserved in the account of Herodotus (III. 89-95), is clearly from his own time, that of Artaxerxes I..., not, as he states, from the time of Darius." In the list the "Gandharians" figure in the empire's seventh province. So Gandhāra around 450 B.C., which Pāṇini is said to know as an independent *janapada*, is found to be in Achemenid possession.

Summing up, we may say: "From every angle Pāṇini's independent Gandhāra has to precede the Behistun inscrip-

46. *Ibid.*, p. 435.
47. In *The Age of Imperial Unity*, p. 43.
48. "The Rule of the Achaemenids", *The Indian Historical Quarterly*, Vol. 25, p. 156.

tion of *c.* 520-518 B.C., and his 'Yavanānī' should be dissociated from Greece."

If chronological curiosity prompts us to ask how far beyond this inscription we need to go for that Gandhāra, the answer is to be drawn from a comparative scrutiny of the records of Darius I. No less than his inscription at Behistun, those set up by him at Persepolis (*c.* 518-515 B.C.), Naksh-i-Rustam (*c.* 515 B.C.) and in addition the Hamadan Gold and Silver Tablet mention Gandhāra, but only the last three mention *Hi(n)du* (*=Sindhu*) which, according to Mookerji's study of Herodotus[49], must have meant a portion of the Punjāb to the east of the Indus as distinct from provinces which take us farther north as far as the river-mouth. The late mention of *Hi(n)du* indicates, as Mookerji[50] opines, "that very probably it was Cyrus [the founder of the Achemenid empire] who conquered Gandhāra which was inherited by Darius as part of his empire while for himself he pushed his conquest farther into the region called *Sindhu*". Between Cyrus and Darius there intervened Cyrus's son Cambyses (530-522 B.C.), but he "was too much occupied by rebellions in his own empire to think of engaging in any movement towards India".[51] On the other hand Cyrus (558-530 B.C.) is credited by Greek and Roman historians with eastern conquests. The best conclusion from their reports is, in Mookerji's eyes,[52] Eduard Meyer's: "Cyrus appears to have subjugated the Indian tribes of the Paropanisus (Hindu Kush) and in the Kābul valley, especially the Gandharians." Hence Pāṇini's Gandhāra must go past some time between 558 and 530 B.C. to be independent.

The only conceivable loophole is the 8-year reign of Cambyses. Gandhāra might have become independent while he was occupied with rebellions elsewhere. But this is a sheer supposition, for which the detailed account of Herodotus of

49. *The Age of Imperial Unity*, pp. 41-42.
50. *Ibid.*, p. 41.
51. *Ibid.*, p. 40.
52. *Ibid.*

Achemenid events from Cyrus onward affords not an inch of ground. Nor, at the commencement of Darius's reign when some revolts took place, do we hear of any in Gandhāra. Even if we surmise one we shall have to acknowledge that it failed just as all the others did. For, in the Behistun inscription very soon after Darius rose to power, Gandhāra stands as part of a roster of twenty-three provinces in a widespread, organized and stable empire. No shred of evidence exists for the recent acquisition of any new province. Thus quite appreciably anterior to this inscription, which records a vast heritage from Cyrus, lies any possibility of Pāṇini's Gandhāra.

But can we even say that the period before Cyrus's conquest of Gandhāra will allow "Yavanānī" to signify what Agrawala and most scholars believe? Unfortunately, a dilemma blocks their path. There was no opportunity for Gandhāra to know the Greek script until Cyrus first came into contact with Greece on defeating Croesus of Lydia in 547 B.C. and conquering that country. If Gandhāra was conquered after this date, then as long as it had enjoyed its independence it had come into no relation with Cyrus and consequently acquired no knowledge of the Greek script from Lydia through him. If the conquest of Gandhāra was earlier than 547 B.C., there was also no chance for its Pāṇini to get at this script, all Persia dividing him from Greece by Persia's own lack of connection with Lydia. Therefore, either way an independent Gandhāra and the Greek script cannot go together during the reign of Cyrus. And, of course, prior to his reign the second horn of the dilemma would be just as sharp. By no means and at no time can we bring "Yavanānī" into rapport with the Greeks instead of with an Indian tribe.

A touch of scepticism may meet us here: "If the Greeks could be involved by Pāṇini's expression, we would have a distant people haunting our mind's eye. But if it refers to the script employed by an Indian tribe, how is it that Pāṇini who lists a substantial number of *janapada*s, including the usual companion of Yona – namely, Kamboja – fails to bring in the

Yona province, a *janapada* called Yavana contiguous to Kamboja?"

The sceptic proceeds on the misconception that Pāṇini set out to give geographical, political, social or cultural information. Pāṇini did nothing of the sort. He compiled just a masterly grammar: his aim was grammatical analysis and linguistic investigation. Whatever finds place in his treatise serves as an example of rules and verbal structures. All the information provided is a by-product. Nor is it likely to be exhaustive under any head. No matter how profuse, it is bound to be selective on the whole. In respect of any topic we should do well to remember Agrawala's observation[53] apropos of a certain species of information: "Names of rivers, forests and mountains are noticed not in connection with any social or historical significance, but as examples of linguistic peculiarity, such as vowel-lengthening (IV.3.117-120) or cerebralisation (VIII.4.4-5)."

At this point we may relevantly comment that comparable to Pāṇini's overlooking of a possible Yavana *janapada* is his overlooking of the Ganges among the rivers, although the *gaṇa* to VII.157 names a river we know as its tributary: Rathaspā, identical with the Rathasthā of the Vedic period and with the modern Rāmagaṇgā which is still in its upper course known as Rahut or Ruput and falls into the Ganges at Kanauj.[54] Again, the omission of a Yavana *janapada* or of Yavanas as a tribe has no momentous overtones any more than has the omission, except for "Yavanānī", of all the other scripts that, for instance, appear along with "Javaṇāṇiyā" (="Yavanānī") in the list of scripts in the *Samavāyānga sūtra* (*Samavāya* XVIII), to which Agrawala[55] alludes. The sceptical touch would be a case of insensitivity to the fundamentals of the Pāṇinian approach.

Moreover, even the Yavana tribe cannot be considered quite out of Pāṇini's sight or definitely divorced by him from

53. Agrawala, *op. cit.*, p. 36.
54. *Ibid.*, pp. 45, 46.
55. *Ibid.*, p. 312.

its usual companion. Back in 1881 Rajendralal Mitra[56] noted that Pāṇini offers "Yavanānī as an example to show the use of the affix *āṇuk* to indicate the writing of the Yavanas". Thus Pāṇini's usage appears not to confine itself to a mere adjectival label: it implies a collectivity called "Yavanas" and so most probably a *janapada* of them. Mitra[57] has also a mention of Kātyāyana, the commentator on Pāṇini, who is always taken to bring out the earlier grammarian's sense and not to import anything alien: "In Kātyāyana's *Vārttika* on Aphorism 175 of the first section of the fourth Book of Pāṇini, the Yavanas are linked with the Kambojas, showing their near relationship." In fact, for this relationship and its suggestion of a *janapada* of the Yavanas neighbouring that of the Kambojas we do not have to depend on implications or *Vārttika*s. Few scholars realise that Pāṇini's *Aṣṭādhyāyī*'s word is not his only reference to the Yavanas. There is a second one which has a perfectly traditional bearing and which, in addition to creating a background of *janapada* and Kamboja-relationship, makes a non-Greek connotation of "Yavanānī" obligatory with full force even apart from the issue of Pāṇini's date.

A.K. Narain[58] remarks: "Like other early Indian sources, Pāṇini associates the Yavanas with the Kambojas." For, as Narain says in continuation, the *Gaṇapātha* (178 on II.1.72) has the phrase: *yavanamuṇḍaḥ kambojamuṇḍaḥ* – "shaven-headed Yavanas, shaven-headed Kambojas." The greatest commentators, like Vāmanajayāditya of the *Kāśikā* and Bhattojidīkshita of the *Siddhānta-kaumudī*, have accepted the phrase as authentic. But what is striking about it is not merely the traditional association of two peoples: it is also the curious way in which the association is couched. Both Narain[59] and Barua[60] observe how the phrase links up with the Purāṇas' ancient Yavanas and Kambojas and other tribes punished by King Sagara: *e.g.*,

56. *Indo-Aryans* (Calcutta, 1881), p. 177.
57. *Ibid.*, p. 190.
58. *The Indo-Greeks* (Oxford, 1957), p. 1.
59. *Ibid.*
60. Barua, *op. cit.*, Part I, p. 99.

the *Harivaṁśa* (XIV.16) tells us: "*Muṇḍam kritva vyasarjayat yavanānāṁ śiraḥ sarvam kambojānāṁ tathai cha*" – "getting the heads of the Yavanas wholly shaved and also those of the Kambojas (he) expelled them."

It is incredible that the Greeks were thought of as having completely shaven heads and incredible too that – as Narain has suggested – Pāṇini's description of shaven-headedness, positively implying no hair at all, probably meant no more than the Greeks' custom of wearing their hair short! A straightforward look should convince us that Pāṇini, like the *Majjhima Nikāya*, is inalienable portion of an old testimony and that this testimony as bearing on the Yavanas' non-Greek origin seems firmly founded.

Confronted by such a situation we may well credit the suggestion made on the discovery of the Aramaic stone-inscription at Taxila but unsupported by any proof so far, that Pāṇini's "Yavanānī lipi" pointed to the Aramaic script.

And, if we attend to the verbal contents of the *Aṣṭādhyāyī*, we see that not a single word appears to have been borrowed from the Greek language whereas some contact with the Semitic tongues is undeniable, on Agrawala's own showing.[61] Among several words which are inexplicable by Sanskrit and can only be compared to Semitic forms, there is *hailihila* (VI.3.38) about some article, which corresponds to the Arabic *halāhila* meaning deadly poison (cf. Hebrew *halūl*, deadly poison). Agrawala conjectures that "the original Semitic form of the word... may have been Aramaic". He attributes its arrival to the prevalence of Aramaic in the Achemenid world, but himself offers a sign in Pāṇini of older Indo-Semitic exchanges with the word *goṇī* mentioned as denoting a container or sack (*āvapana*) made from *goṇa* (IV.1.42), obviously a cloth. "It is unknown in Vedic literature," comments Agrawala, "but occurs in the *Brahmajāla Sutta* XV as *goṇaka*, explained as a woollen cloth made from the hair of long-haired goats. It was probably the same as *kaunakes*, a one-piece

61. Agrawala, *op. cit.*, pp. 124, 146, 220-21.

loin-cloth worn by the early Sumerians and Accadians, and made of suspended loops of wool hanging from a woollen skirt (Marshall, *Indus Valley Civilization*, I.33, 342; pl. 95, fig. 10). The word seems to have travelled to India through commerce in pre-Pāṇinian times."

Here a certain possible confusion of counsel is to be avoided. Otherwise "Yavanānī" may tend to equate Aśoka's Yonas to Greeks. There is a tradition mentioned by Agrawala which associates Pāṇini with a Nanda king. In the current chronology the royal predecessors of Chandragupta Maurya, the grandfather of Aśoka, were a number of kings named Nanda. Agrawala[62] informs us: "Of the kings of Śiśunāga dynasty as given in the *Purāṇa*s Nandivardhana and Mahānanda occur as the last two kings after whom came the base-born Nandas." Then Agrawala mentions the first of the last-named: Mahāpadma – and goes on to say: "According to Tāranātha, Nanda the patron of Pāṇini was the father of Mahāpadma." Leaving aside the exact Nanda-relationship attributed to Pāṇini, we may ask whether the attribution of any relationship is at all justified. In other words, what is the tradition worth?

The two oldest commentators on Pāṇini are Kātyāyana and Patañjali – both of them belonging to the B.C. time. In what Agrawala[63] reports of their comment on Pāṇini we find no connection between the great grammarian and a Nanda king, even though Kātyāyana has a reference to the Nanda monarchy. Agrawala[64] tells us: "In the illustration *Nandopakramāṇi mānāni* (*Kāśikā* on II.4.21) we have an allusion that the weights and measures of the country were standardised for the first time by king Nanda." The tradition by which Agrawala sets store is a very late one, as we can gather from his own reports:[65] "Tārānātha, in his *History of Buddhism* compiled from older sources (1608 A.D.), states that Pāṇini

62. *Ibid.*, p. 464.
63. *Ibid.*, pp. 4-9.
64. *Ibid.*, p. 464.
65. *Ibid.*, p. 462.

lived in the time of a Nanda king. Somadeva (1063-1081) in the *Kathāsaritasāgara* and Kshemendra in the *Bṛhatkathāmañjarī* (11th century) also associate Pāṇini with king Nanda and his capital Pāṭaliputra. The newly discovered *Mañjuśrī-Mūlakalpa,* which Jayaswal placed roughly at about 800 A.D., confirms the tradition that 'king Nanda's great friend was a Brāhmaṇa Pāṇini by name' (Jayaswal's edition, p. 14), and also adds that in the capital of Magadha there were Brāhmaṇa controversialists who gathered at the king's court." Next Agrawala quotes Yuan Chwang (Hiuen Tsang), the Chinese pilgrim. In an earlier context, after writing[66] that the term Śalāturīya applied to Pāṇini preserves the tradition of his original home being at Śalātura, he[67] tells us: "Yuan Chwang visited Śalātura in the seventh century A.D. and found that the tradition about Pāṇini was current there." He writes: "...This is the place where the Ṛṣi Pāṇini... was born" (Beal, *Siyuki,* I, p. 114...). So Yuan Chwang is not only earlier than the rest of the authorities quoted by Agrawala and the next earliest to Kātyāyana and Patañjali but also a witness to the actual tradition prevailing in Pāṇini's own town. Let us see what Agrawala has to transmit:

"Yuan Chwang faithfully repeats the much older tradition contained in the *Mahābhāshya* [of Patañjali] with regard to the spread of Vedic learning in all its offshoots and branches, the origin of grammar, the growth of the Aindra system, the chaos produced by different grammatical schools, and finally the emergence at this crisis of Pāṇini with his new grammar, his eminent qualities and method."[68] "...Yuan Chwang from his record of the tradition as handed down in Pāṇini's birthplace, Śalātura, states that Pāṇini after finishing his work sent it to the supreme ruler, who exceedingly prized it and issued an edict that throughout the kingdom it should be used and taught (*Siyuki,* p. 115). Although the name of the king and that of the town of Pāṭaliputra are not mentioned, he confirms

66. *Ibid.,* p. 9.
67. *Ibid.,* p. 10.
68. *Ibid.,* p. 14.

the tradition of Pāṇini's connection with a royal court and of the patronage bestowed upon him in recognition of his work."[69]

Quite clearly, in the first place the account of Pāṇini's link with a king and his court, whether at Pāṭaliputra or elsewhere, is no part of the earliest testimony, namely, of Kātyāyana and Patañjali, and in the second place even this account as heard by Yuan Chwang in Pāṇini's native town nearly two centuries before the *Manjuśrī-Mūlakalpa* names neither a Nanda nor Pāṭaliputra. It may be of some interest, though not necessarily proving Pāṇini unaware, that the *Aṣṭādhyāyī*, while listing Magadha as a *janapada* (IV.1.170), has no reference to Pāṭaliputra. Speaking of this town, Agrawala[70] quotes only Kātyāyana's *Kāśikā* and not Pāṇini's *Aṣṭādhyāyī*. Since Gandhāra, which contains Śalātura, was a kingdom in Pāṇini's day, is there any need to look – if at all we must – for Yuan Chwang's "supreme ruler" anywhere outside this *janapada* whose eastern capital Takshaśilā and western capital Pushkalāvatī are both indicated by Pāṇini?[71] In any case King Nanda is out of the question and our chronology for Paṇini remains unaffected.

Everything considered, the original Yavanas with their province and their script antedate any possible Greek presence in India.

Of course, this does not mean that at no period in India were the Greeks called Yonas or Yavanas. In the *Mahāvaṁśa* (XXIX.30ff), the *Milindapañhe* and the Besnagar inscription of Heliodorus the Greek-Yona equation holds. But they refer to times later than Aśoka's, and the Greeks figuring in them are either the Bactrian Greeks or the Indo-Greeks who followed the ones from Bactria. Perhaps the Persia-inspired transference of the label from the original Mazdean Yonas was made easier by the possibility that Aśoka's non-Greek Yona tribe of the country round Kandahār had somehow got submerged by the time of those later Greeks.

69. *Ibid.*, pp. 462-63.
70. *Ibid.*, p. 73.
71. *Ibid.*, p. 49.

Such a transference is in itself not more unthinkable than the one that is admitted for post-Greek times in India. Sircar[72] records: "The word *Yavana* was used in medieval Indian literature as a synonym of *mlechchha* and indicated any foreigner... The Muslim rulers of India are often called Yavana...."

If finally in desperation it is asked how "Yona" and "Yavana" come to resemble "Ionia" without the former pair being derived from the latter term through the intermediary Persian "Yauna", the immediate reply can be a counter-query: "Is it not curious to find Darvas, Daradas (Pliny's Dardae), Kiratas (Cirrhadae of the Periplus) and Ramanas (Ptolemy's Rhamnai) listed among ancient Indian tribes and to encounter the Dorians, Dardanians, Cretans and Romans in Europe?" Probably there was an original common stock of terms from which these comparable versions went in different directions with racial movements. Perhaps we may even venture to suppose that the very tribe which became the Ionians in Greece became the Yonas-Yavanas in India after dividing itself on its way out from an ancestral homeland. All this, however, makes no odds to our thesis of ancient India's non-Greek Yonas-Yavanas.

The many-sided perspective our "second thoughts" have opened on the bilingual inscription is indeed alarming and provokes revolutionary questions about Aśoka and his alleged Greek subjects. How they are to be answered is not our present concern. But possibly the answers will emerge of themselves after we have increased the alarming note by elucidating the quite contrasting chronological aspects of the two languages employed – Greek and Aramaic – and inquired whether Aśoka could have really had an equal connection with both of them.

72. *The Age of Imperial Unity*, p. 101, with fn. 2.

PART II

1

Can the Two Texts be considered Contemporaneous?

According to the facts we have marshalled, the Greeks could not have been the Yonas who in Aśoka's edicts no less than in early Indian literature are coupled with the Kambojas. But, failing "Yona", we have in these edicts no other designation possible for the Greeks as Aśoka's subjects. What then are we to think of the Greek text accompanying the Aramaic which, *contra* Benveniste and the modern historical school, we have shown by detailed analysis of his thesis to have been intended for the non-Greek Yonas of Aśoka's empire? Could it be that only the Aramaic text is Aśokan and that the Greek is merely a translation and adaptation of the Aramaic, made by the post-Alexandrine Greek colony of Arachosia? But the region of Arachosia in which Kandahār is situated was within the empire of Aśoka. Have we then to regard the Kandahār of Aśoka's time as having had nothing to do with this colony so that the Aśokan Aramaic text would not be post-Alexandrine at all?

Here comparative linguistics is the field to be explored. We must scrutinize the two texts, examining various other features than their common omission of Brāhmaṇas and Śramaṇas to which we have already attended. Now we must attend closely not only to the characteristics of the thought in the texts but also to those of the language in them, as brought forward by Robert, Dupont-Sommer and Benveniste in the *Journal Asiatique*.

What emerges very prominently from a perusal of Benveniste's study of the Irānian words in the Aramaic version is the impression that, while the Greek has all the signs of a living dialect of the third century B.C., especially the period 275-225 B.C., the Aramaic is much of a riddle. Benveniste[73] notes:

"Even leaving aside the rather unclear *ptytw*, we gain five

73. *Journal Asiatique*, CCXLVI, 1958, I, pp. 44-45.

Irānian words of good standard quality: *patizbata, frabasta, hupatyasti, mazišta,* a high proportion for a relatively short text. The gain is as appreciable as it was unexpected. At the date of the inscription, in the middle of the third century B.C., these words indicate, by their form, an Irānian language of ancient type, like Avestan or Old Persian, and not the Middle Irānian stage: the notation of *pati* with the mute and the final vowel, the notation of the final vowel *-i* in *prbsty,* are the principal proofs of this. To define the dialectal position of the language, we have a significant pointer in the form *mazišta-* which was restricted till now to Avestan.

"From the lexical point of view we attach great importance to the word *hwptysty* (=*hupatyasti*) 'good obedience' which establishes an essential bond between our inscription and that of Taxila. This concordance, in addition to the name *prydrš,* puts it beyond doubt that the inscription of Taxila was also an edict of Aśoka, reduced to a fragment of a few words. As we have noted above, *hupatyasti* is new as composed with *hu-,* but the term *patiyasti* belongs to the language of the Avesta and to the Mazdean vocabulary. It has not survived, to our knowledge, in Middle Irānian....

"This lexical fact agrees then with the dialectal trait which issues from the form *mazišta.* Shall we conclude here that, in the milieu of the third century B.C., the Irānian population settled between Kandahār and Taxila spoke the same language as the Avesta? We need not yet go so far. All that seems allowable to affirm, on the indirect testimony of this inscription, is that the *religious* language coincided with that of the Avesta, and that Mazdeism prevailed in this region. If one reflects that even yesterday we knew nothing of the linguistic and religious conditions proper to this zone of the Irānian world for the period in question, this conclusion, though limited, is not without import."

We can see that Benveniste is trying to be cautious and drawing only a limited conclusion when the signs are wide enough. Earlier he[74] says about *hupatyasti*: "That it should

74. *Ibid.*, p. 42.

appear now at this date..." Evidently there is no reason why the "*religious* language" in the inscription should be that of the Avesta rather than some other less ancient form which we might expect in the milieu of the third century B.C. The common people would be reached much more readily through the latter language. The most likely conclusion from such an abundance of Avestan terms in so short an inscription is that the people living between Kandahār and Taxila in the time of Aśoka did speak more or less the same language as Avestan. If there was a difference from it, the difference is hardly explicable by the kind of Irānian we know of in the Achemenid period, much less in the post-Alexandrine. Benveniste himself speaks of "the rather unclear *ptytw*" which is definitely Irānian but cannot be elucidated in the light of post-Alexandrine or even Achemenid Irānian. And the difficulty seems even greater with the possible alternative reading: *ptytz*. Benveniste[75] confesses: "*ptytz* (or *ptytw*) sets us at the very start face to face with a difficulty which will be in fact the most serious of those we shall encounter in our study." There is also his statement:[76] "The word *'dwšy* (or *'rwšy*), supplied with an Aramaic plural, is not Aramaic. But one hardly ever sees an Irānian word like *'dwš* or *'rwš* that answers to the sense which the context would suggest: 'disagreement, misfortune' or 'bad action, impiety' or a similar notion.... One does not find in Irānian the matter for a useful hypothesis."

Ancient terms or forms appear to be drawn upon and, even when some of them cannot be paralleled in the Avesta for the meanings that seem necessary, it is instructive to realize that these terms or forms which cannot also be paralleled in post-Alexandrine or even Achemenid Irānian have nothing to do with religion. They are not strictly part of a "*religious* language". The word *ptytz* (or *ptytw*) follows the phrase which in Aramaic signifies "ten years" and the word

75. *Ibid.*, p. 36.
76. *Ibid.*, p. 38.

in the same place in the Greek text is "elapsed" or "passed".[77] The word *'dwšy* (or *'rwšy*) should mean, as Benveniste says, "disagreement, misfortune" or else something like "bad action, impiety". So it is not only the religious language of the inscription, that carries the atmosphere of an ancient semi-Avestan tongue. What induces Benveniste to limit his conclusion is just his *idée fixe* that by any means we have to be in the middle of the third century B.C. If we go uninhibitedly by the evidence of the Irānian or non-Aramaic words we should be almost obliged to date the inscription to a period when a semi-Avestan language could be thought of as current. At least – on the basis of Benveniste's linguistic observations – there would be no bar to carrying the non-Greek part of this inscription – and by analogy the whole inscription of Taxila – to a greater antiquity than the Greek part.

The prevalence of a semi-Avestan language for all uses and not only for religious ones in the areas adjoining north-western India in Aśoka's day would best explain some general peculiarities in the dialect of the Shāhbāzgaṛhī and Mānsehrā redactions of his edicts and even in that of the Girnār redaction. Here we are much nearer to Sanskrit than in the other versions, but Mookerji[78] remarks: "As Michelson has pointed out, this dialect cannot be regarded as a mere lineal descendant of Sanskrit. It presents certain forms which establish its affinity to *Avestan* rather than Sanskrit: e.g. *atikrātam* (G); *susrusā, susrusatām* (G) corresponding to Avestan *susrusemno*; G. *sruṇāru*, Shb. *sruṇeyu* and M. *sruṇeyu*, which agree with Avestan *surunaoiti* in structure as opposed to Sanskrit *śṛiṇoti*." What, of course, concerns us is not Avestan rather than Sanskrit forms but Avestan rather than later Irānian. And their presence indicates not only the former's general prevalence we have spoken of: it indicates also the antiquity of the Aśokan dialects involved.

And when we look at the non-Irānian element in the

77. *Ibid.*, pp. 22-23, 36-37.
78. *Aśoka* (Delhi, 1956), p. 248.

Aramaic text – the strictly Aramaic element there – we find in Dupont-Sommer's study several signs of archaism in it. We find him writing things like: "to note the archaic form", "as an archaic *ittafal* of this root", "it may be explained as corresponding to a form archaic (or dialectal)", "this form is altogether unprecedented.... Is it the survival of an archaic form...?"[79] The strictly Aramaic element is itself such as suggests greater antiquity than the time we can assign to the Greek part. Hence one is tempted to suppose that originally – much before the middle of the third century B.C. – the Aramaic version alone of the bilingual inscription was there and that the Greek was put centuries later in the empty space above it. The Aramaic might very easily have been so positioned as to leave empty spaces both above and below.

So much for the linguistic data proper. When we look at the language in relation to the thought we are again led to cut apart the two versions. In section 3 of our Part I we have already quoted Dupont-Sommer: "The Aramaic recension, a little longer, is manifestly closer to the Indian text...." We have also illustrated by one example out of several given by him the shorter and more generalized character of the Greek text. This text has also a distinct Hellenic touch more marked than the Irānian touch of the Aramaic text which, says Dupont-Sommer,[80] the Aramaic scribe has adapted from the original Indian "to a lesser degree than the Greek scribe". The greater length, the more detailed character, the closer approximation of the Aramaic to the original Indian create a *prima facie* case for regarding it as a more fundamental version than the Greek instead of as one tagged on to the latter, as superficially it might appear from the engraving of the Greek above it. The Aramaic seems to be the version to which importance was attached by Aśoka and over which his scribe took conscientious care. It is as if it were the sole version set up by Aśoka. The brevity, the generalized nature, the greater

79. *Journal Asiatique*, p. 25.
80. *Ibid.*, p. 34.

departure from the assumed original Indian, which we observe in the Greek, support the presumption that Aśoka had nothing to do with it and that he had no Greek subjects to whom it could be addressed.

Even in the single instance where the Greek text is longer, Dupont-Sommer cannot bring himself to trace a greater fidelity to the original Indian. Apropos of the Aramaic version – "even those who catch fish" – he[81] comments: "This expression designates evidently the fishermen, who are precisely mentioned in the Greek inscription; the latter equally mentions the hunters and it states precisely that the question is of 'hunters and fishermen of *the King*': these precisions do not figure in the Aramaic text. Perhaps they were absent from the Indian model which, by taking up only the case of the fishermen, may have left it understood that the same thing held, *a fortiori*, for the hunters; according to this hypothesis, the Greek scribe, by mentioning hunters and fishermen, may have wished no doubt to make explicit the passage he was translating."

Dupont-Sommer is so impressed – and rightly – by the fidelity the Aramaic text appears to show to the original Indian that where the former is shorter than the Greek he postulates a similar shortness in the model. But he is loth to give up the idea that the Greek scribe is dealing at first-hand with the original Indian. Here he is at one with all the scholars who have written about the inscriptions: they suppose, on noticing the adaptations of Indian concepts made by both the Greek and the Aramaic texts, that the authors of them do not depend on each other and work from a common model according to the spirit of their own culture. But is it not possible that the adaptation by the Greek scribe is from the Aramaic adaptation? If we can think of him as Hellenizing Indian concepts and turns, we can equally think of him as Hellenizing Irānian or Indo-Irānian ones. Dupont-Sommer[82]

81. *Ibid.*, p. 28.
82. *Ibid.*, p. 24.

writes: "'Piety'... under the pen of the Greek scribe is a transposition of the Indian idea of *dhamma,* just as 'Truth' ...under the pen of the Aramaic scribe." But to adapt *dhamma* to "Piety" is on a par with adapting "Truth" to "Piety" – especially as Dupont-Sommer[83] himself informs us about the word for "Truth" in the Aramaic text: "We translate therefore 'Truth', but this word means practically 'religion, faith, piety'."

Benveniste[84] draws our attention to the sequence "mother-father" and "father-mother" in the Aramaic and Greek texts respectively. About the former he says that it proves for the Aramaic version a direct translation from an Indian model, for repeatedly and always Aśoka writes "mother-father", continuing the old Vedic *dvandva mātára-pitára.* Then Benveniste argues that since the Greek text is in disaccord with the Aramaic and gives the traditional Greek order of the two words, we have a proof that the two versions are independent of each other and both go to a common Indian model. But is there not a slip in Benveniste's logic? If the Aramaic order of the two words establishes a direct derivation from an Indian model, how can the reverse order do the same? Conversely, if the reverse order implies a direct derivation from an Indian model, its difference from the Aramaic text which in this case is exactly like the Indian should also imply a direct derivation from the Aramaic model. Logically, the true inference from the circumstances is that, since the Greek sequence differs equally from the mutually agreeing Indian and Aramaic, it could derive from either.

Even in the instance of the hunters and fishermen, why cannot we take the Greek scribe as making explicit what is in the Aramaic version? When Dupont-Sommer feels bound to equate the latter to the Indian text, we can relate the Greek to the Aramaic just as validly as to the Indian. And actually the Aramaic, by taking up only the case of the fishermen, does

83. *Ibid.,* p. 23.
84. *Ibid.,* p. 42.

appear to leave it understood that the same thing held, *a fortiori*, for all others who kill living creatures. For the words run: "even those who catch fish, these men are subject to prohibition." This seems to imply that there is a prohibition not only against others who take animal lives but even against such men as kill creatures like fishes. There is implicit here everything that Dupont-Sommer imagines the Greek scribe to be making explicit from the Indian model.

Thus, in the matter both of concepts and of linguistic turns, no sign exists anywhere that the Greek scribe, like the Aramaic, worked straight from a non-Greek non-Aramaic model framed by Aśoka.

Only one proper noun – the name of the king – can provoke a doubt to the contrary. Benveniste[85] comments: "The difference between *Piodasses* of the Greek and *prydrš* of the Aramaic shows already that the two texts do not depend on each other. This difference attests two distinct dialectal traditions. The Greek form *Piodasses* is imitated from the Middle Indian *Piyadassi*, with a phonetic peculiarity, the internal *-o-*... On the contrary the Aramaic *prydrš* agrees with those edicts (notably of Shāhbāzgaṛhī) which have the quasi-Sanskrit form *priyadraśi* (Skr. *-darśi*)." Certainly, two distinct dialects are observable in the two forms, but what is implied in the situation cannot be gauged unless we try to reconstruct how the assumed original model could have led to them.

Dupont-Sommer[86] says: "...every Greek colony, from archaic times down to the Byzantine period, had around it the group of those 'Hellenised' by the culture, and it is from them most often that the translators and the interpreters were recruited." Well, then, there would be for the translation and interpretation a "Hellenised" person knowing Greek as well as the Indian language in which the original model came. Similarly, for the Aramaic version, there would be an Irānianized person knowing Aramaic and the Indian language. The

85. *Ibid.*, pp. 37, 38.
86. *Ibid.*, p. 12.

latter go-between was evidently of the region (most probably Shāhbāzgaṛhī) where the quasi-Sanskrit *priyadraśi* was in vogue. The former go-between must be imagined as a man of the region where the Middle Indian *piyadassi* was current.

It is true in general that the Greek transcription of Indian proper names bears touches of a Middle Indian medium – yet not unmixedly in most part. These touches are exhibited by at least two out of the three examples quoted by Benveniste[87] to illustrate one of the ways in which the internal *o* could have entered: *Taprobanè* for *Tāmraparṇī, Sandarophagos* for *Chandra-bhāga, Errannoboas* for *Hiraṇyavāha*. But it is notable that the *r* in the first part of each Sanskrit name, whether intervocal or conjunct, is preserved. On the analogy of *Taprobanè* and *Sandarophagos* and, we may add, *Sandrokottos* (for Chandragupta) we should expect Priodasses or else Piriodasses. Something Sanskritic mixes with something Middle Indian. The initial *Pr* itself of a Sanskritic name is seen preserved in the well-known Prasioi for *Prāchya*, the "Easterners", the people whose capital was *Pāṭaliputra* (Greek Palibothros). Strabo (VI.22), based on Megasthenes, mentions a class of Indian philosophers, the Pramnai, who are obviously the *Prāmānika*s. Piodasses is somewhat of an anomaly.

It is also difficult to understand why a go-between from a place like Mānsehrā or Shāhbāzgaṛhī, near the Greek settlement, an intermediary who would be more likely than a man from an inner province to know Greek, would not be found to help the Greeks. To explain Piodasses as nothing more than the result of a Middle Indian dialectal tradition is too simple, too abstract.

Again, we have to ask whether the Indian model read *Piyadassi* or *Priyadraśi*. Barua[88] has given what looks like the most accurate picture of the way the edicts were prepared for Indian localities : "R.E. III goes to show that the *Yukta*s of the Imperial Secretariat codified the king's orders or messages

87. *Ibid.*, p. 38.
88. *Aśoka and His Inscriptions*, II, p. 28.

under the instructions from the *Parishad* or *Purusha*s acquainted, according to P.E. IV, with the king's desires (*ehaṁdaṁnāni*). And it is clear from R.E. VI that these orders and messages were issued verbally at first by the king. The drafts prepared on the basis of the king's verbal orders and dictations by the different personal agents were bound to vary. We are, moreover, to presume that among the *Yukta*s some were considered competent to prepare the draft for Shāhbhāzgaṛhī, some for Mānsehrā, some for Dhauli, some for Kālsī, some for Yeragudi..." If suitable linguistic drafts of the original which was in the official language (Middle Indian) of Pāṭaliputra were prepared and if the draft for the inhabitants of Arachosia was also first done in an Indian language, it must have been in a linguistic form resembling what used to be prepared for Shāhbāzgaṛhī and Mānsehrā which neighboured this region. Benveniste himself has seen the accordance of the Aramaic *prydrš* with *priyadraśi* of Shāhbāzgaṛhī. Now the question arises : Could Aśoka have sent to Arachosia two linguistically different drafts – one in quasi-Sanskrit and one in Middle Indian – for local translation into Aramaic and Greek? All the adaptations made by the Greeks and by the indigenous Arachosians have been attributed by the scholars to these people themselves: it is reasonable to believe that *prydrš* and *Piodasses* are also due to these people working on the same draft, though possibly in two copies. It seems fantastic to hold that a draft in Middle Indian was especially despatched to the Greeks living in a region close to the provinces where quasi-Sanskrit was the dialect.

Or if we hold that the whole Greek version and the whole Aramaic to have been got ready in Pāṭaliputra itself by competent *Yukta*s, then also there is no reason to hold that the Greek was made from a Middle Indian draft and the Aramaic from a quasi-Sanskrit. Why should an Aramaic-knowing *Yukta* in Pāṭaliputra not work from a Middle-Indian draft, just as the Greek-knowing *Yukta* might be thought to have done? If the indigenous Arachosians could be said to have more acquaintance with the Shāhbāzgaṛhī forms of Indian names and terms, the same must be said of the Greeks of Arachosia. *Priyadraśi* would certainly be more natural to them than *Piyadassi* since they would always be hearing Indian names and terms following the quasi-Sanskrit dialectal tradition popular in the neighbourhood of Shāhbāzgaṛhī and Mānsehrā. The Greek-knowing *Yukta* of Pāṭaliputra might introduce a variation in keeping with the usual run of Greek forms answering to Indian ones: that is, he might mingle Middle Indian with Sanskrit or quasi-Sanskrit as in Taprobanè and Sandrokottos. In that case, he would not exactly write *Priodrasi* or even *Priodrasses* but he would at least write *Priodasses* and not *Piodasses*.

The same would hold if we posited an educated Greek under Aśoka as the writer of the Greek version. To make him capable of *Piodasses* we should have to imagine not only that he was settled in Pāṭaliputra and had learnt the court-language but also that he would be quite unaware of the Prākṛt prevalent in Arachosia side by side with Aramaic and heard by the Greeks there. The possibility that he would know merely the Magadhan Prākṛt and be entirely ignorant of the Arachosian would be still less if we realized, as we must, that he would himself be not a fresh foreigner but the member of a Greek family settled in Arachosia since the time of Alexander's invasion – in other words, for two generations. Even though he might not be master of Arachosian Prākṛt he would be sure to remember what sort of Indian dialect his fellow-Greeks around Kandahār would hear. Writing for the Greeks in Arachosia and not in Magadha, would he choose for Aśoka a form unfamiliar to them instead of one with which they were daily acquainted? What would be his point in confronting them with a form so different from *Priyadraśi* which would be all the while in the air of their province?

There is a small yet not insignificant further matter to be reckoned with. *Piyadassi* is indeed the Indian equivalent of *Piodasses*, but in no inscription of Aśoka's do we find *Piyadassi*. At Kālsī and several dialectically related localities, as well as occasionally at Girnār, we have *Piyadasi*: we never have the form with a double *s*. Of course, the single *s* is an orthographic convention adopted in order to save the trouble of engraving a conjunct which would abound in Prākṛt: the actually spoken Middle Indian for the Sanskrit *Priyadarśi* must have been either *Piyadassi* or else *Piyadāsi*. However, in all copies in Middle Indian of an edict distributed for engraving, the written form would be *Piyadasi* without exception. Such a copy handed for the Greek text to a translator – be he a Hellenized Arachosian in Arachosia itself or a Greek-knowing *Yukta* at Pāṭaliputra or a Prākṛt-knowing Greek there – could never have read *Piyadassi*. And there is no reason why the translator should ignore the universal practice of *Piyadasi* for epigraphs, and, in spite of the same form confronting him in his own copy, Grecize the name as *Piodasses* rather than Piodases. Benveniste[89] has been very scrupulous about the phonetic value of *prydrš*: "The Aramaic script naturally does not let us decide between *priyadraśi* and *priyadarśi*, but as *priyadraśi* is alone attested (to the exclusion of *–darśi*) in the Indian epigraphy of Aśoka, it is for this form that we opt." It is surprising how Benveniste, though never doubting the Greek version to be Aśokan, forgot that *Piyadasi* is the sole attested form in the epigraphs concerned and that it is the form relevant to the discussion of *Piodasses* and that this form would not be apt at all to explain *Piodasses* as an epigraphic fact. Epigraphically, *Piodasses* should be considered non-Aśokan.

When we look closely into all the features of the situation in which *prydrš* and *Piodasses* could come about, the latter hardly connects us to an original Indian model. To accept it at its face-value and speak of a distinct dialectal tradition is to make things over-easy. We cannot explain it by remaining within the direct context of Aśoka and thinking of a Greek translation on his own orders. *Piodasses* has to be independent of Aśokan epigraphy.

How then is it to be explained? Suppose the Aramaic text

89. *Journal Asiatique*, p. 38.

is already there from the past, and the post-Alexandrine Greeks in Arachosia discover it. An interpreter knowing both Aramaic and Greek translates it for them. The Greeks, *vis-à-vis* the alien and unheard-of name *Priyadraśi* as given by the interpreter, will inquire into the identity of the king bearing it. An inhabitant of Arachosia at a period sufficiently removed from Aśoka's will scarcely be able to throw light on the subject. Several Indians will be called in. The interrogation will go on until the arrival of one who hails from Magadha. He will be the most likely to know about the king who called himself "*Lājā Māgadhe*" in the Bābru Edict. Speaking Middle Indian, this man will, in the course of his informative talk, keep repeating to the Greeks a form – *Piyadassi* – which they may represent by *Piodasses*. Naturally they will defer to his greater acquaintance with Indian things and select his version rather than the other. No doubt, the form *Piyadassi* would not be possible in Arachosia as a basis for the Greek version if simultaneously and at the same spot the Aramaic had *Priyadraśi* as its basis and if both were executed in the province during the life-time of Aśoka when he would be well known as Priyadraśi and when the Middle Indian form with a double *s* would never be submitted for any inscription. But *Piyadassi*, at a time different from Aśoka's and from his Aramaic text's, would be easily acceptable and could lead to *Piodasses*.

Thus the bilingual inscription, examined from the standpoint of both linguistic form and message-content, props up definitely the idea provoked by the non-Greek character of Aśoka's Yonas – that the two texts are not contemporaneous. They call out to be placed in epochs distant from each other – the Greek as a late addition in 275-225 B.C. to the Aramaic which was an Aśokan edict set up much earlier, when the kind of language, secular no less than religious, which we find in it was in use instead of the Aramaic current in 275-225 B.C.

2

Aśokan Inscriptions and Later Additions

To suppose an addition made at a later date to an inscription in the far past is not to imagine a state of affairs unique in history. The Allāhābād Pillar Inscription of Samudragupta is right under an old one – and the latter is actually an Aśokan epigraph. The inscriptions of Rudradāman I and Skandagupta are both on the same Junāgarh rock – and they share this rock again with an edict of Aśoka. When two inscriptions of Aśoka himself have neighboured additional matter from other ages, we should not be surprised if a third – of whatever kind – is supposed to have done the same.

The sole novelty in the present instance would be the positioning of a later inscription – an adapted translation or paraphrase of an earlier one – above rather than below the original. But, provided that space was available both above and below, it would be a question of convenience or of end in view or of artistic consideration, whether the one were selected or the other. Granted the space, there is no reason why a later inscription of any sort should follow rather than precede the earlier. Perhaps the Greek's proverbial pride in his own language, together with his equally proverbial eye for artistic effect, would choose the upper space even though the lower might be just as convenient.

A close look at the lines of the Greek text[90] seems to show that the first four lines are less interspaced than the rest, as though the engraver put them one after the other somewhat near lest sufficient space should not remain for the ten more to follow and, then, finding space enough, put those lines a little more apart. If the Aramaic was not already engraved, there would be no need to crowd the lines even slightly, for there is space on the rock for an Aramaic text twice the present length.[91] The tentative crowding would be required

90. *Ibid.*, Plate IV, facing p. 8.
91. *Ibid.*, Plate III, facing p. 6.

only if a fixed height of space were available because the Aramaic stood already there in the middle of the rock. The middle position may itself suggest the original solitary engravement of the Aramaic.

A flood of clarifying light is cast on the situation if we look at another Aramaic message of Aśoka's – the one discovered in 1966 in the valley of Laghman in North Afghānistān.[92] The text, except for two mysterious words (*knpty* and *shyty*), is all in Aramaic but again in a kind of language in keeping with that in our bilingual. Dupont-Sommer[93] informs us: "As the other Aramaic inscriptions of Aśoka show, this Aramaic language is generally of a rather awkward style, and, at times, of an incorrect grammar." In the post-Achemenid post-Alexandrine age and in the proximity of Irān, we should have a very different quality of expression and syntax – hardly the archaic gaucherie and linguistic primitiveness which take us back to the beginnings of a tongue's use and do not at all suggest an Aśoka of 269-232 B.C. But what we are immediately concerned with is how the Laghman text stands on the rock-face.

The text has below it an inscription in quite different characters, a specimen of the famous "petroglyphics" of Laghman.[94] Above, there is a blank space where a Greek translation or paraphrase can easily be introduced. An Aśokan inscription does not always start right at the top of a rock-face and its being in the middle does not imply that it is there because it follows a Greek or any other version of it. Its position allows several possibilities.

If the Greeks were in Aśoka's time as his subjects, why is there in Laghman, which is part of the locality where the Greeks are known to have settled in the wake of Alexander's invasion, no Greek version set up by Aśoka of the Aramaic text although room is available both above and below? The

92. *Académie des Inscriptions et Belles-Lettres*: Comptes Rendus des Séances de l'année 1970, Janvier-Mars, Paris, pp. 163-69.

93. *Ibid.*, p. 163.

94. *Ibid.*, p. 159, Pl. II.

"petroglyphics" must have come much later than the original Aramaic text. Aśoka could have added a Greek version in their place or in the space at the head of the rock-face. The absence of it argues against the Greeks having been present in Laghman in Aśoka's time and against this time having been post-Alexandrine in which the Greeks were actually in Laghman.

The case of this inscription is different from that of the epigraphs of Taxila and Pūl-i-Dārunteh. The latter two are on stones leaving hardly any room for a Greek version below or above the Aramaic. The opportunity provided by the Laghman epigraph and the wasting of it are significant for our contention that just because the Greek in the Kandahār bilingual is above the Aramaic it need not be deemed contemporaneous with it, it may have been put there later. The Aramaic in the Kandahār bilingual, just like the Aramaic at Laghman, has sufficient space above and below for other texts to be accommodated.

Perhaps we shall be asked: "Why should the Greeks of a later age have been interested to put up a version in their own language?" The answer is not far to seek. We know that during the seventy-five years or so after Alexander's invasion they were extremely interested in India and matters Indian. The preserved fragments of the *Indica* of Megasthenes – starting around 302 B.C. in the reign of Sandrokottos – amply attested to the interest: it is an anthology of social, political, economic, military, religious information, and legend after strange legend is collected in it to whet the curiosity of the Western reader. Pliny, Strabo, Arrian have drawn copiously upon the *Indica*. The companions of Alexander have themselves left records from which later writers like Curtius and Arrian have derived abundant material. The absorption of the West in "Indology" continued for centuries. We may hark back to the testimonies of Athenaeus and Epiphanius, cited on page 220. The former reports that Ptolemy II Philadelphus reigning in 285-247 B.C. organized processions in which Indian women, Indian hunting dogs, Indian cows and also

Indian spices on camels were to be seen. We are told by Epiphanius that the Head of Philadelphus's Library at Alexandria was anxious to translate the books of the Hindus. To get a translation done of an old Indian semi-religious inscription discovered in Arachosia and to have it engraved on the same rock as the original – this is precisely what we may expect of the Greek Arachosian colony. Robert[95] tells us that a Greek emigration, in the Hellenistic epoch, always included intellectuals, school-masters, rhetoricians, poets, actors, philosophers, doctors, professors of every sort and every qualification, athletes, artists, marble-cutters, stone-engravers. He[96] adds: "One may be sure that there was in Arachosia, as at Babylon, a gymnasium, with its young men, meeting-place for festivals and conferences and conversations." The cultural character natural to a Greek colony is enough to account – more than ever in a period when Hellenic eyes were keenly turned on India – for the engraving of a Greek recension of an Aramaic inscription in the Kandahār-region.

The one possible objection, in the present context of our discussion, to our separating rather widely in time the two versions is Benveniste's "historical perspective" for the Aramaic version. He[97] writes: "To put this Aramaic text in the historical perspective which accords with it, we should compare it to the documents of Achemenid date found in Egypt. Two centuries after the Great Kings, at the other extremity of the Irānian world, we rediscover the same type of wording, the same titling, the same language equally stuffed with Irānian words. The surprise is just there: that an inscription set up in a region bordering on India and subject to the power of an Indian sovereign should be in the Aramaic language and find its analogues only in the writings of the ancient Persian satrapies. The use of Aramaic shows that we are in reality in an Irānian province, where were maintained the

95. *Journal Asiatique*, p. 13.
96. *Ibid.*
97. *Ibid.*, pp. 43-44.

traditions of the Achemenid chancelleries. One could conjecture it since the discovery of the Taxila inscription. It is now a certitude."

If our own thesis is correct, the Aramaic version still keeps a relationship with the writings of the Old Persian satrapies, but the relationship gets altogether reversed. It is not the documents of the Achemenid times discovered in Egypt that provide the precedents of this version: this version itself manifests a style and texture that are echoed in those documents. The use of Aramaic may show that we are in a province, if not Irānian, at least Irānianized, but not that the traditions of the Achemenid chancelleries are maintained here. Those traditions may have formed themselves on an antecedent practice such as we find in our inscription. We know that Xerxes (486-465 B.C.), Darius I (522-486 B.C.) and even the earlier Cyrus (558-530 B.C.) were masters of Arachosia and other regions west of the Indus, and this mastery continued up to 330 B.C. when Alexander defeated Darius III. We know too that the traditions of the Achemenid chancelleries in the form that Benveniste has in mind do not go beyond Xerxes.[98] They could easily have started after the Persian conquerors had seen ancient Aśokan inscriptions in the territories ruled by them. Or else, if they did not see those inscriptions, they may have got acquainted with the official practice in those territories, inherited from earlier Aśokan times.

In any case, it is not true that only in "the documents of Achemenid date found in Egypt" do we have "the same type of wording, the same titling" as in the Kandahār inscription. Benveniste's "Egypt" is correct, but his "Achemenid date" is not at all binding for the official verbal turns by which he sets store. The most typical expressions of this type in our text are: "our lord Priyadraśi the King" and "our lord the King". The basic formula here is actually found in Egypt 900 years before

98. *Encyclopaedia Britannica* (13th Edition), Vol. XIX, p. 619; also A.T. Olmstead, *History of the Persian Empire* (Chicago, 1948), pp. 244-45.

the Achemenid Xerxes. Leonard Cottrell[99] mentions the urgent appeals which in *c.* 1400 B.C. poured forth for troops into Akhneten's Foreign Office from the Governors of some threatened provinces. The Governor of the coastal city Tunip wrote: "...And when Aziru enters Simyra [another coastal city] he will do as he pleases in the territory of our Lord the King.... For twenty years we have been sending to our Lord the King, the King of Egypt, but there has come not a word, not one." This type of wording and titling continued in later yet still pre-Achemenid epochs, and even outside Egypt. Thus Georges Roux[100] quotes from one Zakir's correspondence with Ashurbanipal (668-631 B.C.): "The disturbance is the fault of the King of Amurru and his land for allowing the money of the king, my lord, to be in the land of Amurru. Let the king, my lord, do as he wishes. The hand of the king, my lord, shall capture him...."

The formula in question was a standard one all over the ancient Orient and the Persian satrapies merely copied it. These satrapies themselves are not required in the least to account for it in Aśoka's Aramaic text. But entirely to cut it apart from the Achemenid Chancelleries, we must bring the pre-Achemenid Orient into relationship with India and demonstrate an early contact of the Aramaic language with this country as well as this country's contact with early Irān's Avestan thought.

3

India, Avesta, Aramaic

There are passages in the Avesta seeming to indicate a political hold by early Irān on Northern India before the Achemenids. As R.K. Mookerji[101] reports, although corroboration or details of this connection have hitherto been lacking,

99. *The Anvil of Civilization* (Mentor, New York, 1956), p. 144.
100. *Ancient Iraq* (Harmondsworth, 1966), p. 312.
101. *The Age of Imperial Unity*, p. 39.

some scholars have taken these passages as genuine evidence. Particularly apt is the *Videvdāt*'s reference to Hapta-Hindu (Sapta-Sindhu) – land of the seven-rivered Indus-system – as one of the countries Ahura Mazda created for his own people. Juxtaposed, the Avestan passages and the Avestan character of the Irānian component in our text may be seen to throw light on each other.

Persia's own contact in pre-Achemenid times with the Semitic world from which the Aramaic language emerged can serve as a background for India's early touch with the latter. Quite famous is the tablet of Ashurbanipal mentioning the Zarathustrian pantheon under the form of Assara Mazas (Ahura Mazda) along with seven good angels and seven bad spirits – the tablet which provides one of the clearest arguments for dating Zarathustra much before Darius I in whose reign a number of scholars are inclined to place him. Sargon II (722-705 B.C.) records in a clay prism the names of two conquered princes: Mazdaku and Mastaku – names derived from Mazda. R. Ghirshman[102] cites the annals of Shalmaneser III to show that the Assyrians knew of the Medes (Madai) in 836 B.C. and of the Persians (Parsua) in 844 B.C.

Information on India's own touch with the Semitic world hails from several quarters. R.A. Jairazbhoy[103] has two interesting bits of it: "The cotton tree was introduced from India into Assyria (*c.* 700 B.C.) by Sennacherib (704-681 B.C.) who is reported to have said that trees that bear fleece were sheared and shredded into garments.... The earliest date [for the Indian peacock's arrival in Assyria] may be 738 B.C., when there is a possible reference to a peacock among the wonderful birds received as tribute by Tiglath Pileser III." A.D. Pusalker,[104] gathering "archaeological evidence" of India's communications with Western Asia, refers to "The figures of apes, Indian elephants and Bactrian camels on the obelisk of Shalmaneser III (860 B.C.)."

102. *Iran* (Harmondsworth, 1954), p. 90.
103. *Foreign Influence in Ancient India* (Bombay, 1963), p. 30.
104. *The Age of Imperial Unity*, p. 612.

The very presence of Semitic tongues in North-western India is attested. We have already quoted from Agrawala two examples of Semitic words in Pāṇini - *hailihila* (VI.2.38) and *goṇī* from *goṇa* (IV.1.42) - which Agrawala inclines to regard as originally Aramaic. He[105] has one further example relevant to our theme: "*Jābāla* denoted a goatherd, and *mahājābāla* (VI.2.38) one who was the owner of a big sheep-run. *Jābāla* does not seem to be a word of Sanskritic origin. It may be traced to a Hebrew word *yobel* or *jobil*, signifying ram's horn, whence 'jubilee'..." But it is not only the number of Semitic (Hebrew, Aramaic or Arabic) vocables to be culled from Pāṇini that is of direct moment here: it is also their chronological pointer. Pre-Pāṇinian all these vocables surely are and if Pāṇini, as we have argued apropos of Agrawala's statement about the grammarian's province Gandhāra having been an independent kingdom (IV.1.169), is earlier than even the first Achemenid Cyrus who started his reign in 558 B.C., India's Semitic contacts go substantially beyond the time usually allocated to Aśoka: the middle of the third century B.C. And with *goṇa* before us we see from Agrawala himself[106] that through *goṇaka* in the *Brahmajāla Sutta* XV we may even link this term, which denotes "obviously a cloth", to *kaunakes*, "a one-piece loin-cloth worn by the early Sumerians and Accadians". The prevalence of Aramaic in India's borderland could indeed be very early.

This should not be surprising when we consider the enterprising character of the Arameans whose language was Aramaic. Their merchants went far and wide. "The Arameans," says Philip K. Hitti,[107] "traded in purple from Phoenicia, embroideries, linen, jasper, copper, ebony and ivory from Africa, and in the 'product of the seas', perhaps the pearls for which throughout the ages the Persian Gulf has been famous." And if we believe, as Hitti[108] does, that several

105. *India as Known to Pāṇini* (Lucknow, 1953), p. 220.
106. *Ibid.*, pp. 220-21.
107. *A History of Syria* (London, 1957), p. 168.
108. *Ibid.*, p. 162.

groups formed parts of the Aramean movement, though not so designated, and that, besides the Khabiru, there were the Akhlamu (otherwise known as the Ahlamu), whose designation "companions" was generic rather than ethnic and must have been first applied to a confederation of tribes – if, with Hitti, we believe that the first mention of the Arameans by Tiglath-Pileser I (*c.* 1100 B.C.), in close association with the word "Akhlamu", merely throws into prominence a people already subsumed under the latter a couple of centuries before, then we have the presence of the Arameans, according to Roux's information,[109] attested in 1400-1350 B.C. in Assyria, at Nippur, and even at Bahrain down the Persian Gulf. Overseas as well as overland the Arameans are likely to have travelled with their language and their alphabet in the direction of Arachosia at a pretty early date.

Here we may also take account of a fact long ago spotlighted by G. Bühler apropos of the Brāhmī script which Aśoka used along with the Kharoshṭhī. Today the undeciphered script of the Indus Valley Civilization is regarded as lying behind Brāhmī, but part of Bühler's contention still has force. He pointed out that a certain proportion of the oldest Brāhmī letters are practically identical with letters on some Assyrian weights and on the Moabite Stone of King Mesa[110] which bears the longest and one of the earliest Hebrew inscriptions.[111] The striking resemblance must have come about by contact of India with the Semites (Hebrews, Arameans, Phoenicians) before and not after the time of the Moabite Stone; for later Semitic forms show no sufficient agreement.[112] The Moabite Stone was erected, as Hitti[113] notes, shortly before 842 B.C. We must, therefore, pass beyond the middle of the ninth century B.C. for the contact of the Arameans and their likes with Arachosia and its neighbourhoods.

109. *Ancient Iraq*, p. 248.
110. Rhys Davids, *Buddhist India* (Calcutta, 1950), pp. 70-71.
111. Hitti, *op. cit.*, p. 196.
112. Davids, *op. cit.*, p. 71.
113. Hitti, *op. cit.*, p. 195.

Bühler's fact about Brāhmī illuminates also the chronology of Aramaic in these places. For, there is no doubt that Brāhmī's companion, Kharoshṭhī, is derived from Aramaic, as Bühler convincingly explicated. However, the question will be put: "Can the antique and archaic nature of the Kandahār Aramaic allow us to go very far back in time beyond the definite date of the Kandahār Greek? Have we historical evidence of great antiquity for Aramaic inscriptions?" Let us see how much we can retreat into the past in this context. Hitti[114] tells us about the earliest epigraphs known. For long the pride of place went to the inscription of King Zakir (*c.* 775 B.C.). But now come earlier specimens. A votive stele, unearthed four and a half miles north of Aleppo and bearing the name of Ben-Hadad I is of *c.* 850 B.C. Older yet is a short inscription from Tell-al-Halaf (Gozen) in North Syria: it dates back to the beginning of the ninth century B.C. Still older epigraphic evidence may be indirectly cited. Hitti[115] brings the information: "The annals of Ramses III (1198-1167 B.C.) give the Aramaic spelling of the name [for Damascus] *Tiramaski* corresponding to Aramaic *Dar*(fortress)-*Mesheq*." So the inscription at Kandahār which has traits tending to place it among very early epigraphs need not be denied its proper antiquity. The Egyptianized echo of the Aramaic for "Damascus" permits, by its promise of epigraphic possibilities, the Aśokan edict to find its true historical perspective.

Perhaps we shall be challenged: "Can our inscription be regarded palaeographically as more primitive than those Hitti has mentioned or even the Egyptian documents of the Achemenids which Benveniste has cited?"

One should not be discomfited very much if the palaeographical pronouncements were unfavourable to one's thesis. Palaeography – the comparative study of old writings – is not an exact science. We may recall Sylvain Lévi's opinion[116] that

114. *Ibid.*, p. 170.
115. *Ibid.*, p. 165.
116. Quoted in English by Vincent Smith in *The Indian Antiquary*, Vol. 31, 1902, p. 196.

palaeographical tests have little independent value (*autorité absolue*) although they may be used as a check (*contrôle*) upon or a guide (*indice*) to the interpretation of positive history. In a narrower context Jouveau-Dubreuil[117] has put palaeography in its place: he has remarked that it is a bad auxiliary to the chronology of Indian history as very often the documents dated in the same reign differ much from each other and thus its evidence would be mainly suggestive or corroborative but at any rate not by itself conclusive.

A.S. Altekar provides us with a significant "slant" on questions palaeographical. Discussing the dynasty known as the Maghas, he[118] mentions that "there is a great controversy about the dates of the rulers of this dynasty". Some scholars think the Maghas date themselves in the Chedi Era starting in 248 A.D.; others go in for the Gupta Era as commonly calculated to begin in 320 A.D.; still others opt for the Śaka Era of 78 A.D. Thus the datings would vary by 72, 178 or 242 years. Altekar[119] favours the Śaka Era for reasons which to his mind outweigh the most impressive-looking palaeographical considerations. What is especially to be marked is that such considerations can be countered within the realm of palaeography itself, for there is no final standard in it. Altekar writes: "The most cogent argument in favour of the Chedi or the Gupta era is palaeographical; there is no doubt that the characters of the Magha inscriptions are almost the Gupta characters. This argument however is not a convincing one; for many of the Gupta forms of characters are to be seen in an inscription of Kanishka, dated in the 14th [Śaka] year (92 A.D.); see *Epigraphia Indica* XXI.2."

Thus, among the factors that are determinative, palaeography has no more force for the Kandahār inscription than for the Magha epigraphs. Determinative are other factors,

117. Quoted in English by Govind Pai in *The Journal of Indian History*, August 1935, p. 197.

118. *A New History of the Indian People*, edited by R.C. Majumdar, and A.S. Altekar (Lahore, 1946), VI, p. 41.

119. *Ibid.*, fn. 2.

chiefly the pre-Pāṇinian presence of Aramaic in the grammarian's Gandhāra leading to Aramaic words in his *Aṣṭādhyāyī* and, most significant of all, his knowledge of the Aramaic script which we have deduced to be the sense of his expression *Yavanānī*. But we have to keep in mind that the language embodied in this script at Kandahār differs widely from the one we meet in the Achemenid Aramaic texts. It differs both in its own forms and in the quality of the Irānian words interspersing it. A further difference in the basis of its texture is gauged from four other Aramaic inscriptions of Aśoka. Those of Taxila and Pūl-i-Dārunteh, which were found many years ago, and the comparatively recent one, a slab broken off from a rock and picked up in the bazaar of Kandahār in 1966 and christened Kandahār II, display Prākṛt as part of this basis. The last-named and the Laghman example provide another and a most unexpected association.

In the former, Dupont-Sommer[120] dwells on the expression KN' joined to the Irānian word *patiasti* which occurs as *hūpatiasti* in the Kandahār bilingual. He says that the interpretation of these letters is very difficult. They cannot be explained by resort to Irānian nor can they be taken as a terminal or else as an independent word: in Aramaic they correspond absolutely to nothing known. Dupont-Sommer asks: "One thinks of the word *kēno* 'right, just, true' attested in Syriac (cf. Hebrew *kēn*; Akkadian *kēnu* 'firm, right', *kettu* 'the truth, the right'); is it a qualifier of *patiasti*: 'the just obedience', an expression equivalent to *hūpatiasti* 'the good obedience', with this difference that the Irānian prefix *hū* would be transformed into an Aramaic pseudo-suffix? It would make of *patiastikēna* a hybrid word, trans-Aramaic, rather monstrous, or the element *kēna* would play, we repeat, the role of a suffix, a role which it never has in Aramaic." Our scholar's puzzlement clearly suggests a strange Aramaic with Syrian affinities.

The Laghman text has an unusual name inscribed at the end – "Wašu" – as that of the "judge" with whose help the

120. *Journal Asiatique* (Paris, 1966), pp. 458-59.

epigraph was made. Dupont-Sommer[121] is perplexed by it. It is not an Indian or an Irānian appellation. Considering the language of the epigraph we should expect it to have an Irānian air about it. But Dupont-Sommer reports: "The name Wašu is not found noticed in the work of Emile Benveniste, *Titles and Proper Names in Ancient Irān* (Paris, Klincksheck, 1966). One encounters in Nabatean, in the inscriptions called Sinaitic, the proper name W'ŠW (*Corpus Inscriptionum Sinaiticarum*, II, 2136, 2315) and also 'WŠW (*ibid.*, 325); one supposes generally that these forms are incorrect for 'WŠW 'Ušu', a proper name extremely frequent in Nabatean (cf. J. Cantineau, *Nabatean*, Vol. II, p. 88 sq.)." Here again the affinities are very odd for a supposedly post-Achemenid epigraph, and the appeal to "the inscriptions called Sinaitic" brings into the picture an epoch remote indeed. William F. Albright[122] informs us that, thanks to "a University of California expedition" in 1948, these "inscriptions prove to date from *c.* 1500 B.C." And, as John Gray[123] informs us, "From the Sinai inscriptions, fragmentary and uncertain as they are, a direct line of development may be discerned to legible alphabetic inscriptions in Syria and Palestine in the second half of the second millennium B.C." The Nabateans do not carry us to such a far past, though they are certainly older than the fifth century B.C. when they are seen pressing "northwards from the oases of the Hajaz" and ousting "the Edomites of Scripture";[124] but geographically they are a far cry from the borderland between India and Irān in the time of the Greek settlement there after Alexander's Indian expedition.

Aśoka's Aramaic inscriptions carry us to a historical period in which not only ancient Avestan Irān but also the Middle East seems to have been directly connected with India, the Middle East of a greater antiquity than the post-

121. *Académie des Inscriptions et Belles-Lettres*: Comptes Rendus des Séances de l'année 1970, Janvier-Mars, Paris, p. 169, fn. 1.

122. *The Archaeology of Palestine* (Harmondsworth, 1961), p. 189.

123. *Archaeology and the Old Testament* (New York, 1962), p. 24.

124. *Ibid.*, p. 16.

Achemenid era where modern historians situate Aśoka and during which the oddities of expression and nomenclature traced by us are out of the question.

On all the counts we have taken into our purview the Greco-Aramaic inscription of Kandahār creates an uncommon chronological background sufficiently wide and clear for us to suggest at least the possibility of attacking in some way or other the evidence which is held to be the strongest in favour of putting Aśoka in 269-232 B.C. – namely, his Edict XIII with its apparent list of the names of five Greek kings who flourished in that post-Alexandrine period.

THE *INDICA* OF MEGASTHENES

A CONTROVERSY WITH R.C. MAJUMDAR

[Reprinted from *Journal of the American Oriental Society*, Volume 80, Number 3, July-Aug., 1960]

Rejoinder to R.C. Majumdar

I. R.C. Majumdar[1] has called for a radical revision of the current attitude of historians towards Schwanbeck's part reconstruction of the lost *Indica* of Megasthenes from passages about India in later classical writers. He presses upon our consideration three points which may be stated thus:

1. When a classical writer offers us a piece of information on ancient India, we should not accept it as derived from Megasthenes unless he is specifically named or it closely resembles what is associated with his name elsewhere. Schwanbeck and, after him, McCrindle who translated his compilation into English have misguided us by doing otherwise.

2. Attaching importance to the testimony of Megasthenes in certain respects, we have allowed some passages to play a crucial role in historical controversies. If they do not pass the above test, we should ignore them and change our minds.

3. We have overrated Megasthenes as an authority. His powers of observation are rather poor and his judgment dubious. We should not rely much on him in any case.

The first point seeks to narrow down the canon for inclusion which Schwanbeck is thought to have adopted. Schwanbeck is charged with two laxities: (1) he admitted passages simply preceding or following those that Majumdar regards as acceptable; (2) he even admitted long passages, including, incidentally, those that closely resemble what is elsewhere associated with the name of Megasthenes or those that simply precede or follow the acceptable ones. To de-

1. *JAOS*, 78 (1958), pp. 273-276.

monstrate how mistaken Schwanbeck was, Majumdar takes up for critical disentanglement two citations: a long one from Diodorus to illustrate the second laxity and a shorter one from Strabo to illustrate the first.

At the very outset we may remark that Schwanbeck is not at all guilty of so loose a canon. He merely risks attributing to Megasthenes at times small bits embedded in matter proved to be his either by parallels elsewhere or by legitimate inference. All citations not included under the title "Doubtful Fragments"[2] have been carefully checked and, if any passage cannot be paralleled, it is admitted not because it precedes or follows any other, still less because it forms the long general context of them, but because it appears to arise logically out of them. Even among the "Doubtful Fragments", the lengthiest and most important – Pliny's "List of the Indian Races"[3] – has been traced, as the footnote informs us, by Schwanbeck to Megasthenes for the most part and yet is not offered as all Megasthenes. The strictness of the canon seems at work here. Majumdar has perhaps been led astray by occasional bracketed statements that Fragment so and so follows or precedes Fragment this or that. Thus Fragment XLI from Strabo[4] carries the Editor's words: "(Fragment XXIX has preceded this)." But it is not allotted to Megasthenes merely for following Fragment XXIX. It also begins, like the latter, with a reference to him: "Speaking of the philosophers he (Megasthenes) says...." Majumdar does not seem to have understood the principles on which Schwanbeck proceeded for matter outside the "Doubtful Fragments". The citations chosen by Majumdar – both of them outside that section – are not in the least likely to put Schwanbeck in the wrong box.

Let us start with Fragment I, from Diodorus (fourteen pages in McCrindle's book).[5] Schwanbeck has entitled it "An

2. J. McCrindle, *Ancient India as described by Megasthenes and Arrian* (Calcutta, 1926), pp. 117-178.

3. *Ibid.*, pp. 129-159.

4. *Ibid.*, p. 97.

5. *Ibid.*, pp. 29-42.

Epitome of Megasthenes". But the name of Megasthenes occurs nowhere. Since others besides him are known to have written on India – even on interior India – Majumdar asks in effect "When Megasthenes is never mentioned, why should we not believe Diodorus to have drawn on others no less than on him?" But we can easily see how little cause exists for this question. We have only to attend to the recurring footnotes or other means by which McCrindle, in the body of his book, makes us hark back to Diodorus from what is undeniably Megasthenes. Again and again[6] we read either "Conf. Epit." or "Conf. Diodorus" and these phrases are followed by numerals answering to those that in Diodorus's fourteen pages stand in small type before the beginning of each sentence. Similarly, footnotes to the "Epitome" direct our attention forward. It should be quite clear to the reader that in the writings of Strabo and some others as well as in Arrian's *Indica*[7] which is avowedly based to a great extent on Megasthenes we have several passages indicating by their substance Megasthenes as the source of Diodorus. Small discrepancies there may be between Diodorus and the rest, but the overall impression is the same. Page after page of Diodorus on matters for which Majumdar[8] holds Megasthenes responsible in Strabo and Arrian – for example, the nearly seven pages[9] covered in the "Epitome" by the legends about Dionysos and Herakles and by the description of the seven "castes" of India – should arrest us from picking out this citation, even if we overlooked the fairly detailed substantiation made by Schwanbeck and McCrindle of their claim. The only debatable point on the whole , as C.H. Oldfather quoted by Majumdar[10] suggests, is whether Diodorus paraphrased directly from Megasthenes or from an intermediary. Old father, unlike Majumdar, does not doubt that Megasthenes is the basis of Diodorus.

6. *Ibid.*, pp. 43, 45, 50, 52, 61, 64, 83, 107, 162.
7. *Ibid.*, pp. 183-227.
8. Majumdar, pp. 275-276.
9. McCrindle, pp. 34-37, 38-41.
10. Majumdar, p. 274.

Not that Majumdar is quite unaware of the presence of Megasthenes. After listing the passages which he considers to be undeniably from him[11] he specifies three of "the most important" whose emanation from him "may be justly questioned", and of course Diodorus's disquisition is there, but Majumdar adds the qualification: "Except the topics and passages included in the above list." What seems to have influenced him to differ from Schwanbeck is just one single piece of information which looks such as Megasthenes with his personal experience of Indian events in the time of Alexander could never have given. But if he had noted what Schwanbeck and McCrindle have been at pains to show, he would have paused before making much of this solitary error.

The error is simply this: Diodorus states that Alexander arrived with all his troops at the river Ganges. Actually, the Hyphasis (Beās), a tributary of the Indus, marked the limit of Alexander's advance. As Megasthenes must have known very well the limit, Majumdar[12] concludes that Diodorus has gone outside Megasthenes. But is the problem as simple as all that? It is possible to look at it differently from two angles.

First, let us recall what Alexander was told about Farther India. He was told that his most formidable foe beyond the Indus-region was Xandrames (or Agrammes) who was king of the Gangaridai and the Prasiai and whose dominions were situated beyond the Ganges. Not only Curtius (IX.II) but Diodorus himself (VII.XVIII) reports this. Plutarch, too, in his life of Alexander (LXII), does so, with small differences of detail like his not mentioning the name "Xandrames" (or "Agrammes") and his reference to the "kings" in place of "king". All of them speak of a huge army of horses, infantry, chariots and elephants, standing on the alert, beyond the Ganges. Plutarch even writes that it was waiting for Alexander and his men. Now, if the enemy on the eastern bank of this river was Alexander's one stumbling-block, is it an

11. *Ibid.*, p. 276.
12. *Ibid.*, p. 274.

unnatural inference that the Macedonian might have moved up to the western bank? In Plutarch (LIX-LXII), after the crossing of the Hydaspes (Jhelum) and the hard-won victory over Porus, the question vexing Alexander's men is simply whether they would allow themselves to be led on to cross the Ganges. To Plutarch, so far as his actual wording goes, no river except the Ganges was part of the boundary to Alexander's advance. It is conceivable that Megasthenes or others representing him did not unequivocally mark the Hyphasis as the limit but only spoke of the great collection of troops on the eastern bank of the Ganges as the force whose threat stopped the Macedonians. Then Diodorus could write as he did – just a step further than Plutarch – without going outside Megasthenes as his direct or indirect source.

What, however, continues to puzzle us here is the fact that emerges when we examine this history of Alexander which Diodorus has recorded elsewhere. The fact is: exactly as does Arrian in *The Anabasis of Alexander* (V.XXIX), not only Curtius (IX.III) but also Diodorus (XVII.XCIV) speaks of Alexander erecting memorials and altars on the western bank of the Hyphasis to mark the limit of his advance. So, to write now of Alexander arriving at the Ganges, Diodorus would have to go not outside Megasthenes but outside Diodorus himself!

Perhaps the best course is to take the text as faulty. At least, the text is such that nothing can be built on it in the controversy Majumdar has raised. It has got to be ignored. Everything considered, we have no reason to doubt that the fourteen pages from Diodorus are all based on Megasthenes. And, consequently, in view of the total omission of Megasthenes's name in each one of them, we are led to adopt the very reverse of the position urged by Majumdar. Instead of ascribing to Megasthenes nothing save what he is openly named as saying or what repeats almost the same thing without naming him, we should credit to him everything that is not explicitly attributed to somebody else.

The more serious of the two laxities charged against Schwanbeck is disproved. How far is the less serious one chargeable? In the citation from Strabo[13] – four pages entitled "Of the Manners of the Indians" – Megasthenes is said by Majumdar to be named in two places only: once at nearly the start in support of a statement and then right at the end in extension of another. Majumdar asks what the purpose here can be if all of Strabo is from Megasthenes: according to him, the second reference is particularly odd because if the first was meant to suggest Megasthenes as the sole authority this was quite superfluous.

To begin with, we may remark that in Strabo's "Fragment" the references to Megasthenes are not only two. Almost in the middle[14] we read: "The same writer says that none of the Indians employ slaves; but Onesikritos says this was peculiar to that part of the country over which Musikanos ruled." As Megasthenes is the only writer already named, "the same writer" is surely he. So we have – contrary to Majumdar's idea – three references to Megasthenes and the second notes a difference of opinion between two writers on a subject about which evidently none else than they have pronounced.

We can take a cue from this. Why should we not hold that, while the information not openly ascribed to Megasthenes was common to several writers reporting independently, the two matters at the beginning and at the end for which he is cited by name were exclusive to him just as the matter for which he and Onesikritos are named was exclusive to the two of them? If nobody except Megasthenes – at least as far as Strabo's knowledge went – gave those bits of information, it would be necessary to quote the authority for them: no authority would be required in points of general agreement between him and the rest.

This probability would be there even if the middle reference were absent and if Majumdar were right in telling us that Megasthenes is only twice named. Moreover, although the middle reference proves directly suggestive, the first bit of

13. McCrindle, pp. 68-71.
14. *Ibid.*, p. 70.

information is enough to set us thinking along the lines we have indicated. For, it is precisely what Megasthenes alone could give: it refers, as Majumdar[15] himself shows by a quotation, to "the camp of Sandrokottos" – Sandrokottos to whom, as Strabo[16] says in another place, Megasthenes had been sent as ambassador.

Majumdar has been hasty to presume that only where Strabo names Megasthenes the information is attributable to the latter's *Indica*.

Our criticism apropos of the two "Fragments" would apply in general to the third which Majumdar mentions when listing the three most important passages that should not be attributed to Megasthenes. But to be quite impartial let us judge it independently.

It is Fragment XXIV from Strabo,[17] describing among other things, as Majumdar[18] puts it, "the Municipal and Military Boards of Administration". McCrindle calls it by a double title: "Of the Administration of Public Affairs. Of the Use of Horses and Elephants." Under the title we read: "(Fragm. XXXIII has preceded this)." Fragment XXXIII is about "the Seven Castes among the Indians" and begins: "According to him (Megasthenes) the population of India is divided into seven parts." Now, Fragment XXXIV has no mention of Megasthenes, and Majumdar must have believed that Schwanbeck ascribed it to Megasthenes because it was preceded by Fragment XXXIII. As we shall see, the sequence has really no determinative force in itself; the Fragment is ascribed to Megasthenes from internal evidence.

This piece has a special interest because scholars have made it a part of the discussion on the age of Kauṭilya's *Arthaśāstra*. Majumdar[19] tells us that a strong argument against dating the *Arthaśāstra* to the time of Sandrokottos who has been identified with Chandragupta Maurya is the absence

15. Majumdar, p. 274.
16. McCrindle, p. 66; also Introduction, p. 19.
17. *Ibid.*, pp. 80-89.
18. Majumdar, p. 276. 19. *Ibid.*

in it of any reference to the Municipal and Military Boards. Naturally, if Fragment XXXIV is not authentic Megasthenes, the discussion on the age of the *Arthaśāstra* would be affected.

The pertinent questions here for us are: (1) Can the information in this Fragment be ascribed to the ambassador at the court of Sandrokottos? (2) Even if it can, could we be sure that it is genuine and not a misconstruction by him?

Although the name of Megasthenes is nowhere in the Fragment, let us bear in mind that Strabo opens it with the words, "Of the great officers of state..." and that it immediately follows what Strabo[20] writes from Megasthenes of the seventh "caste" or "class": "The seventh class consists of the councillors and assessors of the king. To them belong the highest posts of government, the tribunals of justice, and the general administration of public affairs...." The passage about "the great officers of state", some of whom constitute what Majumdar terms "the Municipal and Military Boards of Administration", does no more than elaborate the functions of the seventh "class". This point is brought home to us all the more forcefully when we look at Arrian's version of those functions.* On internal evidence and by the logic of development, can there be the slightest doubt that Strabo's passage under discussion is authentic Megasthenes?

Nor can we look askance at its information as unauthentic, though in places the order of the matters spoken of may differ a little from the traditional Indian. Thus Megasthenes not only has the fourfold division of the army (horse, foot soldiers, chariots and elephants) that is found in Manu and elsewhere; he has given two more constituents – the commissariat and naval departments. But the *Mahābhārata*, we may

20. McCrindle, p. 85.

* *Ibid.*, pp. 218-19: "The seventh caste consists of the councillors of state, who advise the king, or the magistrates of self-governed cities, in the management of public affairs. In point of numbers this is a small class, but it is distinguished by superior wisdom and justice, and hence enjoys the prerogative of choosing governors, chiefs of provinces, deputy-governors, superintendents of the treasury, generals of the army, admirals of the navy, controllers, and commissioners who superintend agriculture."

add with R.K. Mookerji,[21] gives four more, one of which includes the navy and the three others correspond in general to Megasthenes's supplementary components. Because of small variations we can hardly dismiss his Municipal and Military Boards as fictitious. Even Majumdar does not say that no matter if the information be Megasthenes's we should ignore it as inaccurate. What he is concerned with is merely to challenge its accepted status as a culling from the *Indica*. His challenge fails. So, should Kauṭilya here be really at odds with the ambassador to Sandrokottos, the former could not have been writing on the state of things in *circa* 300 B.C.

II. Fragments XXXIII and XXXIV may very aptly lead us to the question: Is Megasthenes on the whole reliable and valuable?

Majumdar[22] brands as "mostly inaccurate and misleading" the description of the seven castes or classes of India. In view of the singular character of the Hindu social system, it should scarcely surprise us that Megasthenes mixed up castes proper and the crafts associated with them. "But his seven classes may truly reflect," as E.R. Bevan[23] points out, "the various activities which a Greek resident of Pāṭaliputra could see going on round about him in the fourth century B.C." As for the information on "the great officers of state", it is not only credible to the utmost but shows a power of acute, direct, detailed observation in an important field. And there is another instance too of Megasthenes contra Kauṭilya, which should help us towards a proper assessment of the Greek writer as an authority on ancient India.

It is well-known that in his description of the city of Palibothra (Pāṭaliputra) he speaks of a massive timber palisade protecting this capital of Sandrokottos and that a remnant of the palisade has been discovered among the ruins of

21. *Chandragupta Maurya and His Times* (Madras, 1943), p. 269.
22. Majumdar, p. 276.
23. In *The Cambridge History of India* (1922), Vol. I, p. 409.
24. *The Wonder that was India* (London, 1954), p. 134.

the city. A.L. Basham,[24] while referring to the account by Megasthenes of "a mighty wooden wall", reminds us of Kauṭilya's mention of earth-work and brick-work for city-ramparts. Then he comments: "The Arthaśāstra advises against the use of wood for fortifications, owing to its liability to fire and rot, but archaeology bears out Megasthenes...." A tremendous compliment it is to Megasthenes that his *Indica* should thus prove right against an ancient indigenous book the *Arthaśāstra*.

Not that we should think him always exempt from error. As with the "seven castes", some misunderstanding by a foreigner is to be expected in places and, if the foreigner happened to be – like most men of the time – fond of strange stories, there was bound to be some spiced reporting here and there. But we must remember that all the strange stories of Megasthenes can be traced to Indian literature and part of his value as a historian lies in his recording of them, for they indicate to us the kind of tradition existing in his day. Even the gold-digging ants, in relation to which Majumdar frames his most serious charge against Megasthenes are, as Bevan[25] informs us, "mentioned in the Mahābhārata...."

Majumdar's charge is based on some words of Arrian. According to Arrian,[26] Megasthenes offered his readers as "strictly true" the "hearsay" about the activity of these creatures which were depicted to be larger than foxes. Majumdar[27] argues that if Megasthenes was uncritical enough not to distinguish between what he actually saw and what was merely told him and could personally vouch for the latter he must be essentially unreliable everywhere. Apart from the sweeping extremism of the argument, there is here a sad want of sympathetic understanding. We have to keep three points in mind.

Firstly, Megasthenes not only had Indian tradition behind him but must also have been influenced by the suggestive

25. *The Cambridge History of India*, Vol. I, p. 396, fn., the *Mahābhārata* reference being: "II, 1860 (Calcutta ed.)."

26. McCrindle, p. 222.

27. Majumdar, p. 276.

term which, as Bevan[28] tells us, the Indians used for gold-dust: *pipīlika*, "ant-gold". Secondly, Arrian himself reports[29] Nearchos as declaring that though he had not seen these ants he had seen many skins of them brought into the Macedonian camp. To be sure, Nearchos and the Macedonian camp were deceived; but what reason had Megasthenes not to feel that this contemporary evidence put the seal of truth on all he had heard? Thirdly, various astonishing animals – some of huge size – had already been observed by the Greeks in India. These ants would be just an addition to the list and hardly more marvellous than they. On no score can Megasthenes be blamed here: his error is quite natural and his assurance to his readers perfectly rational under the circumstances.

Another blunder of Majumdar's[30] is to think that many writers of antiquity – and especially Strabo and Arrian to whom he ascribes a very high degree of critical judgment – had a low opinion of Megasthenes on the whole. The fact is: the censure, right or wrong, of the ancients was directed in the main, as we unmistakably gather from Strabo,[31] against two particular portions of his narrative: his accounts of "fabulous tribes" as well as of fantastic animals and his tales about Herakles and Dionysos. These portions do not at all exhaust his range, and Strabo himself quotes often from him without any scepticism,[32] twice notes without contradiction the support given by Eratosthenes to him[33] and, on one occasion, cites for his own views Megasthenes's authority.[34]

Arrian's condemnation too of what Megasthenes wrote on the trans-Hyphasis country, to which Alexander's expedition had not penetrated, is confined to queer things like the river Silas.[35] But Majumdar[36] is under the impression that Arrian

28. *The Cambridge History of India*, Vol. I, p. 396.
29. McCrindle, p. 222.
30. Majumdar, pp. 276, 277.
31. McCrindle, p. 73, fn. 1; p. 110.
32. *E.g., ibid.*, pp. 52, 54, 65-66, 83-86, 97 (bottom), 103, 106.
33. *Ibid.*, pp. 49, 50-51.
34. *Ibid.*, pp. 107-108.
35. *Ibid.*, p. 202.
36. Majumdar, p. 276.

rejected everything about this region as "absolutely unreliable". Actually, the statement by which Majumdar sets store – "Beyond that limit (the Hyphasis) we have no real knowledge of the country"[37] – is not Arrian's. It stands, like some other words or phrases in the same context, in italics: the italics are meant to indicate the editor's interpolation to save the sense from ambiguity or to effect a smoother transition. If we check with E.J. Chinnock's version[38] we shall easily recognize the interpolations and also realize the need for something like them. But Arrian must not be misconstrued. Surely, he never dreams of rejecting the description of Palibothra which was situated far beyond the Hyphasis.[39] And there is much else he accepts.[40] He is ready even to believe, in spite of its sounding fantastic, the report about the women of Pandaia (evidently the southern kingdom of Pāṇḍya).[41] The true meaning of his warning is that we should use our discretion over accounts of regions where people have not travelled much. The correct position emerges from his remark: "Even Megasthenes, as it appears, did not travel over much of India, though no doubt he saw more of it than those who came with Alexander...."[42]

Ancient writers of eminent critical ability are far from being for the most part scornful of Megasthenes. Their general verdict is really represented by a couple of Arrian's own phrases. In his *Indica* he writes: "Nearchos and Megasthenes, two men of approved character."[43] We read in his *Anabasis of Alexander* (V.v): "Megasthenes and Eratosthenes, who are both approved men." The association with a widely respected author like Eratosthenes whom, as Majumdar[44] observes, Arrian regarded as "the safest authority" is particularly worth noting.

37. McCrindle, p. 202.
38. *The Anabasis of Alexander and The Indica* (London, 1839), p. 405.
39. McCrindle, pp. 209-210.
40. *E.g.*, pp. 200 (bottom), 204 (bottom), 207 (middle), 211, 214-218.
41. *Ibid.*, p. 208.
42. *Ibid.*, p. 200.
43. *Ibid.*, p. 227.
44. Majumdar , p. 275.

To sum up: Majumdar's whole case against Megasthenes breaks down, just as his entire attack on Schwanbeck and McCrindle miscarries.

The Surrejoinder to K.D. Sethna

To reply in detail to Sethna's rejoinder to my very brief paper on Megasthenes would involve the writing of an extensive article which I do not consider necessary. I shall confine myself to the several important points raised by him. My silence as to his other observations should not be taken to mean that I accept them as valid.

Sethna assumes that I have "... perhaps been led astray by occasional bracketed statements that Fragment so and so follows or precedes Fragment this or that..." "Fragment XLI is not allotted to Megasthenes merely for following Fragment XXIX. It also begins: 'Speaking of the philosophers he (Megasthenes) says...' " That I was not "led astray" is clear from my inclusion of the Fragment among the genuine quotations from Megasthenes (cf. p. 275 of my paper, item 10). Therefore, his remark that "Majumdar does not seem to have understood the principles on which Schwanbeck proceeded..." is not correct.

Regarding Fragment I, by Diodorus, Sethna draws attention to the footnotes by which McCrindle "makes us hark back to Diodorus from what is undeniably Megasthenes". I have not ignored these footnotes and have clearly indicated that portions of the Fragment were based on Megasthenes (see p. 276 of my article, item 1). But I expressed my doubt about passages which cannot be clearly traced to "what is undeniably Megasthenes", and cited as an instance one passage which could not possibly be his statement, namely, that Alexander advanced as far as the Ganges. Sethna, after a great deal of discussion, first tries to explain away the passage and then advises us to ignore it and regard the text as faulty. He forgets that such a view was actually held by some classical writers, at least one of whom was a contemporary of

Alexander and his companion (cf. Strabo, 15.1.35). What is then more natural than to suppose that Diodorus based his information on this source? It is certainly a more rational process than to ignore anything for the sole reason that it does not suit a preconceived hypothesis. That Diodorus said something different in another context merely proves that he had several sources of information on which he drew and did not always notice the inconsistencies to which he was led by such isolated passages while writing a large volume. Sethna forgets that I cited the passage as only an instance. There are other passages which are more directly contrary to Megasthenes. For example, Diodorus gives the extent of India as 28,000 stadia from east to west. Since Sethna has so carefully read the footnotes by which McCrindle makes us "hark back to Diodorus from what is undeniably Megasthenes", is it not very surprising that he does not refer to the footnote on p. 48 (Fragment IV), according to which Schwanbeck felt "certain that 16,000 stadia is the only measure Megasthenes gave of the breadth of India". Surely, a seventy-five per cent difference in specific measurements between a book and its epitome calls for an explanation. Again, Diodorus tells us that the Indus was perhaps the largest of all rivers in the world after the Nile (Fragment par. 35). Now, according to Arrian (*Indica,* par. IV) "Megasthenes states that of the two (the Indus and the Ganges) the Ganges is much the larger". In the preceding paragraph of Arrian occurs the statement that "both (the Ganges and the Indus) are greater than the Egyptian Nile and the Skythian Ister even if their streams were united into one". This follows a quotation from Megasthenes and that McCrindle took it as representing the view of Megasthenes is clear from Fragment II which contains a similar statement. It would require great ingenuity to maintain the view that Fragments I and II could both be traced to Megasthenes, correctly. Here, again, I would like to point out that there were classical writers who gave 30,000 stadia as the breadth of India, and it is certainly more reasonable to conclude that Diodorus took his figures from some such writers than that he gave us an epitome of Megasthenes' *Indica*.

The two instances given above, where Diodorus differs categorically on very specific points from Megasthenes, are merely illustrative, and by no means exhaustive. These naturally make one hesitate to take Fragment I as an epitome of Megasthenes, and the hesitation is strengthened by the fact that no reference is made to Megasthenes in this long passage of fourteen pages. But Sethna thinks that by explaining away or ignoring the passage about Alexander's advance to the Ganges it is definitely established "that the fourteen pages from Diodorus are all based on Megasthenes". Once having established this to his own satisfaction, he proceeds to the next step, still more remarkable. Since Megasthenes is not mentioned by Diodorus, though, as he believes, he took everything from that authority, Sethna establishes the general principle, in respect of all classical writers, that Megasthenes must be credited with "everything that is not explicitly attributed to somebody else". These two lead to the final triumphant conclusion, namely that "the more serious of the two laxities charged (by Majumdar) against Schwanbeck is disproved". It is evident that there is a fundamental difference in our outlook and reasoning. Stated broadly, I hold that a thing must be proved to be true before it can be accepted as such, whereas Sethna is ready to accept as true anything which cannot be definitely and unequivocally proved to be false. In view of this it is hardly of any use in discussing Sethna's arguments in further detail.

I would like to say a few words only in respect of Fragment XXXIV, which must be held to be a very important one in view of what I have written (p. 276). Sethna says: "Although the name of Megasthenes is nowhere in the Fragment, let us bear in mind that Strabo opens it with words, 'Of the great officers of state...' and that it immediately follows what Strabo writes from Megasthenes of the seventh 'caste' or 'class'." Now, Strabo's description of the third caste, namely shepherds and hunters, based on Megasthenes, is similarly followed immediately by a long account of elephants and other animals, which is admittedly based on "Megasthenes and other writers". Further Strabo's statement that in his account of the hunters, *i.e.*, the third caste, he mentioned what both Megasthenes and others have said, makes it doubtful whether the details of each caste are wholly derived from Megasthenes. Attention may be drawn in this connection to substantial difference in details given by Strabo and Diodorus in respect of the second, fourth, and sixth castes. These differences are of such a nature that it is difficult to hold that both derived their information from Megasthenes alone. Before passing on to the next topic I need only add that Sethna is right in pointing out that Fragment XXVII really contains three references to Megasthenes, and not two only, as I, through oversight, stated in my paper. But this strengthens rather than weakens my argument. For if all the four pages were taken wholly from Megasthenes, it is hardly likely that three specific references should be made to Megasthenes in support of three distinct statements.

The second part of Sethna's rejoinder concerning the value and authenticity of the account of Megasthenes has not refuted anything that I said. He admits that Arrian's statement, quoted by me, even though added by McCrindle, is really required by the context, and also that Strabo agrees with Arrian in this respect. Thus both clearly indicate their lack of faith in Megasthenes, as other classical writers have done and this is admitted by Schwanbeck himself. His exclusion of Arrian alone from this category of slanders is not wholly correct as I have shown in my paper (p. 276). Sethna's belief that the censure of the ancient writers was directed basically against two particular portions of Megasthenes' account, his apology on behalf of Megasthenes that he was fond of strange stories, and his admission that Megasthenes was not free from error, substantially, though not wholly, meet my point. For it is nobody's position, certainly not mine, that everything that Megasthenes said was false. Sethna might have easily spared us his long discussion to prove the authenticity of the description of Pāṭaliputra, for nobody has disbelieved it. Many other things stated by Megasthenes may be, and possibly are, true. But that does not disprove what I said, in full agreement with the classical writers, about his lack of critical faculty. Sethna unnecessarily takes trouble to point out, in an elaborate discussion, that Megasthenes' information about fabulous races or other incredible stories was derived from Indian literature. This has been fully demonstrated by many others before him. No one suggests that Megasthenes invented them out of his own fancy. The real point at issue is whether a reasonable man, endowed with ordinary critical faculty, should have believed in them and mentioned them as, or as if they were, facts. Discerning persons like Arrian and Strabo had no hesitation in dismissing them as incredible fables. This certainly proves my thesis, namely that Megasthenes "did not possess a very high degree of critical judgment", and nothing that Sethna has said goes against this proposition, or what I generally said about the reliability of Megasthenes. Sethna has tried to explain – unnecessarily, as others have done it before – how or why Megasthenes was misled and to show that there is a substratum of truth in Megasthenes' accounts of Indian society. Sethna has cited the opinion of Mukherji against my criticism of Megasthenes' statement about the seven castes. But Mukherji also states that Megasthenes has made a confusion between castes proper and crafts, and his opinion of Megasthenes in this respect does not appear to me to be fundamentally different from mine, as Sethna supposes. Sethna admits what he regards as the most serious charge brought by me against Megasthenes, namely that he averred as strictly true what he merely heard from others about the gold-digging ants, but asks whether from this single instance we can "declare that Megasthenes always emphasizes as strictly true the things he has heard?" I have never said that he *always* did so; but we may certainly be skeptical about one who is known to have done so once. Again I have never denied *Indica* "a wide mass of factuality or of accurately reported fable", but have stressed the necessity of taking pains to find out what is fable and what is fact in the accounts of Megasthenes, since he did not always distinguish between the two and did not possess a sufficiently critical mind to enable him to do so. I am prepared, along with Sethna, to "admire the pains Megasthenes took to acquaint himself with Indian literature", if he really did so, but feel very sorry indeed that out of that literature he chose to communicate to the world only a number of incredible stories which a man with a modicum of reason and common sense would have no hesitation in rejecting outright as unworthy of belief and having no value in understanding the country of which he was writing the account.

In spite of the elaborate arguments of Sethna I still remain an unrepentant sinner, and again express doubt whether we should place absolute reliance on the statements of an uncritical writer like Megasthenes, even if they were based on his own observations. It is by no means an easy task to report correctly what one sees, and I would draw attention to what Strabo (15.1.2) said about Alexandrine writers: They "made their sojourns together... yet they all frequently contradict one another. But if they differ thus about what was seen, what must we think of what they report from hearsay?" There are no good grounds for the belief that Megasthenes occupied a much higher rank, as a chronicler, than those to whom Strabo refers. At least that remains to be proved by positive evidence, rather than accepted as a belief handed down from old generations of Indologists who had little opportunity and probably less inclination to examine very critically the few sources of information available to them. This is my position and I am unable to share Sethna's satisfaction that "the whole case against Megasthenes breaks down."

A Comment on R.C. Majumdar's Surrejoinder to K.D. Sethna

As Schwanbeck's part reconstruction (translated into English by J. McCrindle) of the lost *Indica* of Megasthenes is of great interest and importance to Indologists, I should like to return to my discussion with Majumdar of its contents and value.[45]

I wrote that Majumdar did not seem to understand the principles on which Schwanbeck had proceeded for matter outside the section entitled by him "Doubtful Fragments". My contention was that because of his misunderstanding he had accused Schwanbeck of two laxities: (1) Schwanbeck admitted passages simply preceding or following those that could obviously be regarded as founded on Megasthenes; (2) he also admitted long passages including, incidentally, those that closely resemble what is elsewhere associated with the name of Megasthenes or those that simply precede or follow the obviously acceptable ones. Unfortunately, in my rejoinder a needed quotation from Schwanbeck got omitted. Not that it was quite indispensable; but it would have brought my criticism to a sharper focus. I now give it to prove that even in framing his smaller accusation Majumdar took his cue from something related only to the "Doubtful Fragments". Naturally, if the smaller is itself invalid for the bulk of Schwanbeck's compilation, the bigger is still less likely to hold true.

The very first passage among the "Doubtful Fragments" is one from Aelian (XII.8). Schwanbeck's second footnote[46] to it runs: "This Fragment is ascribed to Megasthenes both on account of the matter of it, and because it was undoubtedly from Megasthenes that Aelian borrowed the narrative preceding it (Fragm. XXXVIII) and that following it (Fragm. XXV)." In other words, one reason why Aelian here may be brought into rapport with Megasthenes is that his passage itself follows and precedes those about which we are sure. Is it not clear that Majumdar has built a generalisation on this part of the footnote and applied it even to passages outside the "Doubtful Fragments"? If Schwanbeck had actually subs-

45. *JAOS*, 80 (1960), pp. 243-250. Majumdar's original article appeared in *JAOS*, 78 (1958), pp. 273-276.

46. McCrindle, *Ancient India as described by Megasthenes and Arrian* (Calcutta, 1926), p. 118. The "Doubtful Fragments" cover pp. 117-178.

cribed to the canon attributed to him by Majumdar, he would have put the citation from Aelian not among the "Doubtful Fragments" but with the passages outside them.

Apropos of these passages, I charged Majumdar with being perhaps led astray by occasional bracketed statements – which are purely factual – that Fragment so and so follows or precedes Fragment this or that. And, giving an instance, I wrote that Fragment XLI from Strabo was not allotted to Megasthenes merely for following Fragment XXIX but for having a reference to Megasthenes at the very start. Majumdar[47] now comes out and defends himself: "That I was not 'led astray' is clear from my inclusion of the Fragment among the genuine quotations from Megasthenes..." The defence is puzzling. I never said that in spite of Megasthenes being mentioned Majumdar did not accept any consecutive passages! I only said that Schwanbeck did not accept passages just because they were consecutive. Like Majumdar, he accepted them for better reasons which really constituted his canon.

His canon for passages outside the "Doubtful Fragments" is much stricter than Majumdar allows. The admitted matter must be proved to be Megasthenes's either by parallels elsewhere under his own name or by legitimate inference from what is undeniably his. Embedded in such matter there may be small bits about which one is uncertain or which are not in consonance with what some writer or other has specifically attributed to Megasthenes. But surely to let such bits stand on account of their structural relation with the rest is quite different from the laxities that Majumdar lays at Schwanbeck's door.

As for the rest of the points made by me, Majumdar who is usually one of the most understanding and open-minded of historians acts here mainly out of character. He merely reiterates his original positions without caring to consider my arguments. His remarks on Diodorus's supposed "Epitome of

47. *JAOS*, 80, p. 248.

Megasthenes" and on Strabo's passage about the State-officers are the sole part of his surrejoinder where he has thought it fit to controvert me with concrete detail. Nor, except for some expansion over this passage of Strabo, does he go beyond these remarks in the note on Megasthenes, which he has built out of his two articles, for his excellent compilation recently published: *The Classical Accounts of India.*[48]

In controverting me Majumdar scores a genuine success in at least one point. It is certain that Diodorus's statement about Alexander's advance up to the Ganges, which is at variance with his own mention elsewhere (XVII.94) of the Hyphasis as the limit, was, as Majumdar suggests, borrowed from another source than Megasthenes and not due to some ambiguity in him as I had thought. The source is Craterus (or rather pseudo-Craterus) to whom Strabo (XV.I.35) attributes the same statement. Possibly, since Megasthenes gives primacy to the Ganges among rivers and takes the Indus to be larger than the Nile, Majumdar is also not wrong in refusing to connect with Megasthenes the phrase of Diodorus (II.35) that "the Indus is perhaps the largest river in the world after the Nile". But here we are on less firm ground. For, we have no Craterus to fall back upon. Majumdar will never be able to identify the source of Diodorus's phrases. And actually there can be no source if we are to believe Strabo's assertion, in the very passage where he refers to Craterus, that though Craterus's account of the magnitude of the Ganges' width and depth is incredible and though other writers' estimates of them differ, "indeed it is sufficiently agreed that the Ganges is the largest of known rivers".[49] In the absence of any source, an alternative explanation for Diodorus is, to say the least, conceivable.

May we not think his memory here distorted what Megasthenes himself may have written? A sentence from

48. *The Classical Accounts of India*, edited by R.C. Majumdar with maps, editorial notes, comments, analysis and Introduction (Calcutta, 1960), Appendix I, pp. 461-469.

49. *Ibid.*, p. 262.

Arrian (*Anabasis*, V.5) and some words of Strabo completing his assertion about the Ganges in the Craterus-passage have verbal turns which send us back to Diodorus and incline us to suspect a memory-distortion of Megasthenes. Thus Arrian: "The Indus is the largest of all the rivers in Asia and Europe, except the Ganges..."[50] Thus Strabo: "...the Ganges is the largest of known rivers on the three continents, and after it the Indus, and third and fourth the Ister and the Nile..." That Diodorus's memory could play tricks is shown by the very fact that, forgetting to be consistent, he gave in two places of his book two different rivers as the limits to Alexander's advance. It is shown also by the exchange of terms when he speaks (III.39) of Antipater, after Alexander's death, dividing the satrapies anew and giving, from the adjacent kingdoms, "that which lay along the Indus to Porus and that along the Hydaspes to Taxiles..."[51] Majumdar notes in his *Classical Accounts of India*: "...we should read 'Taxiles' for 'Porus' and *vice versa*."[52] In the phrase about the Indus a more complicated transposition of terms may be involved. Further, if there was no source here, differing from Megasthenes and leading Diodorus into an inconsistency and if a memory-distortion of a universal opinion was responsible for his phrase, we should expect the distortion in some form or other wherever he touched on the size of the Indus. And this is exactly what we find even at a great distance from the present phrase. In XVII.85 we read: "...the Indus, the greatest of Indian rivers..."[53] In opposing Diodorus to Megasthenes over the Indus, the Ganges and the Nile, Majumdar has not stopped to examine the case closely, subtly, sympathetically.

Still, in view of the complexity of the case and its somewhat ambivalent look, we may refrain from being too harsh on his easy-going inference. But when he argues that, in the details given by Diodorus and Strabo in respect of the second, fourth and sixth of "the seven castes of India", there are substantial differences of such a nature that it is difficult to

50. *Ibid.*, p. 23.
51. *Ibid.*, pp. 239-240.
52. *Ibid.*, p. 243, fn. 4.
53. *Ibid.*, p. 164.

hold that both Diodorus and Strabo derived their information from Megasthenes, our resistance should be stiffer. Even more stiffly would I receive Majumdar's plea – not properly articulate in the surrejoinder but fully expressed in his *Classical Accounts* – that it is unsafe to take as based on Megasthenes Strabo's supplementary note on the seventh caste, describing the special officers of State and mentioning the Municipal and Military Boards of Administration which have figured prominently in the discussion whether Kauṭilya's *Arthaśāstra* where they are not mentioned belonged to the time of Sandrokottos (Chandragupta) and Megasthenes, the fourth century B.C. And when Majumdar flourishes in my face, as directly contrary to Megasthenes, the report of Diodorus on the dimensions of India, I must uncompromisingly protest.

Let us begin with the accounts of the second caste by Diodorus and Strabo. Except in the form of elaboration or commentary, are there any differences at all? Read the accounts side by side and you will see that they agree exactly.* In connection with the fourth caste[54] the significant

* *The Classical Accounts of India*, pp. 237, 264. Diodorus (II.40): "The second caste consists of the husbandmen, who appear to be far more numerous than the others. Being, moreover, exempted from fighting and other public services, they devote the whole of their time to tillage; nor would an enemy coming upon a husbandman at work on his land do him any harm, for men of this class, being regarded as public benefactors, are protected from all injury. The land, thus remaining unravaged, and producing heavy crops, supplies the inhabitants with all that is requisite to make life very enjoyable. The husbandmen themselves, with their wives and children, live in the country, and entirely avoid going into town. They pay a land-tribute to the king, because all India is the property of the crown, and no private person is permitted to own land. Besides the land-tribute, they pay into the royal treasury a fourth part of the produces of the soil." Strabo (XV.I.40): "The second caste, he says, is that of farmers, who are not only the most numerous, but also the most highly respected, because of their exemption from military service and right of freedom in their farming; and they do not approach a city, either because of a public disturbance or on any other business; at any rate, he says, it often happens that at the same time and place some are in battle array and are in peril of their lives against the enemy, while the farmers are ploughing or digging without peril, the latter having the former as defenders. The whole of the country is of royal ownership; and the farmers cultivate it for a rental in addition to paying a fourth part of the produce."

54. *Ibid.*, pp. 237-238, 267.

difference is only that according to Strabo (XV.I.46) some of the Artisans receive wages and provisions from the king and some pay tribute to the State besides rendering services prescribed by it, whereas according to Diodorus (II.41) "this class is not only exempt from paying taxes, but even receives maintenance from the royal exchequer." However, when we turn to Arrian (*Indica,* XII) we find, on the one hand, full support to Strabo's substance and, on the other, a phrase-construction about those who do not have to pay tribute, which reminds us at once of Diodorus's "not only... but even..." Arrian says: "An exception, however, is made in favour of those who fabricate the weapons of war, - and not only so, but they even draw pay from the State."[55] The general impression is that Diodorus has tapped the same source as Arrian - namely, some report from Megasthenes - but, unlike Strabo who has attended more to the contents than the form of Megasthenes, he has misrepresented his source by extending to the whole caste what is applicable to one section of it.

On coming to the sixth caste we are able to confirm our impression that Diodorus founds himself essentially on Megasthenes. For, now we have in him a replica of Arrian's basic contents over and above his constructional form in general. "The sixth caste", writes Diodorus (II.41): "consists of the Inspectors. It is their province to inquire into and superintend all that goes on in India, and make report to the king, or, where there is not a king, to the magistrates."[56] Arrian (*Indica,* XII) writes: "The sixth class consists of those called superintendents. They spy out what goes on in country and town, and report everything to the king where the people have a king, and to the magistrates where the people are self-governed..."[57] Strabo (XV.I.48) gives us the central point but omits to mention the magistrates as alternatives to the kings: this is hardly a reason for us to look beyond Megasthenes. But

55. *Ibid.,* p. 225.
56. *Ibid.,* p. 238.
57. *Ibid.,* p. 226.

what shall we say of his extra information about the "inspectors... using the courtesans as colleagues, the city inspectors using the city courtesans and the camp inspectors the camp courtesans"?[58] Must we go outside Megasthenes for this detail of the means employed by the inspectors in carrying out their duty? Almost immediately after Strabo has described the officials of the seventh caste he (XV.I.53) begins a sentence: "Megasthenes says that when he was in the camp of Sandrokottos..."[59] It would seem that Megasthenes was well acquainted with the affairs of the camp: the camp courtesans would not have been outside his range of knowledge. But even if Strabo is quoting from somebody else here as well as when he refers to city courtesans, we need not doubt that Megasthenes is the principal source for the whole account in Strabo and Diodorus and Arrian of the seven castes. The differences between Strabo and Diodorus are surely not of a kind that would make us suppose another source except in minor points.

Now for Majumdar's argument apropos of the description (XV.I.50–52) of State-officers.[60] As formulated in *The Classical Accounts of India*[61] it may be summed up as follows. Strabo's description of the third caste, based on Megasthenes, is followed immediately by a supplementary note on wild elephants and other animals, which as Strabo himself says, was based on "both Megasthenes and others". His description of the seventh caste is similarly followed by a supplementary note on the officers. So it is unsafe to take it as based on Megasthenes, even though Strabo does not say that it was derived from others. He does not say this because there is no occasion for it: the note here, unlike the previous one, is not a digression and therefore needs no such comment or explanation.

A better example of *non-sequiturs* would be far to seek. Just

58. *Ibid.*, p. 268.
59. *Ibid.*, p. 270.
60. *Ibid.*, pp. 268-269.
61. *Ibid.*, Appendix I, pp. 465-466.

because part of one supplementary note went outside Megasthenes, another need not do the same. There is nothing in the nature of a supplementary note to suggest such a procedure. The information may very well belong to the same author. Unless we have a reason to think of it as belonging to somebody else, it is not at all unsafe to ascribe it to one from whom the immediately preceding matter is drawn. It would be unsafe only if we found, without the writer's mentioning it anywhere, that a supplementary note had drawn upon somebody else. In the case before us the conditions are quite different. The first supplementary note has not been supplied by us as it belongs in part to sources outside Megasthenes. Strabo has openly informed us of these sources. Hence the second note can be ascribed to such sources only if there is a distinct mention of them. Majumdar's suggestion and warning are illogical under the conditions of the case.

Majumdar himself appears to realise this and consequently brings in the excuse that there is no mention of sources outside Megasthenes simply because the second supplementary note is not a digression. But may we ask what the digressive nature of a note has got to do with mentioning or not mentioning a different author? A digression means nothing more than that some matter not directly pertaining to a subject or to a certain sequence of observations is introduced: the matter can come from the same author, from another portion of his work, without the digression ceasing to be digressive, and in that case no call arises to say where the matter hails from. The call arises solely when a different author has been tapped. Hence a supplementary note, by not being a digression, is not exempted from being characterised as partly dependent on a different author. If it is not characterised as such, the reason is not its non-digressive nature but its having its source in the same pen that is responsible for what precedes it.

All the more would the reason impress us as being this when the supplementary note carries further along an organic line the details of what has been completed in general before it – as indeed the description of the State-officers carries the details of the seventh caste (XV.I.49) consisting of "the advisers and councillors of the king, who hold the chief offices of State, the judgeships, and the administration of everything".[62] Besides, this description is of the same type as the one which Strabo supplies to us not very much later (XV.I.58-60), dealing with the philosophers whom he has broadly mentioned (XV.I.39) as constituting the first caste. The passages developing the details of the first caste begin: "Speaking of the philosophers, Megasthenes says..."[63] The whole supplementary note on the philosophers is acknowledged by Majumdar[64] to be built on Megasthenes. The one on the State-officers, analogous to it and beginning "Of the officials..."[65] has nothing to make any part of it non-Megasthenes. Moreover, if we look at the text starting from the place where the digression (XV.I.42-45) about wild animals ends, we see that it commences with the words: "Let me return to Megasthenes and continue his account from the point where I left off."[66] And in between these words and the conclusion of the passages describing the officers of State we get nobody else's name. All the odds are in favour of Megasthenes being, if not the sole, at least the fundamental and predominant source for the entire second supplementary note.

Let us now take up the report of Diodorus on the dimensions of India. Majumdar[67] writes: "Diodorus gives the extent of India as 28,000 stadia from east to west... Schwanbeck felt 'certain that 16,000 stadia is the only measure Megasthenes gives of the breadth of India'. Surely, a seventy-five per cent difference in specific measurements between a book and its epitome calls for an explanation... I would like to point out that there were classical writers who gave 30,000

62. *Ibid.*, p. 268.
63. *Ibid.*, p. 273.
64. *Ibid.*, p. 469.
65. *Ibid.*, p. 268.
66. *Ibid.*, p. 267.
67. *JAOS*, 80, pp. 248-249.

stadia as the breadth of India, and it is certainly more reasonable to conclude that Diodorus took his figures from such writers than that he gave us an epitome of Megasthenes' *Indica.*"

Now here is a confusion of several kinds. First, the reference to Schwanbeck's certainty that 16,000 stadia is the only measure Megasthenes gave of India from east to west omits to accompany itself with a mention that, as both Arrian (*Indica,* III) and Strabo (XV.I.11) show, this measure Megasthenes gives to the east-west extension "where shortest" or "at its minimum".[68] How can a contradiction be affirmed between Diodorus and Megasthenes unless the former also is proved to be offering us the shortest or minimum extension?

Diodorus's exact words (II.35) are: "The extent of the whole country from east to west is said to be 28,000 stadia, and from north to south 32,000."[69] And, a little before these words, we have his assertion that India is in shape a quadrilateral. Evidently, if the east-west and north-south extensions differ, the quadrilateral is not equal on all sides. In this inequality Diodorus is at one with all classical writers. But what about the opposite sides of the quadrilateral? Does Diodorus look on them as equal? No other classical writer can be said to do this – either before or after him. The most plausible course for us is to understand Diodorus's measurements as the longest or maximum since he is talking of "the whole country". Then there can be no contradiction of Megasthenes, for the latter leaves it perfectly possible that the longest or maximum, as distinguished from the shortest or minimum, stretch from east to west should be 28,000 stadia.

What we have called "the most plausible course" becomes the inevitable one on our probing further into Majumdar's confusion. He does not realise that the term "breadth" is used by Megasthenes differently from other classical writers. Arrian (*Indica,* III) tells us that Megasthenes "calls the breadth

68. *The Classical Accounts...,* pp. 216, 248.
69. *Ibid.,* p. 232.

of India its extent from east to west, though others call this its length..."[70] Thus what is to be understood as breadth from others – namely, the extent from north to south – cannot be put side by side with Megasthenes's "breadth". But Majumdar has done just this. Apropos of Diodorus's 28,000 stadia from east to west and Megasthenes's minimum breadth of 16,000, he brings in 30,000 stadia as having been given by some classical writers as India's breadth and concludes that Diodorus must have followed in the footsteps of such writers. But may I ask what classical writer has offered 30,000 stadia for India's east-west extension which Majumdar is discussing? The answer is: None at all. 30,000 stadia occur only in the context of India's north-south extension – normally understood as its breadth by ancient geographers – and they occur too not without connection with Megasthenes himself! Hipparchus is quoted by Strabo (II.I.4) as writing: "...two competent authorities, Deimachus and Megasthenes, who state that in some places the distance from the southern sea is 20,000 stadia and in others 30,000."[71]

Perhaps Majumdar in part defence of his slip will try at least to keep Megasthenes out by citing Strabo's own direct reference (XV.I.12) to Megasthenes and Deimachus: "They put the distance from the southern sea to the Caucasus at 'above twenty thousand stadia', although Deimachus says that 'at some places the distance is above thirty thousand stadia'..."[72] But even if we confine the larger number to Deimachus and consider Hipparchus instead of Strabo mistaken, we get "20,000 stadia" or "above twenty thousand stadia" as Megasthenes's north-south measurement and we may legitimately take them as answering to his 16,000 for the east-west minimum: they apply "in some places" from north to south and make the smaller of the two opposite north-south sides of the Indian quadrilateral. Indeed, Arrian (*Indica*, III) confirms our interpretation and reports Megasthenes in

70. *Ibid.*, p. 216.
71. *Ibid.*, p. 283.
72. *Ibid.*, p. 248.

precise terms when he tells us that according to Megasthenes India's extent from north to south "is, where narrowest, 22,300 stadia".[73] Thus, in respect of not only east-west but also north-south, room is left by Megasthenes for a maximum stretch greater than his own figures. But if what Strabo attributes to him as well as to Deimachus marks the minimum, the "above thirty thousand stadia" in some places which he attributes to Deimachus alone must mark the maximum. These evidently correspond to Diodorus's 32,000 – and with very particular precision by analogy if we note that "above twenty thousand stadia" is really equal to 22,300. The correspondence proves Diodorus's 32,000 to be the maximum north-south measurement and accordingly his 28,000 the maximum east-west one. Then our case for the non-contradiction between him and Megasthenes gets absolutely established both for the stretch from north to south and for that from east to west.

Of course, if we could go beyond the non-contradiction of Megasthenes's minimum figures by Diodorus's maximum and produce Megasthenes's maximum to tally with the latter's, our refutation of Majumdar would be quite complete. But we have no indisputable knowledge of Megasthenes's maximum. The writers who come after Diodorus and refer to Megasthenes in their geographical accounts are silent. Yet it should be evident that while speaking of minimum east-west and north-south extensions Megasthenes must have thought of maximum ones to compare them with. And there is the double fact that all maximum figures other than those of Diodorus are associated with other names than Megasthenes and Deimachus – for instance, 19,000 east-west and 16,000 north-south with Eratosthenes (*vide* Strabo, XV.I.11) – and that the maximum figures of Diodorus are the only ones that go higher than not merely Megasthenes's east-west minimum but also his north-south. In view of this double fact, those figures of Diodorus are as if left over for Megasthenes and

73. *Ibid.*, p. 216.

Deimachus and seem just the maximum measurements they may have given. Nor is Diodorus's omission of the name of Megasthenes on a par with any ordinary omission: it is such as would not create a presumption against Megasthenes for those figures. Does not the entire account of India by Diodorus omit his name even though several parts of it are unmistakably based on him, as Majumdar[74] himself admits? The bare omission here has no force against our thesis if other factors are in our favour: the omission is precisely what we should expect in spite of Megasthenes being the source of the information. In addition, as we have seen, we have Hipparchus – a writer preceding Diodorus in time – associating a maximum north-south extension of 30,000 stadia with Megasthenes no less than Deimachus. All things considered, may not both of Diodorus's measurements be an echo of Megasthenes?

Here Majumdar[75] will most probably repeat from his surrejoinder the gibe: "It is evident that there is a fundamental difference in our outlook and reasoning. Stated broadly, I hold that a thing must be proved to be true before it can be accepted as such, whereas Sethna is ready to accept as true anything which cannot be definitely and unequivocally proved to be false." But here Majumdar would be, just as he was in his surrejoinder, unfair. There is no question of a general principle. I hold exactly what he does, but I plead always for attention to the particularities of a case and submit that in certain contexts we may have a sufficient accumulation of probabilities – made up of some pointed positives and many permissive negatives – to justify acceptance of a view even if it is not in the strict sense proved. Majumdar himself has been at times ready to entertain views for which strict proof has been lacking and even the accumulation of probabilities has been less than I have in favour of a rapport between Diodorus and Megasthenes. I am referring to his

74. *JAOS*, 78, p. 276; *JAOS*, 80, p. 248; or *The Classical Accounts...*, p. 469.
75. *JAOS*, 80, p. 249.

inclination – quite creditable in my eyes – to accept, until definitely and unequivocably disproved, the historicity of Vikramāditya of Ujjainī whom Indian tradition persistently makes the founder of the era of 57 B.C. as well as a victor over the Śakas.

Of course, in suggesting a rapport between Diodorus and Megasthenes, I am not implying that Megasthenes was right in his measurements. Obviously he was wrong – and more so than the other writers, all of whom were wrong. But in this matter too there are certain details to be observed in order to see it correctly.

We have already said that India was thought of as an unequal quadrilateral. Strabo (XV.I.11) makes it plain that when Megasthenes mentions 16,000 stadia he means the northern side of the quadrilateral, running from east to west. And we learn also from Strabo (XV.I.11,12) that Megasthenes's "above 20,000 stadia" from north to south are the western side which Strabo refers to as running "from the Caucasian Mountains to the southern sea".[76] This means, as he adds, the course of the Indus from those mountains (the Himālayas) to its outlets, a course conceived by all ancient writers as directly southwards. Now, the Indus-region is the one region which Alexander traversed and measured and, going by his measurements, Eratosthenes (Arrian, *Indica*, III; Strabo, XV.I.10,11) puts the course of the Indus at 13,000 stadia. Why did Megasthenes, who must have been familiar with Alexander's measurements, increase the number to 22,300 stadia – that is, by over 9,000 stadia? The question is all the more challenging when we realise that his number for the northern side is exactly the same as what Eratosthenes took from the Register of Days' Journeys (Strabo, XV.I.11).

Majumdar will cry out that this demonstrates perfectly the general idiocy and unreliability of Megasthenes. But, unlike any other mistake on the part of Megasthenes, this seems utterly inexplicable: it is something which is as impossible for

76. *The Classical Accounts...*, p. 248.

him as the assertion that Alexander reached the Ganges. And yet, while that assertion in Diodorus can be found outside Megasthenes, this is traceable to him from all accounts: it is at the same time impossible for him and indubitably his. In the context of the figures given by his predecessors it must remain a unique riddle and cannot be used as a stick to beat him with.

However, there is one statement of Hipparchus, reported by Strabo (II.I.4), which might supply a clue. It tells us that the account given by Deimachus and Megasthenes, of the north-south stretch being 20,000 stadia in some places and 30,000 in others, "agrees with the ancient charts of the country".[77] What charts could these be? Surely not Alexander's, from whose 13,000 stadia for the course of the Indus Megasthenes's measurement differs widely. Could it be that Megasthenes, as also Deimachus, founded his figures on information gathered from the Indians themselves of his day and that he chose on the strength of it to ignore Alexander's measurements? The words of Hipparchus would appear to suggest such a procedure. And indeed what else than indigenous information, by which he laid so much store, could have led Megasthenes to set these measurements aside?

Now we come to what may properly be considered as Megasthenes's faults. How shall we appraise Majumdar's second attempt to disparage him? In the surrejoinder he has not added any argument that was not already challenged in my criticism of his original article. But in Appendix I to his *Classical Accounts of India* he tries to fill some of the gaps he has left here. Thus, to meet a point of mine, he makes a remark after quoting Schwanbeck's comments on whatever censures the ancient writers had passed on Megasthenes. He writes (p. 467): "Schwanbeck's comments on these observations are interesting. He says: 'The fact is they find fault with only two parts of the narrative of Megasthenes, – the one in which he writes of the fabulous races of India, and the other

77. *Ibid.*, p. 283.

where he gives an account of Herakles and the Indian Dionysus; although it so happens that on other matters also they regarded the account given by others as true, rather than that of Megasthenes.' The first part of this comment is unwarranted, and is contradicted by the last part."

Well, we can understand a writer falling into serious inconsistency in different portions of his work, but surely we may hesitate to imagine that Schwanbeck should so flagrantly contradict himself in one and the same breath, and this too in a discussion involving no intricate argumentation. The first thing to bear in mind is that he is not talking of the same attitude in the two parts of his sentence. In the first he is talking of a direct fault-finding; in the second of a general distrust. So there is no contradiction as such. The next thing is to inquire what exactly the word "other" means. It could do duty for "all other"; but it could just as well connote "some other". If the former implication is chosen, the whole of Megasthenes loses value, though in two different ways and not, as Majumdar thinks, in a single manner. If the latter, there are certain portions of Megasthenes that lose value, and these portions exceed those concerned with fabulous races and Herakles and the Indian Dionysus but they do not cover everything of Megasthenes and may leave a good deal of him as valuable. Whether we should choose the sense of "all other" or that of "some other" must depend on the total evidence we possess of the opinions held about Megasthenes by the ancient writers.

Do these writers always express a low opinion of him? Do they brush aside, in one fashion or another, all that he has said? The answer can only be No; for otherwise Arrian (*Anabasis*, V.5; *Indica*, XVI) whom along with Strabo Majumdar[78] classes as a discerning person would not speak of Megasthenes as a distinguished authority and a man of approved character.[79] Schwanbeck himself, elsewhere in his

78. *JAOS*, 80, p. 250.
79. *The Classical Accounts...*, pp. 25, 231.

essay on Megasthenes's *Indica,* quotes Arrian in favour of Megasthenes. So, in the passage cited by Majumdar, he is bound to mean "some other" and imply that certain portions of Megasthenes were neither directly found fault with nor passed over with a general distrust but considered as valuable. Majumdar's attempt to prove Schwanbeck absurdly self-contradictory betrays a lack of perspicacity.

And his sweeping cry of "unwarranted" to Schwanbeck's statement that ancient writers found fault with only two parts of Megasthenes's narrative stands without any kind of proof – unless he means nothing more than that Arrian may be said to find fault too with Megasthenes's account of the river Silas in which nothing could float and of the gold-digging ants about which he had learnt from hearsay. But I may remind Majumdar that Strabo (XV.I.38), a discerning person, draws our attention to atmospheres so thin that no winged creature can fly in them and to certain rising vapours which tend to attract to themselves and "gulp down", as it were, whatever flies over them just as amber does with chaff and the magnet with iron; and his final verdict on the river Silas is: "perhaps there might also be natural powers of this kind in water."[80] I may in addition point out to Majumdar that it is only when Strabo (XV.I.57) comes to Megasthenes's stories about strange peoples that he speaks of his "going beyond all bounds to the realm of myth"[81] and it is only in reference to Megasthenes's statements about Dionysus that he (XV.I.58) remarks: "Now these statements of Megasthenes are mythical and refuted by many writers, and particularly those about the vine and wine..."[82] Finally, let me mention again that Strabo quotes Hipparchus as calling both Deimachus and Megasthenes "two competent authorities".

The truth about ancient writers' judgment on Megasthenes is that they gave him a sufficiently high place in regard to some subjects, while criticising him severely or moderately in

80. *Ibid.,* p. 263.
81. *Ibid.,* p. 272.
82. *Ibid.,* p. 273.

regard to others. Majumdar's failure to see it is not likely to spread to unprejudiced Indologists. Perhaps what has prejudiced him is the discrepancy already noted by us between Megasthenes and Kauṭilya whose *Arthaśāstra* Majumdar, it is well known, is anxious to put in the time of Sandrokottos to whom Megasthenes had been sent as ambassador by Seleucus Nicator.